THIRD EDITION

CREATING
STANDARDS-BASED
INTEGRATED
CURRICULUM

THIRD EDITION

CREATING STANDARDS-BASED INTEGRATED CURRICULUM

The Common Core State Standards Edition

SUSAN M. DRAKE

CORWIN
A SAGE Company

CORWIN
A SAGE Company

FOR INFORMATION:

Corwin
A SAGE Company
2455 Teller Road
Thousand Oaks, California 91320
(800) 233-9936
www.corwin.com

SAGE Publications Ltd.
1 Oliver's Yard
55 City Road
London EC1Y 1SP
United Kingdom

SAGE Publications India Pvt. Ltd.
B 1/I 1 Mohan Cooperative Industrial Area
Mathura Road, New Delhi 110 044
India

SAGE Publications Asia-Pacific Pte. Ltd.
3 Church Street
#10-04 Samsung Hub
Singapore 049483

Acquisitions Editor: Carol Chambers Collins
Associate Editor: Megan Bedell
Editorial Assistant: Sarah Bartlett
Production Editor: Cassandra Margaret Seibel
Copy Editor: Cate Huisman
Typesetter: C&M Digitals (P) Ltd.
Proofreader: Jennifer Gritt
Indexer: Jean Casalegno
Cover Designer: Lisa Riley
Graphic Designer: Karine Hovsepian
Permissions Editor: Jason Kelley

Printed in the United States of America.

Library of Congress Cataloging-in-Publication Data

Drake, Susan M., date

Creating standards-based integrated curriculum : the common core state standards edition / Susan M. Drake. —3rd ed.

p. cm.
Includes bibliographical references and index.

ISBN 978-1-4522-1880-9 (pbk.)

1. Interdisciplinary approach in education—United States. 2. Education—Curricula—United States. 3. Education—Standards—United States. I. Title.

LB1570.D695 2012
375.000973—dc23   2012009206

This book is printed on acid-free paper.

12 13 14 15 16 10 9 8 7 6 5 4 3 2

Contents

List of Figures

Chapter 3

Chapter 4

Chapter 5

Chapter 6

Preface

When you walk down the ramp to board an airline, you can often see a fascinating set of billboards that originated with the HSBC "your point of view" advertising campaign. The advertisements feature a set of images that use different words to describe the same image. For example, the exact same image of a baby is repeated three times with the words *love, legacy,* and *expense* on its belly. Or you may see the image of a bottle of water with three different captions: *healthy, fashionable,* or *wasteful.* Which one is it?

Similarly, two images can be juxtaposed to challenge the viewer's perceptions. The first image may be a high-heeled shoe with label of *pleasure* written across it. The second image is a hot chilli pepper featuring the word *pain.* Directly beside this is a repeated image of a high-heeled shoe. This time the word *pain* describes the shoe. The next image repeats the chilli pepper with the word *pleasure* written across.

I am always startled when I see these ads. There are so many images that we can see in so many different and sometimes contradictory ways. The HSBC advertisements capture the complexity of the world we live in. We can't look at the world from one lens. To really understand phenomena in our modern world, we need to see with a wide-angle lens that captures the world from many different perspectives. As educators we need to focus on our disciplines at the same time as we need to step outside of their boundaries to capture the real world.

BALANCING RIGOR AND RELEVANCE IN THE 21ST CENTURY

The world is changing dramatically as we move deeper into the 21st century. As education adapts to these changes, three themes prevail. Like the HSBC ads, two of these themes may seem contradictory at first glance—accountability and relevance—but they are two sides of the same coin. This book is about how to create a curriculum that honors both themes through creating a standards-based interdisciplinary curriculum. The third theme is the 21st century context. Although we are well into this new century it is becoming more and more apparent that the world is changing in fundamental ways and education must change with it. This book then sets curriculum and assessment in the 21st century context—a context that is decidedly different than the one in which most teachers were educated.

The 21st century is an age of accountability. The essence of accountability is to determine that teachers are teaching what they are supposed to teach and that students are learning what they are supposed to learn. Standardization is a way of determining such accountability. Student success is largely measured by standardized large-scale testing whether at the local, regional, statewide, national, or international level. These data can be helpful in determining a system's next steps (Wiliam, 2010). There have been many critics of the unintended consequences of large-scale testing, however, such as narrowing of the curriculum, teaching to the test, and even manipulating the situation to produce better scores (Volante, 2006). But how can we ensure that teachers teach what they are supposed to teach? The state standards are the starting place for this role. Yet state standards have been uneven across the country with some states having much more rigorous standards than others. Thus it has been impossible for students to move from one state to another, for example, and be assured that they have acquired the same skills and knowledge as their peers in their new locale.

A challenge with curriculum in an age of accountability is that students are motivated by the need for a high grade rather than learning for the sake of learning. Paradoxically, this is occurring at a time when there is more to learn than ever in the history of the planet and knowledge is increasing exponentially. Memorization and regurgitation are no longer enough. Students need to acquire the 21st century skills, for example, that include the 3Rs but go far beyond them. Thus, it is crucial that curriculum is relevant and meaningful to ensure that students reach their full learning potential. As well, the culture of grading needs to be replaced by a culture of learning.

Adopting the Common Core State Standards can lead to a balance between accountability and relevance. These standards are generally receiving positive reviews as rigorous and developmentally appropriate given that they are research-based and have input from an international context. The role of these standards is to maintain consistent, high-quality education across states. At the same time, no one is dictating how these standards are to be met. In principle, educators are free to be creative in how students meet the standards. This freedom to be creative allows educators to design curriculum that is relevant to students in a local context. This book will focus on creating engaging curriculum using the standards as a guide.

The catalysts for the rapid changes occurring in the 21st century are usually connected to technological innovation and access to the Internet. Younger people have grown up with these innovations, and working with them is second nature. One only has to witness a two-year-old playing with an iPod Touch or an iPhone to see this intuitive phenomenon in action. These young people are the *digital natives* (Prensky, 2001). In contrast,

Prensky calls the older generations *digital immigrants*—no matter how adept digital immigrants are with new technology, they will never be fully at ease with it.

In the fall of 2011, the freshman class of 2015 entered college (Watters, 2011c). Most of the members of this class were born in 1993. According to Beloit College's annual Mindset List for the Class of 2015, these young people were "the first generation to grow up taking the word 'online' for granted and for whom crossing the digital divide has redefined research, original sources and access to information, changing the central experiences and methods in their lives." (http://www.beloit .edu/mindset/2015/).

The *NMC Horizon Report K to 12 Edition* (New Media Consortium, 2011) reports on how technology is changing teaching. The report predicts key trends based on current realities. Technology is

- Increasingly easy to access
- Not based in the school server but in the cloud
- Profoundly affecting how we communicate
- Raising expectations to learn 24/7 from anywhere
- Increasing the perceived value of innovation and creativity

According to this report, cloud computing and mobiles will be implemented in schools within 12 months. In three to five years, game-based learning and open content will be widely adopted. In four to five years, personalized learning will be the order of the day, where students will design their own learning experiences to match their personal learning styles.

These are indeed rapidly changing times. It is unlikely that these students will be satisfied with teaching styles of the 20th century. This book then sets a meaningful, yet accountable, curriculum for the 21st century.

FROM THE FIRST TO THIRD EDITION

It is a strange experience to have previously written seven books on integrated curriculum. It may appear as if I simply write the same book over and over again, but this is far from the reality. I find myself wrestling with new ideas and ways to resolve new issues emerging from the latest policy mandates. For each book, I have been fortunate enough to connect with or have access to some of the finest educators on the planet. Their efforts are awe inspiring, and I continually learn from them.

The evolution of this book parallels the pendulum swings between the accountability and relevance approaches. The 1998 book offered a smorgasbord of the best in interdisciplinary curricula from the late 1980s and early 1990s. Integrated curricula were a popular response to reports such as *Turning Points* (Carnegie Corporation, 1989) in the United States and *Rights of Passage* (Hargreaves & Earl, 1990) in Canada. These reports targeted adolescents who were not motivated to learn. Essentially, there was a call for curricula that were more relevant for young people. For many, interdisciplinary curricula provided an answer.

During this period, there was a great deal of exciting work happening in classrooms across North America, and many engaged students and educators were involved in innovative processes. The 1998 book offered samples of the wide range of models that emerged during this time. In short, someone could use the book and sample the state of the art in interdisciplinary models without going to several different books to discover each one.

But around the mid-1990s, the climate in education changed. The pendulum swung swiftly and dramatically. Critics of education noted that students still were not achieving at desired levels. There were renewed fears that North American students would not be able to compete in the global economy. Suddenly, there was a shift from finding relevance in the curriculum to ensuring accountability in the system. How could we know when students were achieving at satisfactory levels? The answer, of course, was the development of standards and standardized tests to ensure that the standards were being addressed adequately.

It has been a bumpy road in education since that time, as educators have tried to come to terms with accountability measures. One of the first things to disappear with the new mandates was the interdisciplinary approach. Many of the "gurus" of the late 1980s and early 1990s declared that integrated curriculum was dead and shifted to areas deemed more appropriate to accountability efforts.

Across North America, the associations representing the disciplines created the standards—regardless of whether they were at the national, state, provincial, or regional level. Teachers were busy addressing the disciplinary standards (usually there were too many in each discipline) and preparing students for the large-scale tests that were disciplinary in nature. The results of these tests were important. In many jurisdictions, a teacher's reputation was affirmed or broken by the results. Funding for the school could also be affected. For most teachers, integrated curriculum was a thing of the past. Moving through the standards of each separate discipline was the order of the day. Even those who had experienced success with integrated approaches in the past had trouble seeing any light.

During this time, I never stopped believing in the power of integration as a motivating learning tool. Perhaps it was because I had the luxury of working at the university level with practicing teachers and graduate students who were taking a course in innovative curriculum or innovative assessment. Working on these graduate credit courses, the teachers enjoyed playing with new ideas without scrutiny from their district colleagues or administrators and with the added reward of a course credit.

THE SECOND EDITION

As I began to update the first edition of this book, however, I realized that I was actually creating a completely transformed and different work. One cannot approach interdisciplinary work in a standards-based environment simply by adding standards to the late-1980s and early-1990s models (which had not previously dealt with standards). To simply match standards to activities looked good but did not really get at creating a curriculum that was deeply anchored in standards, nor did it align interdisciplinary work with assessment and instruction. Because the accountability process demanded such a different approach to curricular design, I found myself writing what seemed to be virtually a new book entirely.

Consequently, very little from the 1998 edition appeared in the second edition in 2007. I did describe again the three approaches to integration as a framework for understanding the range of possibilities for integration: multidisciplinary, interdisciplinary, and transdisciplinary. But in essence, apart from this central organizing principle, the second edition was a new book from cover to cover.

THE THIRD EDITION

Now, five years later I am writing a third edition. The context has changed again. The pendulum seems to be coming to rest between relevance and accountability. The Common Core State Standards offer a shared language and opportunities for collaboration across many jurisdictions. They provide the potential for accountability that is consistent but also gives teachers the much-needed flexibility to design meaningful curriculum. The basics of standards-based curriculum design found in the second edition are still the same in this third edition; this method was and continues to be sound.

There are some differences in this edition. I have adopted slightly different language for key terms in order to try to match the language being used in the field. Big Understandings has changed to Enduring Understandings, and a Big Assessment Task is now a Rich Culminating Assessment Task. A Big Question is now an Essential Question. Big Skills are 21st Century Skills. It is always an educated guess what terms will become popular over the next few years. For example, I decided on 21st Century Skills as I think that this is a widely used term that people recognize. On the other hand, there are a number of critics in the field who strongly dislike this term, and they may prevail; if so, I would have been wiser to call these skills something else like Essential Skills.

In this edition you will find that some of the process has been reordered. I have done this after working with many educators with the second edition and finding things that I thought could be improved. In this edition, you will also find 21st century teachers in real classrooms who are working with the Common Core State Standards and integrating the curriculum. Almost all of the examples are new; the six profiles of exemplary programs are also new.

I am also very aware of what is not in this book. I did not include a list of the published research that supports interdisciplinary work. That would have read like a long laundry list, and in my experience, such a list has done little to convert anyone. Fortunately almost every example that is in this book comes with some accompanying quantitative measure of success. This type of evidence is new for the field and is the result of educators implementing integrated programs in an age of accountability.

I have not included a list of the potential pitfalls of trying to do integrated approaches or how to avoid these pitfalls. For example, there may be structural obstacles such as scheduling that inhibit this type of work. But, in my experience, educators can be their own advocates and find creative ways around the obstacles. I also did not address the differences between working alone and team teaching. These are indeed very different contexts, and each has its own problems and its own rewards. I have found that where there is a will, there usually is a way. I focused on the process of standards-based design, which is similar from kindergarten through college. With a clear process, some of the obstacles, whether one is working alone or collaboratively, are naturally removed.

Acknowledgments

The writing of this book has been a fascinating experience. Writing at a time when interdisciplinary curriculum may seem to have gone underground, I discovered that this is simply not true. Integrated approaches are everywhere—one only needs to look to find them. I am deeply grateful to the exemplary educators featured in this book who are dedicated to making school a wonderful experience for their students. I thank each and every one of them, not only for their contribution to this book but also for their tireless efforts to bridge accountability and relevance.

I was indeed fortunate to work with insightful educators who understood integrated curriculum at a deep level. Terry Whitmell created many of the figures in this book. Often, she would challenge my fuzzy thinking and then help me to clarify it. Joanne Reid, who once taught with me at the high school level, acted as a critical friend. Like Terry, she is a strong conceptual thinker who cuts through fuzziness like a knife. Elizabeth Rothmel also challenged me with insightful comments. I am indebted to the late Tessa Torres-Dickson who showed me that with persistence it is possible to implement integrated curriculum in the most challenging of circumstances.

I met Carol Collins shortly after the second edition of this book was published. She became my third editor at Corwin. It was Carol who encouraged me to rethink this book in the light of the Common Core State Standards. The more deeply I explored the Common Core from a both a philosophical and practical perspective, the more I could see that Carol was right. The Common Core offered an excellent fit with integrated curriculum. I am thankful to Carol for the foresight to see the future and for steering me down the right path.

Thanks to Corwin's Sarah Bartlett and Megan Bedell, Sanford Robinson and Julie Gwin, as well as Gem Rabanera, who spent a great deal of time on this manuscript. A special thanks to Cate Huisman for her detailed and thoughtful editing of this third edition; to Cassandra Seibel, project editor; and to C&M Digitals for graphic creation.

Finally, I thank my family and friends who have lived through all the ups and downs of writing this book. Thanks to Tamara Bahry for her great photography skills. Thank you to Scott, Addie, Katie, Jack, Odessa, and Max Paterson for constantly teaching me how young people learn. And thanks most of all to Michael Manley-Casimir for his patience, love, and support.

About the Author

Susan M. Drake is a full professor in the Department of Graduate and Undergraduate Studies in Education at Brock University, St. Catharines, Ontario. She earned a PhD in curriculum from the University of Toronto. She has taught at all levels of education. She taught physical education and health as well as English for 18 years at the high school level. She worked on school improvement teams at the elementary level and spent one year as an elementary teacher. Also, she was a partner in a private adult education company that provided organizational development, consulting, and adult learning courses.

Today, Susan teaches curriculum and assessment courses to undergraduate students who will soon be entering the teaching field as well as students seeking their master's and doctoral degrees. As a researcher, she seeks out educators who are involved in exemplary practices, as she believes that a good practice makes good theory. This is Susan's eighth book on the topic of curriculum integration, and she has published more than 66 articles and 12 book chapters. She coauthored *Meeting Standards Through Integrated Curriculum* (2004) for ASCD with Rebecca Burns. Also, she authored *Creating Integrated Curriculum* (1998) for Corwin and *Planning for Integrated Curriculum: The Call to Adventure* (1993) for ASCD. She has led interdisciplinary curriculum design teams from the school to the provincial level. Susan travels extensively and has done workshops and presentations across North America and in Europe, Asia, and Africa.

Introduction

Personally Seeking Rigor and Relevance

I am not one to whom accountability comes naturally. For me, it is relevance that has been central to my teaching. If the curriculum isn't relevant, students will not learn. If the students do not learn, there is not much point in teaching. This is a simple axiom, but it is one that I believe now as strongly as when I began teaching more than 40 years ago.

I suspect this belief in relevance is based primarily on my own experiences both as a student and as a high school teacher. I was not a student who loved school. I can remember only one teacher who really turned me on to learning. I was in Grade 5, and Mr. Griffin made Marco Polo's adventures come alive. I was actively involved in classroom activities and filled with brilliant images of the Orient dancing through my head. Perhaps that is why I longed to travel the world—to have my own adventures. But apart from this one experience, school was boring and unrewarding.

Blessed with a good memory, I could memorize what I needed to know for the tests. Thus, I passed the tests and even skipped a grade. My teachers taught a lot of things, but I did not learn what I was supposed to learn. Although I passed the tests, I quickly forgot what I had memorized and regurgitated. Today, I hesitate to play games like Trivial Pursuit because so many of the things I learned in school are gone. The knowledge that had once been so important to test and make sure I could regurgitate had disappeared as surely as if my mind was a sieve. It seems like the only things I truly remember are the things that I have needed to use in later life.

As a teacher, I was even more aware of the necessity for relevance. I was not a natural disciplinarian. To this day, young people laugh if I try to discipline them with a stern, hard voice. Instead, to capture my audience, I must make the curriculum so relevant that students want to learn. Only then can I bypass the need for strong classroom management skills. As a result, I spent hours trying to devise the most interesting lessons to capture the interest of my students. Most important, I was always trying to connect the curriculum to the students—their lives and their interests.

In hindsight, I see that I stumbled into interdisciplinary curriculum as a desperate classroom management tool. My first attempt is still vivid in my mind. I was having trouble making the Grade 10 English lesson engaging. As it happened, I taught physical education to the girls as well as English. One day, I was teaching body language as a communication tool. The girls already knew a folk dance, and I asked them to teach the dance to the boys without any words or music. Everyone got quickly involved. They had never had an English lesson quite like this one. In fact, the experience was so unique that the word somehow spread like wildfire to students sitting in other classrooms. Before the dance class was over, there were many students who had somehow left their own classrooms and were vying for a position to press their noses against the classroom door window. The girls found it extraordinarily difficult to teach the dance without being able to talk. When the boys attempted the dance with the music for the first time, we all collapsed in laughter.

Today, I still believe that students will really learn only when the curriculum is relevant to them, and this does not mean relevant because the material is on the next test or it is something they will need to know in the next grade. But now, like everyone else, I am immersed in the accountability movement. In reality, I can no longer rely on simply creating engaging learning experiences for students. The instructional activities also need to meet the standards. My students might have loved to folk dance in English class, but did they really learn the intended knowledge and skills? While I hoped and believed they did, I had no real way to measure it other than my own assessments and perceptions.

Since the mid-1990s the accountability movement has permeated all aspects of education. My personal challenge became how to make a relevant curriculum accountable. I knew it could be done—although sometimes it seemed impossible. I have spent over two decades learning how to do it. After the second edition was published in 2007, I continued to follow innovative programs around the world. In the last year I have immersed myself in technology so that I could begin to understand the new world that today's students inhabit. This third edition is the result of these journeys.

LESSONS LEARNED

For years, I have worked with educators to develop interdisciplinary programs. My experiences have been overwhelmingly positive. I also know many teachers are reenergized by the process. And when teachers implement these types of programs, they usually have the same positive results as others before them. My mistake in the early 1990s was not to spend all my time and energy with the excited and reenergized teachers all around me who were ready and willing to try integration. I vowed not to repeat this mistake again. No more convincing or cajoling.

Thus, this book does not deal with obstacles and does not attempt to prove the worth of interdisciplinary approaches. It is for the educators who are ready and willing to embrace such an approach. As teachers work with standards and become more comfortable with them, they too see the bigger picture. They realize that to address and assess all the standards, they need to integrate the curriculum. They recognize that there is increasingly more and more information for students to manage. But they can also see that when they focus on what is most important to Know, Do, and Be, students have a way to manage it. This is particularly true for a time when educators are learning how to implement the Common Core State Standards.

THE CHAPTERS AHEAD

Each of the chapters ahead concludes with both discussion questions and suggested activities. The discussion questions center on building personal meaning for the concepts introduced in the chapters. The activities are intended to build on each other. If one engages in the activities from chapter to chapter, most of the pieces for a standards-based curriculum will be completed. By Chapter 6, the reader will be able to put the pieces together to create a standards-based interdisciplinary curriculum. It is recommended, then, that readers work with standards that are relevant to them and that they use these standards to address the activities throughout the book.

Chapter 1 explores possible definitions for integrated curriculum. In this book, the terms *integrated* and *interdisciplinary* are used interchangeably when talking about such curriculum in general terms. The chapter provides an overview of interdisciplinary education since the 1930s. A rationale is offered. Fusion, multidisciplinary, interdisciplinary, and transdisciplinary approaches to integration are described. Finally, we look at how these approaches are affected by the standards movement—how they are similar and how they are different.

Chapter 2 explores the basics of the accountability movement. All the strategies discussed in this chapter can be used for both disciplinary and interdisciplinary work. There is a brief review of the purpose of standards and some of the challenges they pose. The quality of standards has improved over the years, and we look at how we can design a rigorous and relevant curriculum and still meet these standards. To this end, we need to engage in two-dimensional thinking—seeing both the Big Picture and the more focused disciplinary picture at the same time. From a wide-angle lens, we look at creating a Know/Do/Be (KDB) Umbrella and then use the backward design process. Shifting to a zoom lens, we unpack individual standards to see what they actually require of students. Finally, we look at curriculum mapping as a precursor to integrating the curriculum.

Chapter 3 offers six integrated curriculum programs that are exemplars in the field today. These programs show that integrated curriculum can be both accountable and engaging. One example is at an elementary school, two are at middle schools, and three are at high schools. These programs are located in various regions across the country. All six of these examples have something unique to recommend them and are worth reading about regardless of the grade level you work with.

Chapter 4 explores the groundwork that needs to be done in preparation for the backward design of an integrated curriculum. What do we want students to know, do, and be? How can we make connections across the subject areas? This question is first addressed from the wide-angle lens looking at the Big Picture. When we look at the Big Picture, we ask what a student needs to learn to live successfully in society and to be college- and career-ready after graduation. We want students to learn deeply through the lens of Big Ideas and Enduring Understandings. We want students to be able to demonstrate 21st Century Skills such as research, critical thinking, and communication skills. Finally, we want them to be productive citizens in a democratic society who hold and act on a positive set of values.

At this point, we zoom in on the design of curriculum units. How do we identify the broader and more abstract Know, Do, Be (KDB) in specific curriculum documents? What broad-based standards target what we are intending to be learning outcomes? We look at creating the KDB Umbrella and an exploratory web. A scan and cluster process is described for recognizing the Know and the Do in standards. There is an exploration of how to develop Essential Questions. Essential Questions act as a bridge across the disciplines. There is a comparison of Essential Questions and topic questions. A wonderful example of how to create Essential Questions is offered. The connection between standards, Essential Questions, and Enduring Understandings is also explored.

Chapter 5 begins with exploring the concept of interdisciplinary assessment. What is interdisciplinary assessment? How do we use it? Who is responsible for teaching the interdisciplinary skills and concepts? The rest of the chapter addresses the second question of backward design. How do we know when students have learned what we want them to learn? The difference between assessment tasks and assessment tools is described. There is an example of an interdisciplinary Rich Culminating Assessment Task and its accompanying assessment tool. This example comes from an innovative interdisciplinary high school program in Adelaide, Australia. The Rich Culminating Assessment Task must be connected to the KDB Umbrella. Two examples are provided to show how teachers can make this connection. In one example there is a focus on teaching and assessing Big Ideas and Enduring Understandings. In another example there is a focus on the process for creating the Rich Culminating Assessment Task.

In Chapter 6, we examine how to create the daily instructional activities. This is the last question of backward design and is intended to ensure alignment of the curriculum, standards, and assessment. In this chapter, specific ideas for creating engaging instructional activities are given. Learning principles are suggested as a fundamental consideration for planning. The focus is on generating engaging and challenging assessment tasks that are aligned with standards. This leads to engaging and challenging activities. The assessment tools connect us back to the KDB. Chapter 6 puts all the pieces together to design a standards-based curriculum. The process is the same for every grade level. In this sample, a Grade 5 curriculum unit on conservation is featured to illustrate the principles of developing the curriculum.

Finally, in the Epilogue, I explore 21st century learning. As we move deeper into the 21st century, education promises to change. The changes that I explore here are already happening in some parts of North America. The nature of these changes suggests that integrated approaches to curriculum will become a standard method of instruction.

DISCUSSION QUESTIONS AND SUGGESTED ACTIVITIES

As you work through the discussions and activities, please note that you would be wisest to choose a relevant grade level and set of standards and use them for all the activities in the following chapters.

Discussion Questions

1. What is your personal experience of the relationship between accountability and relevance?

2. Does the author's personal experience with curriculum integration shed any light on your understanding?

3. Do you think the author is doing the wisest thing when she says that she will no longer "water the rocks"?

4. Think of a time when you have been involved in a change effort. Resistance is considered a normal part of change. How do you personally respond to change? In what ways have you noticed that others resist change? What factors helped to facilitate the change?

Suggested Activities

Examine the advertisements for HSBC that are described in the Preface. What is the most important point in these ads? Create new advertisements with a similar theme for elementary, middle, and secondary schools. For further information, look at http://theinspirationroom.com/daily/2007/altruism-or-consumerism-your-point-of-view-at-hsbc/.

1

What Is Interdisciplinary Curriculum?

What is *integrated* or *interdisciplinary curriculum?* A definition is particularly elusive. The HSBC advertisements on the first page of the Preface offer examples of the essence of interdisciplinary approaches—making connections and looking at things from more than one perspective. In this book, the terms *integrated* and *interdisciplinary* will be used interchangeably to generically describe a curriculum that connects the various disciplines in some way. In this chapter, we will explore different definitions of interdisciplinary curriculum and what they mean in practice.

Educators can conceive of curriculum integration in a wide variety of ways, and its implementation can be unique in every setting. Virtually any combination of subjects can be integrated given the will of the teachers involved. Perhaps one teacher teaches several subjects through a universal concept or theme. Or perhaps a team of teachers combines areas of expertise. This is one of the pitfalls of interdisciplinary approaches—they cannot be standardized or rarely even replicated by another set of teachers who wish to do the same thing. On the other hand, one of the greatest appeals of integration is this lack of a standardized definition. Teachers can be creative. They can set the curriculum in a relevant context. They can craft it around the needs of their students. They can even ask for students' input into what students want to learn. The ways to make connections across subject areas are limitless. This is both frightening and exhilarating for teachers.

This chapter will explore the roots of integrated curriculum from the early 1930s through late 1980s and early 1990s. This exploration will offer a good starting point for the rationale for educators to implement such curriculum and what it might look like. The second part of the chapter explores the context of the 21st century and how the rationale for integrated approaches has expanded. In each section, examples from real classrooms/schools are included.

The last part of the chapter will show how current interdisciplinary approaches are different from, yet similar to, their predecessors of the past.

WHY INTEGRATE THE CURRICULUM?

Integrated curriculum is not a new phenomenon. Influenced by the philosophy of John Dewey (1938, 1966), the progressive movement was popular in education and promoted an integrated curriculum that would motivate students because it was relevant and followed the principles of constructivism. Dewey advocated for balancing the needs of the learner with the demands of the subject content and of living in a democratic society. According to the principles of constructivism, the learners construct their own knowledge and bring prior learning to the situation. Learners learn by doing, not by memorizing facts. The instruction is student-centred. They also learn by conducting rich and relevant real-world inquiries and explorations to promote deep learning. In social constructivism, learners learn through social collaborations (Vygotsky, 1978).

The project method was a hallmark of the progressive movement. Students learned by doing, and their learning was demonstrated by the completion of an inquiry project. Projects were experience-based, offered student choice, and were presumably more motivating than having information transmitted to a passive learner. Collaborative group work was undertaken with the understanding that the group took full responsibility for its learning. These projects were the forerunners of project-based, problem-based, and challenge-based learning.

An important longitudinal study called the Eight-Year Study demonstrated that high school students educated under the progressive philosophy were successful at university (Aikin, 1942). The study was lead by renowned educators Ralph Tyler and Hilda Taba. Success was ascertained by comparing 1,475 matched sets of students over eight years on 18 variables. High schools were encouraged to adopt constructivist methods, and universities dropped their standardized admissions requirements during this time. The variables measured included grade point average, academic honors, objective thinking, and resourcefulness. The results indicated that graduates of the 30 schools in the study "did a somewhat better job than the comparison group" (Aiken, 1942, p. 112). The graduates from the schools that had embraced progressive methods and were most interdisciplinary were "strikingly more successful" than their matches and than students from all the other schools in the country (p. 113). The graduates from the least innovative schools showed no consistent differences from their counterparts.

The results of the Eight-Year Study have largely been forgotten, perhaps because World War II took precedence or because later educators were traditional in their philosophy (Kahne, 1995). But approaches that were interdisciplinary in nature did not entirely disappear. The National Association for Core Curriculum, for example, supported integrated approaches, as did the National Middle School Association (2004). In 1989, the Carnegie Corporation's report *Turning Points* reported that students were not doing well enough to be productive citizens of the 21st century. The fault lay, in part, in the lack of relevant curriculum. Young people were not learning, because they could not find personal meaning in their studies. During the late 1980s and early 1990s, the nation turned to more integrated approaches set in real-world contexts to provide more relevant curriculum.

At the time, there was a strong rationale for interdisciplinary approaches. Advocates argued that to capture students' interest, the curriculum should be set in the real world. Since the real world was not separated into disciplines, neither should the curriculum be. An interdisciplinary approach would eliminate duplication found across subject areas. Research about how students learned best seemed to favor integrated curricula. According to brain research, the brain thrives on variety and processes most effectively when it makes connections (Caine & Caine, 1997; Jensen, 2005). Also, interdisciplinary approaches left open the possibilities of applying popular learning theories such as multiple intelligences and learning styles. Integrated approaches allowed for teacher creativity and honored them as intelligent agents of education.

It was a time when the potential of the Internet was just being realized. The exponential explosion of knowledge offered yet another reason to adopt an approach that did not attempt to teach "everything." Supporters claimed that interdisciplinary approaches allowed for studying a concept in depth as opposed to breadth. It was also becoming increasingly clear that knowledge did not belong in carefully defined boxes called "disciplines." Some of the boxes were already overflowing and were subdivided into subdisciplines, such as in biotechnology, medical physics, and astrophysics in the sciences. In fact, knowledge in the disciplines seemed to overlap into a messy, interconnected, and interdependent blur.

Some jurisdictions leapt into interdisciplinary approaches. In Ontario, for example, the new curriculum documents mandated integrated curriculum for students in grades K to 9. Few people actually knew how to develop an integrated curriculum. They were confounded by the lack of a clear definition or clear direction. Also, practitioners encountered all the predictable problems that go with any major change. In short, these were turbulent times. During this period, I was very involved helping people understand, design, and implement such curricula across North America.

Critics complained that there was little quantitative evidence to support integrated approaches—which was true to some extent, as most research was anecdotal. Generally the research supported the Eight-Year Study conclusion that students taught an integrated curriculum do no worse academically, and sometimes do better, than students taught traditionally. But, students taught an integrated curriculum were more engaged and motivated, had better attendance, created fewer discipline problems than students taught traditionally, and teachers were more satisfied with their jobs and experienced a positive work climate. (See, for example, Bolack, Bialach, & Dunphy, 2005; Curry, Samara, & Connell, 2005; Ferrero, 2006; Flowers, Mertens, & Mulhall, 1999; and Vars, 2001a, 2001b.) The examples offered in these works and this book add strong quantitative support for integrated approaches to the existing research base.

Although many of these compelling reasons for curriculum integration remained, the age of accountability entered the American educational landscape in the mid 1990s. It was a time of standards, standardized testing, and back to the basics and the disciplines. It was not until a decade into the 21st century that a clear call for relevance was heard again. By 2010, the age of technology had altered the landscape sufficiently that it was clear that education had to be different. For one, curriculum had to be *both accountable and relevant.* States rallied together to create the Common Core State Standards for language, mathematics, and science. This provided a basis for a common language and common understanding of what students should know and do across most of the country and thus insured a wider basis of accountability.

The Common Core Literacy Standards articulate what literacy looks in English and language arts classes, but also there are standards for literacy in science, literacy in history/social studies and literacy in technical subjects. Theses standards recognize that there are general reading and writing skills but that students need to perform these skills somewhat differently in different subjects. Thus, literacy is the responsibility of a variety of different subject area teachers to prepare students for college and university. To teach literacy in science, for example, it makes sense to use science content while focusing on literacy skills. This is a natural opening for an integrated approach.

STEM stands for science, technology, engineering, and mathematics. STEM programs can be found across the country and focus on student engagement to foster interest in later school years and in careers. STEM acknowledges that all four "subject areas" are interconnected and that a high level of skill is necessary to prepare students to live and work in the 21st century. Students need an education that is practical and connected to the real world. Similarly, the Common Core Stare Standards in mathematics want students to understand math and be able to use it for problem solving in the real world. The Framework for K–12 Science Education also includes science, engineering, and technology as the fundamental aspects of science education. Again, it is hard to see how teachers will not need to integrate the four areas of STEM.

In keeping with the Common Core State Standards, Root-Bernstein & Root-Bernstein (2011) write that STEM should turn into STREAM to add the arts (A) and thinking skills (T) to the STEM concept. They claim that skills needed by artists are also needed by the scientists: visual thinking, recognizing and forming patterns, getting a feel for systems, and using manipulatives such as tools, pens, and brushes. Writing is an art that requires thinking tools such as acute observation, use of analogies and metaphors, and translation of feelings and hunches into a communicable form. They claim that scientists and mathematicians also need these skills. Mastery of the English language is a prerequisite for scientific success and improves success in STEM courses. Statistical studies show that the most successful scientists are also writers.

Many classrooms and schools are adapting to the emerging realities of the 21st century. The disciplines exist and are clearly identifiable, but there are also many aspects of these classrooms and schools that are interdisciplinary. Descriptions of 21st century classrooms tend to have the following characteristics:

- Real-world context
- Project-based culminating assessments
- Ongoing formative assessment
- 21st century skills
- Character/leadership education
- Concept-based learning
- Global perspective
- Collaborative learning
- Personalized learning

APPROACHES TO INTEGRATION

Robin Fogarty (1991) offered 10 different interpretations of curriculum integration, as shown in Figure 1.1. Applying her chart, teachers could make sense of their own practices in light of the 10 possibilities. For example, most elementary teachers were already teaching similar skills such as literacy across the curriculum. Teachers in the higher grades could see how different skill sets appeared in different subject areas. This opened the door to new understandings of the potential for integration.

Fogarty's 10 positions did not exactly fit my own experience as the leader of a provincial curriculum team developing integrated curriculum. For me, her last two examples were not integration, because students experienced connections during independent studies.

Figure 1.1 Robin Fogarty's 10 Approaches to Integration

1

Description
The traditional model of separate and distinct disciplines, which fragments the subject areas.

Fragmented
Periscope—one direction; one sighting; narrow focus on single discipline

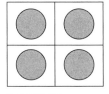

Example
Teacher applied this view in Math, Science, Social Studies, Language Arts, OR Sciences, Humanities, Fine and Practical Arts.

2 OPERA GLASSES

Description
Within each subject area, course content is connected topic to topic, concept to concept, one year's work to the next, and relates idea(s) explicitly.

Connected
Opera Glasses— details of one discipline; focus on subtleties and interconnections

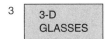

Example
Teacher relates the concept of fractions to decimals, which in turn relates to money, grades, etc.

3 3-D GLASSES

Description
Within each subject area, the teacher targets multiple skills, a social skill, a thinking skill, and a content-specific skill.

Nested
3-D Glasses— multiple dimensions to one scene, topic, or unit

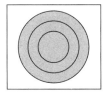

Example
Teacher designs the unit on photosynthesis to simultaneously target consensus seeking (social skills), sequencing (thinking), and plant life cycle (science content).

4 EYE GLASSES

Description
Topics or units of study are rearranged and sequenced to coincide with one another. Similar ideas are taught in concert while remaining separate subjects.

Sequenced
Eyeglasses—varied internal content framed by broad, related concepts

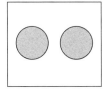

Example
English teacher presents an historical novel depicting a particular period while the History teacher teaches that same historical period.

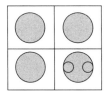

(Continued)

Figure 1.1 (Continued)

5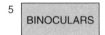

Shared
Binoculars—two
disciplines that
share overlapping
concepts and skills

Description
Shared planning and teaching take place
in two disciplines in which overlapping concepts or
ideas emerge as organizing elements.

Example
Science and Math teachers use
data collection, charting, and
graphing as shared concepts that
can be team-taught.

6

Webbed
Telescope—broad
view of entire
constellation as
one theme,
webbed to the
various elements

Description
A fertile theme is webbed to curriculum contents
and disciplines; subjects use the theme to sift
out appropriate concepts, topics, and ideas.

Example
Teacher presents a simple topical
theme, such as the circus, and
webs it to the subject areas.
A conceptual theme, such as
conflict, can be webbed for more
depth in the theme approach.

7

Threaded
Magnifying Glass—
big ideas that
magnify all content
through a
metacurricular
approach

Description
The metacurricular approach threads thinking skills,
social skills, multiple intelligences, technology, and
study skills through the various disciplines.

Example
Teaching staff targets prediction in
Reading, Math, and Science lab
experiments while Social Studies
teacher targets forecasting current
events, and thus threads the skill
(prediction) across disciplines.

8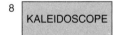

Integrated
Kaleidoscope—new
patterns and
designs that use the
basic elements of
each discipline

Description
This interdisciplinary approach matches
subjects for overlaps in topics and concepts
with some team teaching in an authentic
integrated model.

Example
In Math, Science, Social Studies,
Fine Arts, Language Arts, and
Practical Arts teachers look for
patterning models and approach
content through these patterns.

9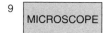

Immersed
Microscope—
intensely personal
view that allows
microscopic
explanation as all
content is filtered

Description
The disciplines become part of the learner's
lens of expertise; the learner filters all content
through this lens and becomes immersed in
his or her own experience.

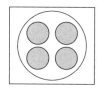

Example
Student or doctoral candidate has
an area of expert interest and sees
all learning through that lens.

10

Networked
Prism—a view that
creates multiple
dimensions and
directions of
focus

Description
Learner filters all learning through the expert's
eye and makes internal connections that lead to
external networks of experts in related fields.

Example
Architect, while adopting the
CAD/CAM technology for design,
networks with technical programmers
and expands her knowledge base,
just as she had traditionally done
with interior designers.

SOURCE: Adapted with permission of the publisher from *Integrating Curricula with Multiple Intelligences: Teams, Themes, and Threads* by Robin Fogarty and Judy Stoeher © 1995 by SkyLight Training and Publishing, Inc., from the chart on page 24, © 1991 by Robin Fogarty, extrapolated from "Design Options for an Integrated Curriculum" by Heidi Hayes Jacobs in *Interdisciplinary Curriculum*, ASCD, 1989.

My team's definition of integration shifted as we worked on creating a curriculum document (Drake, 1991). We experienced three major shifts that felt profound. These shifts included changes in philosophy, in our perceptions of how knowledge and skills were interconnected, and in our ideas about assessment. Most important, our task of creating integrated curriculum was startlingly different depending on which shift we were in. We discovered that we were not the first people to experience these three different positions, and there was a common language for them—multidisciplinary, interdisciplinary, and transdisciplinary.

Were any of these positions superior to the others? At that time, I was convinced that one position was not superior to another, but that each orientation offered advantages in different contexts and for different purposes (Drake, 1993). In the 21st century context, all approaches need to be standards-based, and this controversy is not really relevant. Each approach is as valid as another as long as it honors accountability mandates.

No matter the approach, connections are made around a topic, theme, concept, problem, or issue. There is some controversy about what makes a better organizer. Educators claim that organizing curricula around a topic like "pioneers" or "bears" leads to superficial curricula, because teachers could do a trivial activity like counting the number of bears in a picture book and claim to have added "math" to their unit. To ensure depth, a curriculum needs to be organized around richer concepts. In Chapter 3, the development of rich concepts is discussed in detail.

DEGREES OF INTEGRATION

As was shown in Figure 1.1, there are different ways to approach integration. One of the major theoretical questions of the late 1980s and early 1990s was whether the approaches were hierarchal. Many theorists agreed that there was definitely a range of approaches that appeared to be hierarchal in that they became more and more integrated (Drake, 1993; Erickson, 1995; Jacobs, 1989). A common way to see this hierarchal range is illustrated in Figure 1.2. Four of these approaches will be explored here.

Fusion

One of the first steps on the integration ladder is fusion. Here, something is fused to the already existing curriculum. Technology, for example, which is often infused across the curriculum, is often an integral part of project-based learning where the use of technology goes beyond a WebQuest or Internet research to "students are expected to use technology in a meaningful way to help investigate or present their knowledge" (Milentijevic, Ciric, & Vojinovic, 2008, p. 1131). Environmental awareness and/or character education are often fused into different subject areas at all levels of the curriculum. In Ontario, for example, teachers are mandated to infuse environmental awareness into every subject at every grade level. In the United States, there is some movement in this direction.

Figure 1.2   Different Approaches to Integration as a Hierarchy

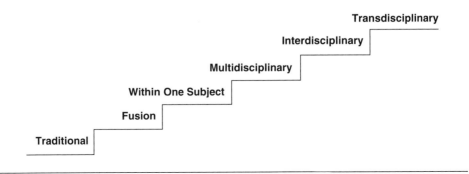

At Fullerton IV Elementary School in Roseburg Oregon, math is fused to history, art, music, and the computer lab from K to 5. Math is considered to be problem solving and a way to communicate. Students, for example, create musical scores thinking of mathematical patterns. In art, they design shapes and consider symmetry. Studying history, they research the Titanic. A part of this study is to go outside and discover how long the boat was (882 1/2 feet) by estimating and then measuring. There is a part-time math coach who helps train the teachers. Since the new math curriculum was introduced in 2000, test scores have soared, and 98% of students are at or above grade level. This rise in scores occurred in spite of the fact that the percentage of students qualifying for free lunch rose to 60% during the same period. Students interviewed on YouTube report that math is their favorite subject (http://www.youtube.com/watch?v=E91gAjunqOM).

Physical activity can be fused into academic classes. New York state law requires that students get 120 minutes of physical activity a week, but one district in Rochester had to eliminate many physical education teachers. The remaining teachers at School 35 have embraced the idea of fusion, recognizing the research that says physical activity will stimulate the brain, and learning will be easier. Teachers find ways to introduce movement into their classes. They have students act out vocabulary words, have warm-ups during announcements, and take breaks to play Nintendo Wii or the popular video game *Dance Dance Revolution* (Lankes, 2011).

Groups representing teachers of history built a case for infusing history into reading programs and instruction at large (King & Zucker, 2005; Manzo, 1996). Why? An unintended consequence of the No Child Left Behind Act was that the emphasis on improving reading and math test scores pushed history into a marginalized position. This is still true with the Common Core State Standards. Teachers looking for more time to spend on language and math activities tend to pinch it from social studies, art, and physical education. Social studies teachers say that as a result, students are not learning how to be engaged citizens of their community. The infusion of history would mean that it is taught in every class.

Multidisciplinary

In the multidisciplinary approach, disciplines remain very distinct, but deliberate connections are made between or among them. See Figure 1.3 for a graphic of an organizing center. At the elementary level, students may visit different learning centers to study a theme. For example, students may study "communities" and engage in disciplinary activities, rotating through a social studies center, a language arts center, an arts center, a math center, and a science center. In high school, the students may study a similar theme in their different classes for different disciplines. A typical example is students studying the American Civil War in history and simultaneously reading *The Red Badge of Courage* in English. The civil war theme may arise in drama class and visual arts or other subject areas. Sometimes this is called a *parallel curriculum.* The same subject matter is taught at the same time in different disciplines. Figure 1.4 shows a planning template for a parallel curriculum.

From the multidisciplinary perspective, teachers do not need to make very many changes. Content and assessment remain firmly within an intact subject. Generally, students are expected to make the connections among subject areas, rather than the teachers having taught them explicitly.

Yet within this multidisciplinary perspective, there are also degrees of integration. A common approach is to create an integrated final project that students work toward in different subject areas. At Harmony Magnet School in Strathmore, California, there is a focus on integrated curriculum and two different pathways students can choose: engineering and performance arts. The work is project–based, and students demonstrate proficiency by doing. In the engineering track, students conduct experiments on corrosion. In geometry they focused on tensions and load bearing. In engineering they used this knowledge to create virtual models of a bridge. Three years after the school opened, every 10th grader passed the California High School Exit Exam in math, and 98% passed in English language arts (Hoachlander & Yanofsky, 2011).

Figure 1.3   Multidisciplinary Organizing Center

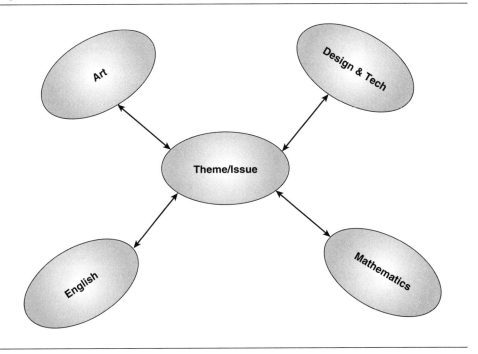

Figure 1.4   A Planning Template for Parallel Disciplines

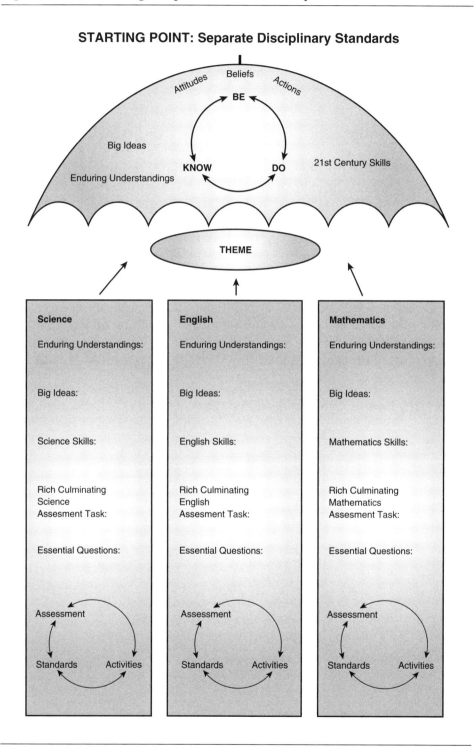

In Chapter 3 there is a description of the Stamford HP Catalyst Project at Scofield Middle School in Connecticut. This is essentially a multidisciplinary project where students complete a rich assessment task and learn about different aspects of the topic (water quality) in different subject areas.

Interdisciplinary

The interdisciplinary curriculum makes more explicit connections across the subject areas. Again, the curriculum revolves around a common theme, issue, or problem, but interdisciplinary concepts or skills are emphasized across the subject areas rather than within them. For example, the unit may be organized around a universal concept, such as conflict or change, or may emphasize generic research skills. In Chapter 3 you will see that the three high schools that are profiled are basically interdisciplinary in nature. See Figure 1.5 to see an organizing center for interdisciplinary curriculum. A planning template for such a curriculum is in Figure 1.6.

It is easy to see how the Common Core State Standards fit interdisciplinary work. With the emphasis on literacy in different subject areas and on understanding informational texts, educators will need to teach subject content at the same time as they teach literacy skills. Murray and

Figure 1.5   Interdisciplinary Organizing Center

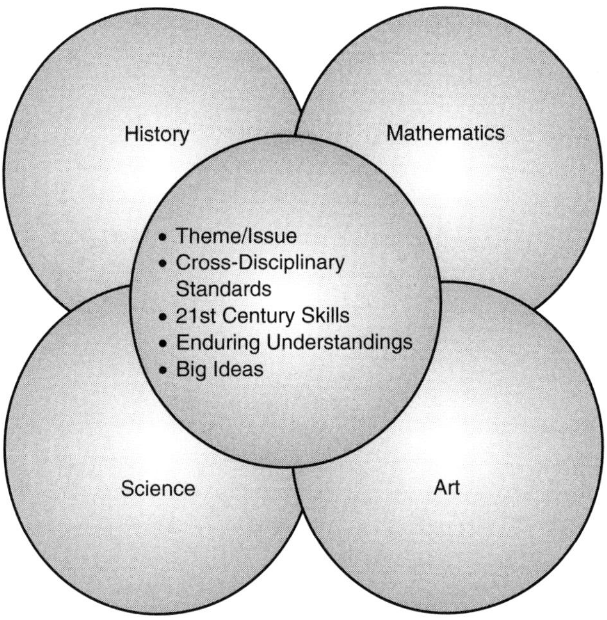

Figure 1.6   A Planning Template for Interdisciplinary Curriculum

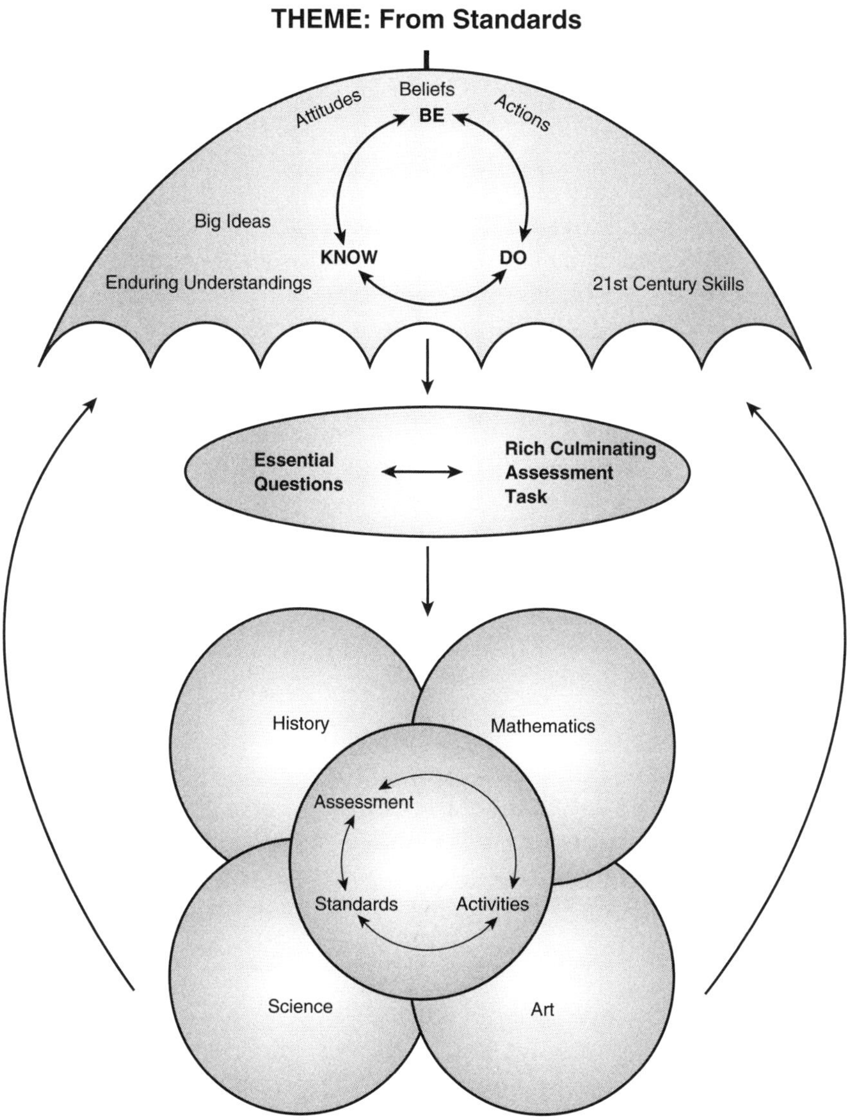

THEME: From Standards

History · Mathematics · Science · Art

Assessment · Standards · Activities

Essential Questions ↔ Rich Culminating Assessment Task

BE · KNOW · DO · Attitudes · Beliefs · Actions · Big Ideas · Enduring Understandings · 21st Century Skills

Bellacero (2008) describe how they integrated math and writing for the National Writing Project for Grade 8 students. They had students look at gossip magazines to discover the writing style of the genre. Then they personally created math stories that were written in the gossip style. One article was entitled "Hypotenuse Caught in Love Triangle," and another was "Polynomial Weight Loss System." Students modeled this approach and wrote their own articles. Ongoing assessment was done as students created their articles. Teachers were amazed at the quality of the writing and how imaginatively students integrated math successfully into their stories.

John Hersey High School in Chicago (suburban, middle class, mostly white students) and Chicago International Charter School Northtown Academy Campus (low-income, minority, urban students) implemented an interdisciplinary curriculum that also integrated traditional expectations (Ferrero, 2006). Through a vertical mapping of the curriculum, teachers carefully mapped the skills and content necessary to meet the ACT college readiness standards and pass standardized diagnostic assessments. Students were grouped by ability to learn the core content and master these skills. These skills were considered the foundation for higher order thinking and necessary for all students to participate fully in the integrated units and hands-on projects.

The success of this interdisciplinary/traditional approach was dramatic. Hersey's average ACT test scores rose from the 60th percentile in 2000 to the 75th in 2005. Student growth on benchmarked performances rose approximately 71%. For every 100 students who entered Grade 9 requiring remedial help, more than 50% enrolled in college prep or honors courses by the Grade 11. Most gains were in reading and writing where the model was most fully developed. Northtown's students were similarly successful.

Transdisciplinary

The transdisciplinary approach begins with a real-life context. It does not begin with the disciplines or with common concepts or skills. What is usually considered most important is the perceived relevance for the students.

An influential educator in the transdisciplinary area is James Beane (1993, 1997). He advocates that the curriculum be developed from the interests of the students themselves. For him, these questions can be categorized as personal growth or social issues. Brown (2006) also recommends that students create their own curriculum based on their own questions. He suggests that in this way, students will learn and apply higher order thinking skills that prepare them for the world of work. His experience demonstrates that students can and do ask substantive questions that revolve around the following:

Environmental issues

Making and managing money

Future technology

How to make the world a peaceful place

Prejudice

Power—who has it and how is it managed?

Crime and violence

What does the future hold for me?

The Alpha program at Shelburne Community School in Shelburne, Vermont, offers an exemplary example of what can happen when Beane's (1993, 1997) and Brown's (2006) philosophies are applied. Operating since 1972, this alternative, multiage middle school has withstood the test of time. This program is highlighted in Chapter 3. Two examples of programs that occurred at Shelburne Community School before 1993 are "Adopt a Business" and "The Big Alpha Circus," both well described by Stevenson and Carr (1993). These are rich examples of integrated curricula. More recent detailed descriptions of the process are also available (Drake & Burns, 2004; Smith & Myers, 2001). Figure 1.7 shows a transdisciplinary organizing center, and Figure 1.8 offers a planning template.

The International School of the Americas is a magnet school of about 450 high school students in San Antonio, Texas. In 2009, over 8% of the senior class earned National Merit Scholar recognition with two semifinalists, four Commended Scholars, and three Hispanic Scholars. This school is intent on providing students with the academic knowledge and skills to work in a global context and "to change the world" (Albright & Breidenstein, 2004). The school offers a rich, integrated curriculum. All students participate in travel expeditions, community service, and a career-exploration internship, and all create final portfolios of their learning in their final year. Students choose an international challenge and conduct research, prepare an informative webpage, design and implement a service-learning project, and present their findings to a panel of community judges. Topics they have covered range from homelessness to teen alcohol abuse. Each grade visits a specific destination to learn firsthand about an international issue. As freshmen, for example, they travel to Heifer International Airport in Arkansas, where they live for four days experiencing the challenge of economic need and learning about sustainable economic development. Sophomores learn about different cultures by travels within and outside the United States. In the junior year, they visit the significant points in the civil rights movement in Alabama to investigate the concept of justice. In the senior year, they go to

Figure 1.7   Transdisciplinary Organizing Center

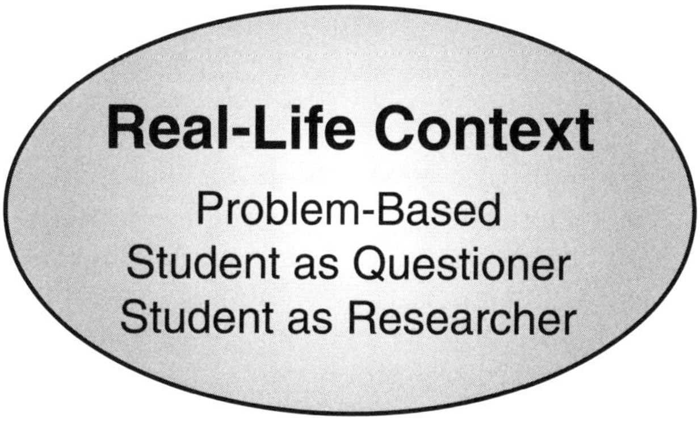

Figure 1.8   A Planning Template for a Transdisciplinary Curriculum

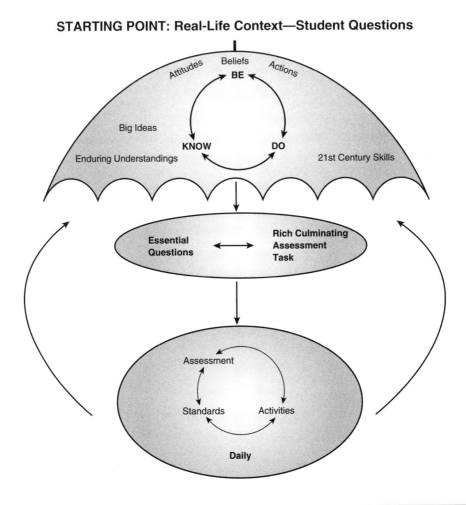

Washington D.C. to more fully understand the government of the United States and compare it to that of other countries around the world.

Problem-based learning (PBL) is often transdisciplinary. Grounded in the project method of the progressive education era, PBL begins with a problem or question rather than with a discipline or a set of disciplines. Much like integrated curriculum, PBL is difficult to define in a concise way. Dr. Helen Padgett, past president of the International Society for Technology in Education and director of professional development for Technology Based Learning and Research at Arizona State University, knows a great deal about integrating technology into the curriculum to improve student learning and achievement. She describes three versions of PBL: project-based learning, problem-based learning, and challenge-based learning (Rillero & Padgett, 2012).

Project-based learning is an instructional strategy in which students work from an engaging question and produce a product that addresses that question. Problem-based learning is student centered and involves an ill-structured problem set in real-world context. Students need to define what they need to learn, and teachers act as facilitators. Challenge-based learning (CBL) begins with a Big Idea and is followed by the creation of an essential question, a challenge, guiding questions, activities, and resources; it creates a process for finding and articulating the solution to a challenge (http://ali.apple.com/cbl/). CBL tackles real-world problems using technology commonly used in daily life and sharing the results with the world. Both PBL and CBL can be transdisciplinary in nature, as a real-world problem or concept is not bound by a discipline.

Research on PBL confirms its effectiveness. Three classes of students underwent a highly controlled experiment at the middle school level. There were three different conditions to learn the same material. Some students learned by a teacher lecture. Other students completed PBL projects covering the same material collaboratively. Still other students did PBL as individuals. The problems were ill structured. The student population was very diverse both ethnically and in socioeconomic status. Results showed that under both PBL conditions the students acquired deeper comprehension and were better able to apply concepts in new settings than the students who learned through a lecture.

Searching on the Internet showed me how project-based learning and problem-based learning are often considered to be the same thing. The Buck Institute for Education has a very helpful website to understand project-based/problem-based learning offering a wide range of resources (http://www.bie.org/about/). Some of these projects remain in one discipline. Others involve many disciplines. The criteria for a rigorous project are as follows:

- It has a relevant and meaningful topic.
- It has a driving question, created by students, that is open-ended, complex, and linked to standards.
- Students choose the topic, question, resources, and product.
- It requires use of 21st Century Skills.
- It requires real inquiry and questioning.
- It involves ongoing feedback and revision.
- Student work is publically presented. (Larmer & Mergendoller, 2010)

A synthesis of a large number of meta-analyses of PBL research on problem-based learning indicated that PBL was superior to traditional education for long-term retention of knowledge, skills development, and the satisfaction of students. In contrast, traditional education was more effective for short-term retention of knowledge (Strobel & van Barneveld, 2009). Also, students who had been taught with PBL learned more of the

21st Century Skills than did their counterparts taught traditionally (Ravitz, Hixson, English, & Mergendoller, 2011).

CBL, as mentioned above, is a good example of 21st century learning. A pilot project on CBL involved 321 students (primarily in grades 9 and 10), 29 teachers, and seven schools, with 16 subjects represented. A resulting white paper describes CBL as "a new teaching model that incorporates the best aspects of problem-based learning, project-based learning and contextual teaching while focusing on real problems faced in the real world" (Johnson, Smith, Smythe, & Varon, 2009, p. 7). Challenges in this project are global in nature, addressing issues such as war, or the sustainability of global water supplies. The teacher acts as a coach, and use of the Internet is an integral part of the learning—whether for research or for global connections such as interviewing experts in other countries.

Two examples from the white paper illustrate how challenges and CBL can look in the classroom. Mooresville High School in North Carolina chose "war" as the Big Idea it would pursue. Their Essential Question was, "What is war and how does it affect society?" The challenge was to use World War I as a reference point to tell the story of war and its impact on society. The 49 students who participated researched World War I and created a multimedia website, including movies and podcasts, to tell the story of war. The site has a WebQuest to help visitors learn more and a video to promote the website (http://www5.mgsd.k12.nc.us/staffsites/worldwarone).

The second example comes from Manor New Technology High School in Manor, Texas, where students explored the Big Idea of "sustainability of food." Their question was "What are the effects of your food consumption?" The challenge was to inspire positive changes in food consumption choices. Thirty-seven students and five teachers spent a week to research what impact the production and distribution of food had on the environment. They also looked at healthy and nonhealthy foods and how to make good choices. They created a "Mythbusters"-like video to show what they learned and encourage healthy choices.

Interviews and journal entries were the primary sources of data used in the pilot study, and they captured "virtually every aspect of the process, with perspectives representing faculty, support staff, administration and, of course, students" (Johnson et al., 2009, p. 13). Fully 100% of students reported satisfaction. Teachers reported that students exceeded expectations. Twenty-eight of 29 faculty reported that students embraced the work and worked well together collaboratively; 75% noted positive change with their students. Students believed that they had learned 21st Century Skills, and 80% thought that their project had made a difference. The projects that students perceived to the most relevant were of the highest quality. Students did not complete the two projects that they found the least relevant. The research was supported by the New Media Consortium (http://www.nmc.org), an international group composed of hundreds of universities, colleges, research centers, museums, and other organizations interested in learning, such as Apple and Hewlett-Packard.

A SUMMARY OF THE DIFFERENT APPROACHES TO INTEGRATION

In the 21st century, the concept of multidisciplinary, interdisciplinary, and transdisciplinary approaches can still be helpful in order to understand different starting places. The process of creating interdisciplinary work has changed since the 1980s and 1990s, because teachers must teach to the standards. Although it may seem to be the same process on the surface, decidedly, it is not.

In an age of accountability, the different approaches of integrated curricula blur as teachers apply the standards-based principles to integration. There are certain rules that seem to go hand in hand with accountability mandates. These rules begin with the requirement that the teacher must cover the standards and prepare students for required standardized tests. Across North America, the process of designing down or mapping backwards is very popular for designing any curriculum, whether it be within a discipline or interdisciplinary. At the same time, curriculum designers can use the best teaching and learning strategies to enable the students to meet the standards.

Figure 1.9 shows how the different approaches blur when a teacher plans using the standards-based rules.

In this chapter, we have looked at different approaches to integrated curriculum. The first part dealt with how these positions looked in the late 1980s and early 1990s. Then we looked at how these positions changed with the advent of standards and standardized testing. In the next chapter, we will begin to explore how to create interdisciplinary curricula.

Figure 1.9   Comparing and Contrasting the Different Interdisciplinary Approaches

How do various approaches differ?		
Approach	**Starting Point Intentions**	**Primary Assessment Concern**
Fusion	A focus that is embedded into all school life. Some examples are environmental stewardship, international education, and social-emotional learning.	Assessment remains subject specific.

(Continued)

Figure 1.9 (Continued)

Approach	Starting Point Intentions	Primary Assessment Concern
Multidisciplinary	The concepts and skills of the disciplines	Disciplinary concepts and skills
Interdisciplinary	Common concepts and skills across the disciplines	Common concepts and skills across the disciplines
Transdisciplinary	Real-world context, student-generated questions, use of life skills	Authentic assessment in a real-life context
What is the same among all approaches?		
Fusion	• Mapping backwards design—using standards • Exemplary teaching/learning strategies • Set in a student-relevant real-world context as much as possible • Performance demonstrations as well as standardized assessment • Assessment for learning (see Chapter 5)	
Multidisciplinary		
Interdisciplinary		
Transdisciplinary		

DISCUSSION QUESTIONS

1. How does a brief history of curriculum integration help your understanding?

2. Examine Fogarty's 10 approaches to integration. Describe any that you have experienced either as a student or as an educator.

3. What is the main difference among multidisciplinary, interdisciplinary, and transdisciplinary approaches?

4. Discuss Figure 1.9 and its implications for curriculum design.

SUGGESTED ACTIVITIES

1. Read the examples for multidisciplinary, interdisciplinary, and transdisciplinary curricula. Using your local standards and the Common Core State Standards, select a content area and theme for an integrated unit based on two or more subjects. How would this unit look if you taught it from the multidisciplinary, interdisciplinary, and transdisciplinary perspectives?

2. Using Figure 1.9, describe how these three different approaches to the same unit would be similar and how they would be different.

2

Accountability and Two-Dimensional Thinking

The goal of this book is to help readers design curricula that meet the current needs for both relevance and accountability. This is particularly important at a time when educators across North America are thinking deeply and collectively about what education should look like, as most states set about implementing the Common Core State Standards. This chapter explains some of the basic practices that ensure that any curriculum—be it disciplinary or interdisciplinary—follows accountability mandates. It begins with a brief discussion of accountability, the role of standards in curriculum planning, and some challenges teachers experience with standards. It follows this with an exploration of the Big Picture and the Know/Do/Be Umbrella. The focus then zooms into the micro level to unpack the standards themselves. A "design-down process" is described as the template for aligning interdisciplinary work with standards. Finally, an approach to curriculum mapping is offered as a precursor to any curriculum design and one that is useful for interdisciplinary work.

WHAT IS ACCOUNTABILITY?

Accountability is an umbrella term that generally refers to educators acting in accordance with how the public has determined they are to act and to achieve what they are expected to achieve. Darling-Hammond (2004) stated that political, legal, bureaucratic, market (school choice), and professional accountability influence educational policy. No single form of accountability stands alone. Intelligent accountability reflects this interconnectedness. Intelligent accountability is transparent, focuses on helping schools, increases individual and collective capacity building, involves shared responsibility, and is interventionist in only extreme cases of need; external and internal accountability seem almost seamless (Hargreaves & Shirley, 2009). Darling-Hammond (2010) calls for reciprocal intelligent accountability. That is, school systems demonstrate their accountability not only to the public but also to educators and students by providing adequate resources for good teaching.

Yet increasingly since the mid 1990s, accountability has meant a focus on standardized educational procedures, prescribed curricula and texts, and test-based strategies tied to tracking. This approach to accountability has not been particularly successful. Convincing evidence shows some of the unintended consequences of high-stakes testing are the narrowing of the curriculum, the failure of grade retention to increase student success, and the encouragement of students to go into special education classes or to drop out of school (Au, 2007; David, 2011). When the stakes are high—funding or one's reputation—teachers can resort to ineffective teaching practices such as "teaching to the test." Students may do better on the tests by remembering material in the short term. But, in the long term, the content is easily forgotten, and there has been no real understanding of the material.

Today, the United States is falling behind many other countries in international rankings (Ravich, 2011). The Common Core State Standards are a response to a perceived crisis in education. The success of the Common Core State Standards, however, will depend upon how they are translated into curriculum and are assessed: Without a collaborative process to develop curricula, it is likely that vested interests such as test and textbook publishers will take over (David, 2011). In this book, we explore how students can meet the prescribed educational standards through an interdisciplinary curriculum that opens the curriculum rather than narrows it.

WHAT IS A STANDARDS-BASED APPROACH?

An effective standards-based approach adopts the following premises for both disciplinary and interdisciplinary work:

A design-down curriculum planning process is used.

The focus is on what students will do, not what the teacher will do.

Standards, teaching strategies, and assessment are aligned.

The standards are observable and measurable.

The assessment of standards is embedded in instructional strategies.

Big Ideas and Enduring Understandings act as an umbrella for the content. They reappear in the curriculum at different levels and in different subjects (e.g., change, interdependence, conflict, objectivity, and causality).

21st Century Skills (complex performance skills) reappear year after year and across subject areas (e.g., literacy, problem solving, and technological skills). For example, in the English language arts, the design of the Common Core State Standards is to "create a staircase of increasing text complexity," so each year students build their skills with increasingly complex texts.

The teacher is free to teach in any style as long as the standards are met.

With each new version of curriculum documents, the standards usually improve. There is a clearer consensus on what students need to know and do, and the standards themselves are articulated more clearly. With the advent of the Common Core State Standards, there are similar goals for all states committed to using them. These standards are internationally benchmarked and have had been vetted by educators, parents, and national math and English organizations. Although these standards exist only in language and math (with science soon to be released) and will be revised over time, they eliminate many of the problems of different standards for each state, such as these:

Uneven quality of standards from different regions

Too many standards created at too many levels of education

Not all standards worth achieving

Some ambiguous standards

Some standards too narrow and irrelevant to facilitate any deep understanding

Often, the challenge is not in the standards themselves but in our assumptions about how to work with them. It takes thoughtfulness and patience to fully understand what a standard is asking a student to know, do, and be. Teachers often "cover the standards" in the same spirit that they cover the content. It is quite easy to check off a standard as completed, when it has not really been addressed thoroughly or it is peripheral to the learning. It is also easy to overlook any new skills that need to be taught to achieve a standard. As well, some teachers assume that once a standard is taught, it has been learned. And although all students should achieve the standard, not all students can achieve the standards in the same way at the same time.

TWO-DIMENSIONAL THINKING

A major challenge today is designing a curriculum that is both relevant and accountable. Accountability can be achieved, in part, by the alignment of the curriculum. Alignment means that the standards, content, assessment, and instructional strategies are coherent and make a complementary fit. An aligned curriculum is sometimes called a *seamless curriculum.* Curriculum planning needs to be thoughtful, with a systematic process for continually checking to ensure that all parts are interconnected. Alignment is a commonly identified strategy for improving student performance (Elmore & Rothman, 1999; Mitchell, 1998; Ohio State Department of Education, 2001).

For optimum student success, the day-to-day curriculum must be both aligned *and* relevant. To create such a curriculum, teachers need to work in two dimensions at the same time. Martin (2007) calls this "integrative thinking." Curriculum designers need to focus both on the Big Picture and the disciplines simultaneously. Figure 2.1 shows a variety of metaphors for this two-dimensional or integrative thinking.

THE KNOW/DO/BE UMBRELLA

To begin to create curriculum that is both relevant and accountable, teachers need a sense of the Big Picture. In a very general sense, what does a K–12 curriculum look like? Are some subject areas more important than

Figure 2.1   Two-Dimensional Thinking

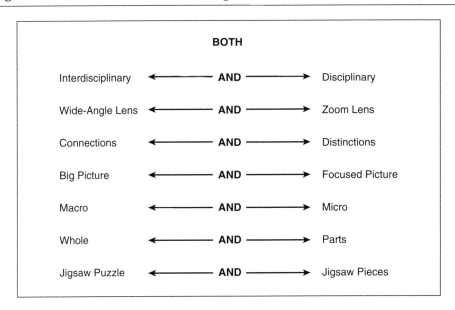

others? Do certain knowledge and skills reappear throughout the curriculum from K to 12? What is most important to learn? Where does the "affect" or student behavior fit into the Big Picture?

An overall view of the purpose of education emerges when one reads all the K to 12 subject documents from one jurisdiction using a wide-angle lens. Having done this for several jurisdictions, I am aware that mandated guidelines are quite similar in many ways. Typically, the purpose embedded in the documents is to educate students to be productive citizens in a democratic society. Vermont's framework offers a good example. "Every Vermont student should become a competent, caring, creative, productive, and responsible citizen committed to learning through life" (State of Vermont Department of Education, 2005, p. A5). *Vermont's Framework of Standards and Learning Opportunities* (ibid.) can be accessed through http://www.state.vt.us/educ/new/html/pubs/framework.html.

One way to think about the Big Picture—what students need to Know, Do, and Be across all subjects—is to view it as an umbrella over the K–12 curriculum. This umbrella represents the core purpose of education and covers all the subject areas, providing the framework within which curriculum must be developed. Figure 2.2 shows the Know/Do/Be (KDB) Umbrella and its relationship to subject areas.

In most jurisdictions, this umbrella is not explicit. *Vermont's Framework of Standards and Learning Opportunities* (State of Vermont Department of Education, 2005) provides a thoughtful overview of the entire

Figure 2.2   The KDB Umbrella

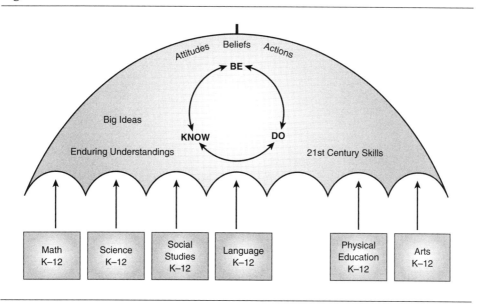

curriculum framework. The framework acts as an umbrella for the various disciplinary standards. The framework is divided into "Vital Results" and "Fields of Knowledge." The Vital Results are interdisciplinary and clearly lead toward students becoming productive citizens. The Vital Results include communication, reasoning and problem solving, personal development, and civic and social responsibility. Students can work toward these results in every subject area. They are the skills and qualities that are considered so important for students to learn that they act as an umbrella for K–12 subject area content. Figure 2.3 offers an overview (an interpretation) of Vermont's framework of Vital Results viewed as a KDB umbrella.

The Ontario Curriculum Grades 11 and 12 Interdisciplinary Studies guideline (Ontario Ministry of Education, 2002) offers a different view of the Big Picture. This document allows teachers to bring together two or more existing courses to create a new entity—an interdisciplinary credit. This credit can be issued for the university-bound stream or at the applied level. There is no restriction as to what existing courses can be integrated. The standards of such a course transcend the boundaries

Figure 2.3   An Overview of Vermont's Curriculum Framework Seen as a KDB Umbrella

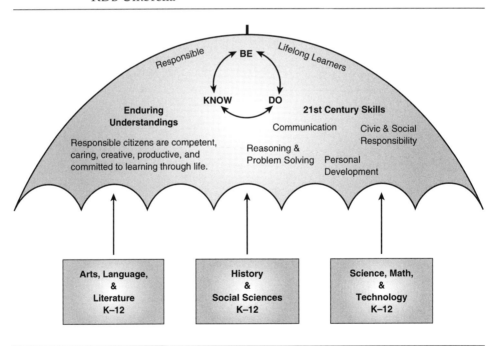

SOURCE: Based on Vermont's Framework of Standards and Learning Opportunities (State of Vermont Department of Education, 2005).

of disciplines and are unique to interdisciplinary work. They revolve around an interdisciplinary approach to

Theory and foundation

Processes and methods of research

Implementation, evaluation impacts, and consequences

Figure 2.4 shows a KDB umbrella for any credit course developed under this plan.

A sample curriculum from the Ontario Curriculum Centre is available online at http://resources.curriculum.org/csc/library/profiles/11/pdf/IDC3OB.pdf. This sample course is called Introduction to Information Studies, and it integrates the arts, business studies, English, guidance and career education, social studies, Canadian and world studies, science, and technological studies. It examines the evolution and impact of information, communication, and computing on society from the beginning of writing to the development of the Internet. It was developed by teachers for teachers in partnership with the provincial boards of education and disciplinary associations and was funded by the ministry. It is well worth exploring this sample as a framework for interdisciplinary work.

Figure 2.4   A KDB Umbrella Based on the Ontario Curriculum Grades 11 and 12 Interdisciplinary Studies

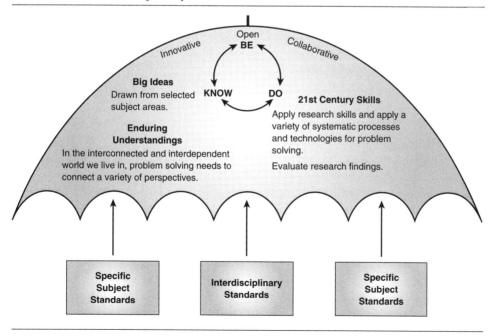

DESIGNING DOWN

A process called "designing down" or "mapping backward" (Wiggins & McTighe, 2005) is a popular and sound way to align disciplinary and inter-disciplinary curricula. Indeed the Common Core State Standards were created using a form of a design-down process. These standards were mapped backwards from what students needed to know and be able to do to be ready for college and careers.

I have adapted the design-down approach for interdisciplinary work using the KDB umbrella as the framework. Backward design involves addressing four basic curriculum design questions. These questions are the following:

1. What do we (I) want the students to know, do, and be (KDB)?

2. Can standards be clustered in meaningful ways that cut across the curriculum?

3. What is acceptable evidence to show that students have achieved the KDB?

4. What educational experiences will enable the students to demon-strate achievement of the KDB?

Often, the first question is not asked with enough emphasis. Educators spend a lot of time working on effective assessment and teaching/learning strategies, but they neglect to ask if what they are teaching and assessing is really significant. Understandably, most teachers accept what is dictated to them in policy documents. These documents rarely help teachers address the question of relative significance—although the Common Core State Standards have clustered related math standards together and given them a cluster heading to signify what is most important about this group of standards. It is up to individual educators to really determine the KDB in their local context—a context that allows for designing a curriculum that is relevant to their particular learners. It is also important that these goals be set in a larger context. Thus, we must ask, what is really worth knowing, doing, and being in the 21st century?

The second question asks how subject areas are connected. Although many guidelines do recommend interdisciplinary connections, they often do not make these connections explicit. I think there is a very practical reason for this. Most documents are discipline based, and there is no one unifying framework as in Vermont. The documents are created for the most part by disciplinary specialists. These exemplary educators no doubt recognize how interdisciplinary connections can enrich their discipline but to create the subject guidelines, they focus on the area of their specialization rather than the Big Picture.

In reality, there are a great many natural connections when you read different documents, but often teachers only read and think about one document and the grade level that they are teaching at. Many of the connections have not been made explicit. Big Ideas and Enduring Understandings do cross subject areas. Patterns, for example, can be found in math, science, arts, history, social studies, and language. We also find that the 21st Century Skills are represented; for example, standards involving communication skills are found in all documents. Now this connection has been made explicit by the Common Core State Standards for Literacy in History/Social Studies, Science, and Technical Subjects. This is an interdisciplinary approach to literacy. The "Be" of Know/Do/Be is not necessarily that easy to find in these documents, but one of the characteristics of a Common Core anchor standard is "collaboration" for students at grades K to 12.

The third question revolves around acceptable evidence to show that the students have learned what they were supposed to learn. For Wiggins and McTighe (2005), this involves developing a core assessment task that demonstrates the core learnings (Enduring Understandings, Big Ideas, and 21st Century Skills). Core learnings also involve the skills that are necessary to know to demonstrate the understanding of content. For example, if students are required to do a PowerPoint presentation to communicate their knowledge of content, they may also need to learn the skills needed to create and deliver a PowerPoint presentation. Wiggins and McTighe stress the importance of performance assessments. We cannot know that students know something unless they can do something with what they know (as opposed to taking a pen-and-paper evaluation such as a standardized test). This second question moves into the area of assessment instruments. We need tools to accurately measure different degrees of student learning. A good rubric, for example, can tell us at what level a student is achieving.

The fourth question revolves around creating daily learning experiences that will enable the student to achieve the KDB. Learning activities are aligned with standards, and appropriate assessments are integrated into these activities. Each instructional activity has a purpose in designed-down curriculum.

DESIGNING DOWN AND INTERDISCIPLINARY WORK

In this book, Chapters 4 and 5 address the three basic questions of backward mapping or designing down. I have presented the process as linear, because this is a way to make a complex process understandable. In reality, it is not linear in practice even in disciplinary work. As educators work with one particular step, they need to be able to see the whole, and when they work with the Big Picture, they need to be able to see the parts. This iterative process requires two-dimensional or integrative thinking.

To create the whole, we need more than the four fundamental questions of mapping backward. We need strategies that link the parts together and allow us to move back and forth between the macro and micro elements of curriculum design. To keep the flow of the book, these strategies are introduced throughout the book. The strategies include the following:

Scan and cluster for the KDB

Exploratory web

Essential Questions

UNPACKING THE STANDARDS

To understand standards at a deep level, it is necessary to use a zoom lens. The KDB offers a way to unpack or deconstruct a standard. This is not as simple as it sounds. It is very easy to check off a standard as met because it is touched on peripherally during a teaching activity. When one unpacks the standards, it is amazing how complex some of them are. Also, many of them assume that a student already has the skill necessary to achieve the standard. For example, when a student is asked to write an essay that presents a good argument, the teacher needs to be sure that the student has the skills to write such an essay.

To analyze the standards, it is helpful to look at the nouns and verbs. The nouns indicate the Know. The verbs indicate the Do. Confusing the issue, some procedural skills such as the scientific method are both a concept and a skill, so procedural knowledge must also be taught. Also, it is informative to look at whether a Be is explicit or implicit in a standard.

Consider the following preK–12 standards based on *Vermont's Framework of Standards and Learning Opportunities* (State of Vermont, 2005) as presented in Figure 2.5. The verbs have been italicized and the nouns underlined as a way of beginning the task—much like the parsing of a sentence.

In interdisciplinary work, math and English language arts are often considered to be process skills. The content for these subjects comes from other subject areas. Thus the standards are treated a little differently for math and English language arts than they are for other subject areas. In English literature there are many Big Ideas and Enduring Understandings. As you can see from the unpacking in Figure 2.6, the Common Core standards are very dense, and if teachers actually teach to them, the students will be very prepared for college and careers at the end of high school.

Figure 2.5   Unpacking the Standards

	Know (Nouns)	Do (Verbs)	Be
Identify the positive and negative effects of technology.	The positive and negative effects of technology	Identify	Students must make a value judgment on what is negative or positive so they can utilize technology in a way that benefits society.
Students *evaluate* music and music performances.	Evaluation criteria for different categories of music and musical performances	Evaluate	Values are implicit and embedded in the evaluation criteria, so students need to apply these values when they evaluate music and musical performances. They must also be open-minded.
Students *understand* the processes of scientific investigation and design; they *design, conduct, discuss,* and *evaluate* such investigations.	Scientific investigation processes, procedural steps, how to evaluate their performances, how to communicate these processes	Design, conduct, communicate, and evaluate scientific investigations.	Values are implicit; if students follow these procedures, they will conduct "unbiased" investigations that move them closer to the "truth," so objectivity is valued.
Students *understand* the effects of interactions between human and physical systems and *comprehend* the resulting changes in use, distribution, and the significance of resources.	The effects of interactions between human and physical systems Cause-effect cycles	Ambiguous—understanding is vague and does not require a specific skill.	Values are implicit; this topic moves into areas such as the human destruction of the environment. Value judgments about results are also necessary.
Students *know* that religious and philosophical ideas have influenced history.	Religious and philosophical ideas, the influence of these throughout history	Nothing	None are identified, although this is a value-laden topic, so it should engender discernment.

SOURCE: Based on Vermont's Framework of Standards and Learning Opportunities (State of Vermont Department of Education, 2005). Retrieved November 16, 2005, from http://www.state.vt.us/educ/new/pdfdoc/pubs/framework.pdf.

Figure 2.6   Unpacking the Common Core State Standards for English
Language Arts and Mathematics.

	Know	Do	Be
Cite the <u>textual evidence</u> that most strongly *supports* an *analysis* of <u>what the text says</u> as well as *inferences* drawn from the text. (Reading, Grade 8, Informational Texts)	Evidence in a text Analysis in a text Inferences	Identify/do the analysis. Choose the strongest evidence to support an analysis of the text's position. Draw an inference and show how it supports the analysis.	Critical thinker Literate
Gather relevant information from <u>multiple authoritative print and digital sources,</u> *using advanced searches* effectively; *assess* the *strengths and limitations* of each source in terms of *task, purpose, and audience; integrate information into the text selectively* to *maintain the flow of ideas, avoiding plagiarism* and overreliance on any one source and *following* <u>a standard format for citation.</u> (Writing, Grades 11–12, Research to Build and Present Knowledge)	Relevant information Authoritative print and digital sources Task, purpose, and audience Strengths and weaknesses Plagiarism Standard format for citations	Gather relevant information. Use multiple sources. Do an advanced search. Assess strengths and weaknesses for task, purpose, and audience. Integrate information into the text. Maintain flow of ideas. Avoid plagiarism and overreliance on once source. Follow standard format for citation.	Competent researcher Technologically literate Ethical
Paraphrase portions of a text read aloud *or information presented* in <u>diverse media and formats</u>, including *visually, quantitatively, and orally.* (Speaking and Listening, Grade 4, Comprehension and Collaboration)	Understand the text, visual images, numbers, and oral presentations.	Express understanding by paraphrasing the text.	Orally literate Listener Visually literate Numerate

	Know	Do	Be
Follow precisely a <u>multistep procedure</u> when *carrying out experiments, taking measurements,* or *performing technical tasks.* (Reading for Science and Technical Subjects, Grades 6–8, Key Ideas and Details)	Multistep procedure Details of the experiment Measurement Details of technical task	Follow multistep task. Do an experiment. Take measurements. Perform technical tasks.	Scientifically literate Logical Numerate
Use the <u>four operations</u> with <u>whole numbers</u> to *solve problems.* (Operations and Algebraic Thinking. Grade 4)	Whole numbers Addition Subtraction Multiplication Division	Solve problems. Use four operations with whole numbers.	Numerate
Solve <u>real-world problems</u> and <u>mathematical problems</u> involving <u>volume of cylinders, cones, and spheres.</u> (Geometry, Grade 8)	Conceptual understanding of volumes of cones, cylinders, and spheres and resulting formulas	Solve real-world and mathematical problems.	Able to reason abstractly and quantitatively Numerate
Represent data with *plots* on the <u>real number line</u> (dot plots, histograms, and box plots). (Statistics and Probability, High School, Interpreting Categorical and Quantitative Data)	Data Dot plots Histograms Box plots Real number line	Represent data with plots on the real number line and with dot plots, histograms, and box plots.	Objectivity Making sense of numbers Ethical

SOURCE: Based on content from the Common Core State Standards, National Governors Association Center for Best Practices and Council of Chief State School Officers, http://www.corestandards.org.

CURRICULUM MAPPING

Curriculum mapping is a popular strategy used by schools and districts to align the curriculum. Essentially, it is a process for recording the content, skills, and assessment actually taught over a distinct learning period or the course of a year. The purpose is to create a seamless curriculum. It is usually done one discipline at a time. Nevertheless, it is an excellent way to begin to think about integrating the curriculum, since it identifies gaps and connections.

How do you curriculum map? Hale (2008) offers plan with three steps: contemplation, planning, and implementation. Contemplation is the process of reviewing what is being taught and comparing that with what the standards require. It is also a time to compare and discuss with colleagues if this process is being done collaboratively in a setting such as a division meeting. Gaps and redundancies are identified. Teachers also "contemplate" what is most important for students to know, do, and be. Planning involves committing to paper what will be taught and assessed during the week, month, and/or year. Finally implementation is actually teaching what is on the plan—with collaborative ongoing discussions about how this is working with other colleagues working with the same map (Miller, 2004).

Mapping is often done at division meetings. It takes time, but it is worthwhile time. Since it is usually done collaboratively, it is a positive step toward building a professional learning community (Truesdale, Thompson, & Lucas, 2004). The conversations that teachers have deepen their understanding of standards and the development of a seamless curriculum. Maps are created horizontally and vertically for each subject area. The process is set out in detail in *Keys to Curriculum Mapping* (Udelhofen, 2005). Jacobs's *Getting Results With Curriculum Mapping* (2004) offers helpful examples of American educators who are mapping in their contexts. The *Curriculum Mapping Planner: Templates, Tools and Resources for Effective Professional Development* (Jacobs & Johnson, 2009) is a useful book and offers a big picture on curriculum mapping for a school as a systematic all-encompassing process. The book begins with establishing the school vision, offers tools for the process, and includes implementation strategies. It also allows for assessment data to inform the process, integrates literacy strategies into the map, and considers the 21st century learner.

Vertical Mapping

Vertical maps are interesting in that they provide a picture of how the content, skills, and standards are connected and build on each other over the years. In some jurisdictions, curriculum guidelines outline the standards for one strand in one discipline over succeeding years on one page. It is very helpful to read through this progression in content and skills in the same strand in the same subject area.

The Common Core Language Arts and English College and Career Readiness Anchor Standards are laid out so that it is fairly easy to see how a standard develops from Grade 1 to Grade 12. A quick look at Figure 2.7 shows that the key areas are identical from K to 12 for Reading, Writing, and Speaking and Listening. These are the general, cross-disciplinary literacy expectations that students must meet to success in college or in workplace training programs. Standards for each grade are tied to the developmental level of children in that grade. From an interdisciplinary perspective, it is interesting to see that research and media skills are embedded into every aspect of the curriculum rather than being put in a separate section. The use of language conventions is in a separate part of the document.

Viewed on one page, there is a lovely simplicity with this pattern. Students learn the same skills from K to 12. Obviously each skill needs to be presented differently over the years to allow for the developmental process. Figure 2.8 is a vertical scan that shows how one skill develops over time. Hopefully, the students (and teachers) will recognize patterns as they move through the grades so that they can develop metacognition about their learning. As well, they need to understand how the Common Core Anchor Standards are interconnected with each other and with reading, writing, speaking, listening, and language conventions. To do this, teachers need to work with the Big Picture and the focused grade picture at the same time.

Figure 2.7   College and Career Readiness Anchor Standards, English Language Arts K–12

Grade Level and Skill	Key Area 1	Key Area 2	Key Area 3	Key Area 4
Reading Grades K–12 English language arts Grades 6–12 Literacy in science, history/social studies, and technical subjects	Key ideas and details	Craft and structure	Integration of knowledge and ideas	Range of reading Level of text complexity
Writing Grades K–12 English language arts Grades 6–12 Literacy in science, history/social studies, and technical subjects	Text types and purpose	Production and distribution of writing	Research to build and present knowledge	Range of writing
Listening and Speaking Grades K–12 English language arts	Comprehension and collaboration	Presentation of knowledge and ideas		

SOURCE: Based on content from the Common Core State Standards, National Governors Association Center for Best Practices and Council of Chief State School Officers, http://www.corestandards.org.

Figure 2.8   Vertical Scan—Reading Standards for Informational Texts

Common Core Anchor Standards for Reading (Informational Texts) Craft and Structure # 6: Assess how point of view or purpose shapes the content and style of a text.				
Kindergarten →	**Grade 3** →	**Grade 6** →	**Grades 9–10** →	**Grades 11–12** →
Name the author and illustrator of a text and define the role of each in presenting the ideas or information in the text	Distinguish their own point of view from that of the author of a text	Determine an author's point of view or purpose in a text and explain how it is conveyed in the text	Determine an author's point of view or purpose in a text and analyze how an author uses rhetoric to advance that point of view or purpose	Determine an author's point of view or purpose in a text in which the rhetoric is particularly effective, analyzing how style and content contribute to the power, persuasiveness, or beauty of the text

SOURCE: Based on content from the Common Core State Standards, National Governors Association Center for Best Practices and Council of Chief State School Officers, http://www.corestandards.org.

Looking at the Mathematics Common Core State Standards through the lens of a vertical scan shows a similar pattern. There are some basics that are taught at all levels for all topics, and there is also a progression in the development of skills from K to 12. The Standards for Mathematical Practice are woven through the skills taught at each grade. They are as follows:

1. Make sense of problems and persevere in solving them.

2. Reason abstractly and quantitatively.

3. Construct viable arguments and critique the reasoning of others.

4. Model with mathematics.

5. Use appropriate tools strategically.

6. Attend to precision.

7. Look for and make use of structure.

8. Look for and express regularity in repeated reasoning.

At the same time there is a progression in skills over the years. Figure 2.9 follows the mathematical strand for geometry.

Figure 2.9   Vertical Scan—The Progression of a Mathematical Skill Over Time

Kindergarten ⟶	Grades 1–3 ⟶	Grade 6 ⟶	Grades 9–12 ⟶
Identify and describe shapes–– (squares, circles, triangles, rectangles, hexagons, cubes, cones, cylinders, and spheres)	Reason with shapes and their attributes	Solve real-world and mathematical problems involving area, surface area, and volume	Similarity, Right Triangles, and Trigonometry • Understand similarity in terms of similarity transformations • Prove theorems involving similarity • Define trigonometric ratios and solve problems involving right angles • Apply trigonometry to general triangles Circles • Understand and apply theorems about circles • Find arc lengths and areas of sectors in circles Expressing Geometric Properties With Equations • Translate between the geometric description and the equation for a conic section • Use coordinates to prove simple geometric theorems algebraically Geometric Measurement and Dimension • Explain volume formulas and use them to solve problems • Visualize relationships between two-dimensional and three-dimensional objects Modeling With Geometry • Apply geometric concepts in modeling situations

SOURCE: Based on content from the Common Core State Standards, National Governors Association Center for Best Practices and Council of Chief State School Officers, http://www.corestandards.org.

Vertical mapping can be done with the same categories as horizontal mapping. Figure 2.10 provides a sample template of a vertical map.

Vertical maps can also be used to focus on how the same skills and concepts are spiraled through the curriculum at increasingly sophisticated levels. Judy Zaenglein, who has now retired from Penn State at

Figure 2.10   A Generic Vertical Curriculum Map for One Discipline

School:					
Subject:					
Year	Standard	Enduring Understandings Big Ideas	21st Century Skills	Essential Questions	Assessment
1					
2					
3					
4					
5					
6					

Harrisburg, shared a wonderful strategy she used with her students. She had teachers line up against the wall in order of the grade level they taught. Then, together they chose a Big Idea or 21st Century Skill, and each person told how he or she dealt with it at his or her grade level, going from the lowest grade to the highest. This way, the teachers got a real sense of a continuum and were ready to map with a Big Picture in mind.

Horizontal Mapping

There is no one formula to map the curriculum. Different educators may map in different ways for different purposes. It is important to capture the information that is most useful for making curriculum decisions and that the map is clear in its intention. Usually, there is a horizontal map for each discipline. Most maps include the time frame (full year or unit), content, skills, standards, and assessment. Figure 2.11 offers a sample template showing these categories.

Another way to plan for the year is to look what Big Ideas are in the curriculum standards and plan around those for the year. Figure 2.12 shows a creative way to plan for the Big Ideas that cover a third-grade curriculum for two thirds of a year. This map was created by Sharlene Annie Lee, Barbara J. Johnson, and Judi Watkins of Campbell Park Marine Science Magnet Elementary School, Florida.

Teachers in different subject areas can create maps of what is most important to know and do (and be). Figure 2.13 shows a sample of one unit from an excellent curriculum map for a Grade 11 science unit. Seonaid Davis of Havergal College, Toronto, Ontario, created this map using the Ontario curriculum guidelines.

Mapping for Potential Integration

Curriculum mapping often leads to integration projects. Teachers see firsthand the overlap in curriculum standards and unnecessary duplication in their curriculum plans. During the process of implementation of the Common Core State Standards, many states are doing a variation of curriculum mapping as a first transition step. For this type of gap analysis, educators identify the gap between their own state standards the Common Core ones (see, for example, Kendall, 2011). This is a perfect time for educators to identify possible places for connections across subjects.

Interdisciplinary connections can be included on disciplinary curriculum maps. This makes it easier to talk about potential connections. Figure 2.14 shows a map created with the explicit idea of moving into interdisciplinary work. The KDB Umbrella was created before the disciplinary map. Thus the standards are deconstructed to identify the Know (Enduring Understandings and Big Ideas) and the Do (21st Century Skills). The Be is implicit in the standards. Potential connections to other subjects are included.

Figure 2.11   A Generic Horizontal Curriculum Map for One Discipline

Curriculum Map					
School: Subject: Grade Level:					
Time Frame	**Sept/Oct**	**Nov/Dec**	**Jan/Feb**	**March/ April**	**May/June**
Essential Questions					
Know Big Ideas Enduring Understandings					
Do 21st Century Skills					
Be					
Standards					
Assessment					

Figure 2.12 Two Units of the Third-Grade Yearlong Conceptual Map

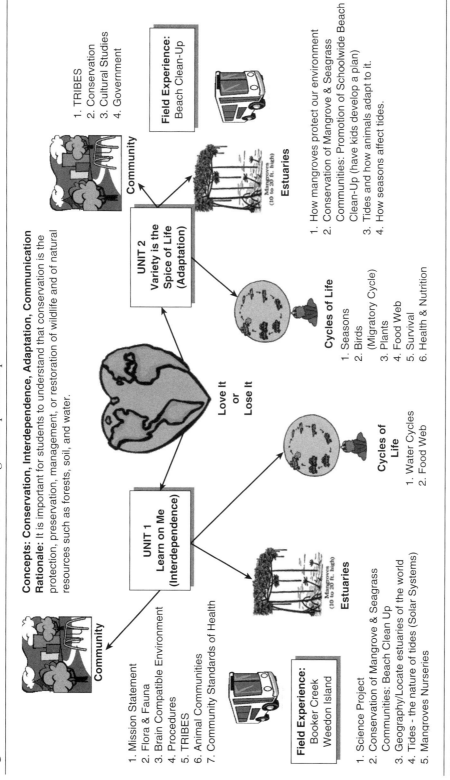

Concepts: Conservation, Interdependence, Adaptation, Communication

Rationale: It is important for students to understand that conservation is the protection, preservation, management, or restoration of wildlife and of natural resources such as forests, soil, and water.

Community

1. Mission Statement
2. Flora & Fauna
3. Brain Compatible Environment
4. Procedures
5. TRIBES
6. Animal Communities
7. Community Standards of Health

Field Experience:
Booker Creek
Weedon Island

Estuaries

1. Science Project
2. Conservation of Mangrove & Seagrass Communities: Beach Clean Up
3. Geography/Locate estuaries of the world
4. Tides - the nature of tides (Solar Systems)
5. Mangroves Nurseries

UNIT 1
Learn on Me
(Interdependence)

Love It
or
Lose It

Cycles of Life

1. Water Cycles
2. Food Web

UNIT 2
Variety is the Spice of Life
(Adaptation)

Cycles of Life

1. Seasons
2. Birds (Migratory Cycle)
3. Plants
4. Food Web
5. Survival
6. Health & Nutrition

Community

1. TRIBES
2. Conservation
3. Cultural Studies
4. Government

Field Experience:
Beach Clean-Up

Estuaries

1. How mangroves protect our environment
2. Conservation of Mangrove & Seagrass Communities: Promotion of Schoolwide Beach Clean-Up (have kids develop a plan)
3. Tides and how animals adapt to it.
4. How seasons affect tides.

SOURCE: Sharlene Annie Lee, Barbara J. Johnson, and Judi Watkins.

47

Figure 2.13 A Sample Curriculum Map for Grade 11 Biology

Understanding Inheritance Patterns—Grade 11 Biology—9-Week Unit—Second Unit of the Year

Standards	Big Ideas	Enduring Understandings	Key Skills	Essential Questions	Assessment	Key Teaching/ Learning Strategies.
Scientific Investigation Skills Demonstrate scientific investigation skills **Genetic Processes** D1. Evaluate the importance of some recent contributions to our knowledge of genetic processes, and analyze social and ethical implications of genetic and genomic research D2. Investigate genetic processes including those that occur during meiosis, and analyze data to solve basic genetics problems involving monohybrid and dihybrid crosses D3. Demonstrate an understanding of concepts, processes, and technologies related to the transmission of hereditary characteristics	Change and continuity	DNA is the universal code for life: It enables an organism to transmit hereditary information and along with the environment determines an organism's characteristics. The genetic code maintains the continuity of the species over generations and allows for gradual change.	**Inquiry Skills** Using the Punnet square to solve genetics problems Using probability to solve genetics problems Using the chi-squared test to determine significance **Communication Skills** Report writing—summarizing data and suggesting solution to the problems	How can we predict inheritance, or to what extent is it possible to predict inheritance patterns? Why do we see the patterns that we see?	**Assessment for/as Learning** To be embedded into the ongoing teaching/ learning **Assessment of Learning** *Fly Lab Investigation* Students will investigate the inheritance pattern of selected genotypes in fruit flies using simulation software. *Genetic Disorder Oral Report* Genetic symposium—students will research and report on a genetic disease and prepare an oral report. *Family Tree Analysis* Students complete a three generational tree. *Genetics Unit Test*	Intro to genetics: alike but different Chromosomes and karyotypes Meiosis Meiotic error and life cycles and meiosis Mendel's First Law, as demonstrated in "blue people" Family tree—pedigree analysis Chi-squared test of significance Sex-linked traits Fly lab Mendel's Second Law Variations of dominance—trumpet fly Genetic-symposium report Review for genetics test Genetics symposium

SOURCE: Seonaid Davis.

48

Figure 2.14 A Sample Curriculum Map That Focuses on Connections in One Unit of Grade 11 Biology

September/October	Essential Questions/Topic Questions	Interdisciplinary Connections	KNOW (from standards)	DO (from standards)	BE
Unit: Diversity of Living Things	*Essential Questions* How are structure and function related? How is evolution supported? *Topic Questions* Why are there so many different living things? Who are the "Masters of the Universe"?	*Art* Microscope skills Line drawing Representational art *Geography* Plant/animal species unique to certain parts of the world (evolution, structure) Continental drift *Math* Equations to support evolution Hardy-Weinburg law *Technology* Simulation of natural selection *History/Philosophy* Eugenics Genetic disease Pedigrees (hemophilia) Russian Revolution *English* Report writing Persuasive writing	*Enduring Understandings* The structure of an organism allows it to fulfill its function. Evolution is supported by substantive evidence. *Big Ideas* Structure and function Evolution 1. Classification 2. Features of three domains and five kingdoms 3. Intro to evolution and natural selection 4. Characteristics of bacteria and viruses 5. Bacteria in health and disease 6. Immune system	21st Century Skills *Scientific Method* Microscope skills Microbiological skills Independently plan, conduct, and report Experiment on bacteria Formal lab writing Persuasive Essay	*Critical Thinker* *Objective* when doing experiments and lab writing *Persuasive* when writing persuasive essay *Collaborative* Work cooperatively

BENEFITS OF CURRICULUM MAPPING

Curriculum mapping can have powerful results. Lachowicz (2004) describes a two-year curriculum mapping commitment in the Alternative Education Program, a branch of the Allegheny Intermediate Unit No. 3 in Pittsburgh, Pennsylvania. After they mapped their curriculum, teachers became more reflective and held higher expectations for themselves and their students. They understood the standards more fully and used them to develop activities that required higher order thinking. They shifted from writing instructional strategies that began with verbs such as *review, explain,* and *demonstrate* to ones that began with verbs such as *compare and contrast, predict, discover,* and *create.* Assessment techniques became more sophisticated, and the teachers focused on the alignment of assessment, content, and strategies. Finally, they discussed starting points for content integration.

Mapping naturally leads to a clearer view of both the discipline in focus and the Big Picture. Consider some typical teachers' comments:

Mapping allows me to identify the essential elements of the curriculum.

It's easier for me to modify activities from year to year.

I focus teaching and learning activities and assessments to address what is really important.

I can build on my colleagues' work.

Mapping allows me to concentrate on teaching students what they do not know.

Mapping helps me cluster standards to integrate where appropriate and to articulate essential questions.

Social studies is a good place to begin curriculum mapping because it encourages integration.

We can share resources more easily. (Miller, 2004)

In this chapter, we have explored some basic steps that ensure that the curriculum is aligned. The teachers will be teaching what they are mandated to teach. Presumably, the students will be learning what they are mandated to learn. What may be missing in these recipes for accountability is the relevance factor. Many people, myself included, believe that if the curriculum is not relevant to students, they will not learn it in a way that sticks. Advocates of interdisciplinary approaches to curriculum believe that integration is the route to relevance. But what does interdisciplinary curriculum look like in an age of accountability? The next chapter explores this question.

DISCUSSION QUESTIONS

1. Discuss the different types of accountability. How do these play out in your local context?

2. Discuss Figure 2.1 and how two-dimensional thinking plays out in curriculum planning in your context or experience.

3. For many teachers, the backward design process is difficult to follow. They prefer to identify good teaching strategies first and then go on to design the curriculum. What is the difference when teachers do use backward design?

4. Curriculum mapping is a good preparation for integrating the curriculum. What are the advantages? Can you see how it might fit in your context?

5. What do Figures 2.7, 2.8, and 2.9 tell us about the nature of standards?

SUGGESTED ACTIVITIES

1. Explore the Common Core State Standards and create a KDB Umbrella for each subject area.

2. Look up your state standards on the Internet. Is there a framework that acts as a KDB Umbrella? In other words, has the state identified the most important knowledge and skills that they expect a student to demonstrate from K to 12? Have they done this for a selected group of grades (e.g., 9–12)? Have they done this for individual subjects such as science and geography?

3. Look up another state's standards, and compare them to yours. In what ways is the framework the same? Different?

4. Unpacking the standards is an important skill to ensure that you are actually teaching what each standard requires. Using relevant standards, choose one or two standards from each subject, and create a chart comparable to Figure 2.5 or 2.6. Deconstruct the Know, Do, and Be.

5. Create a horizontal map such as the one in Figure 2.14 for a subject area of your choice, and identify potential curriculum connections.

3

Snapshots of Exemplary Integrated Programs

This chapter offers six snapshots of exemplary integrated curricula. One snapshot is at the elementary level, two are at the middle school level, and three are at the high school level. The examples come from across the country—from Florida to California, from Philadelphia and Detroit to Connecticut and Vermont. The snapshots are from one private school, two public schools, and three public charter schools. The most established program began in 1972; the newest program brought in its first students in 2011. These snapshots provide evidence curricula can be integrated in an age of accountability.

SCOFIELD MAGNET MIDDLE SCHOOL, STAMFORD, CONNECTICUT

The Stamford HP Catalyst Project

https://sites.google.com/site/stamfordhpcatalystproject/

Scofield Magnet Middle School is one of five middle schools in the Stamford Public Schools district in Connecticut. Students receive admittance to the school through a lottery process and come from all parts of Stamford. Led by Principal Jan Rossman, the school addresses the students' physical, social, and emotional needs to further intellectual development. Rossman says that an interdisciplinary approach is the way that the school does business, with a special emphasis on science, math, and technology.

Contaminated water was a local concern, as the landfill across from the school in an affluent neighborhood contained pesticides. Assistant Principal

Bryan Olkowski described this as a teachable moment. The teachers asked themselves how students could explore this local problem in a way that connected science, social studies, language arts, technology, and math. They applied for a Hewlett-Packard Innovation in Education grant and were successful. With the $300,000 they received, they purchased laptops, software, and water testing equipment.

In social studies, 200 Grade 8 students learned about the history of the local watershed going back to the Industrial Revolution. In language arts, they took the role of journalists to report about the contamination; they met with reporters to learn the methods of investigative journalism. In science, they learned water-testing procedures and proceeded to examine water samples taken from several different locations of the river that starts with the feeder brook that runs behind the school. They studied the water cycle, pollution, and the impact of water quality on human life. In math, they looked at data points, gathered data, and found coordinates on a map.

In the second year, Grade 7 students were added to make the total number of students involved 400. Laptops were integrated into all levels of the curriculum. Eighth grade students went on a hiking trip on the Appalachian Trail to collect soil samples. They learned the relationships between soil quality, elevation, and temperature. Students learned how to use GPS (global positioning system) monitors to plot points along the trail and GIS (geographic information system) technology to create a map of water quality in Stamford. GIS technology can take more sophisticated measurements than Google Earth. Teachers had to train to learn how to work with GIS technology too.

Teachers developed the curriculum with community environmental agencies. Students learned how the local watershed is maintained and began to understand the importance of being informed local citizens. Their final presentations showed the community how actions can improve the environment (Parry, 2010).

How did the students respond? Testimonials found in the second-year report showed that students enjoyed their learning. Student surveys confirmed this. Students also saw the connection between math and science in the real world and art, social studies, language arts, and music. Was the curriculum accountable? All curriculums addressed the Connecticut state standards and the National Educational Technology Standards. Scores on the Connecticut Mastery Test (CMT) showed that the number of students who performed at Below Basic or Basic level was reduced, while the number who performed at or above Proficient level increased. Over two thirds of the students performed at or above Proficient level. Significant gains were seen in the Hispanic group, whose average score on the Science CMT increased by 10 percentage points in the at/above goal category, while the white subgroup witnessed an

8.1% increase in the Science CMTs in the same category. A detailed first- and second-year report can be found at the school's website at http:// stamfordpublicschools.org/content/64/76/3888/4322/default.aspx.

Pleased with the success of this project, these educators wrote another grant for the Hewlett-Packard Catalyst Initiative. This grant focuses on creating a global network for developing effective approaches to STEM (science, technology, engineering, mathematics) education. The goal is to create international "sandboxes" of innovation to explore how students can use their technological and creative ingenuity to address social challenges locally and internationally. The HP Catalyst website can be found at http:// www.hp.com/hpinfo/socialinnovation/education.html#catalyst.

The school was awarded an HP Catalyst Grant totaling $160,000 to continue with their local initiative while collaborating with the middle school attached to Shandong University, Jinan, China. The focus was, "How do we get more kids interested in STEM?" They used the funding to further develop ideas on the water testing unit and provide professional development for teachers. Professional development took the form of summer institutes like the G. E. Developing Futures Conference. As well, some teachers got to go to an international conference supported by Hewlett-Packard in India to share ideas with other innovators.

The school had previously developed a sister school relationship with Shandong University Middle School in Jinan, Shandong province, China. This was a formal relationship where the Scofield principal went to China to sign the official sister school agreement. In March 2011, two Scofield teachers also traveled to Jinan to build upon the established sister school relationship. These educators taught Chinese teachers and students how to conduct water quality testing at the Black Tiger Spring in Jinan.

In September 2011, three teachers and 16 students from China traveled to the United States and stayed with host families in Stamford, where they participated in science lessons with the Grade 8 American students. The American students intend to visit China as well. All students worked with experts and learned skills and techniques relevant to science and future environmentally related careers. They tested, for example, pH, salinity, and dissolved oxygen in samples from various locations, using GPS, HP Mobile Calculating Lab probes, HP calculators, notebook computers, and GIS software to document their findings. Students and teachers in both schools are learning from each other about water quality and how to improve it.

As well, they are learning about each other's culture. School in China is very different, with up to 72 students in a class (Herbert, 2011). The Chinese students know some English, and the Stamford students are studying Chinese. In 2011, Scofield Middle School won a silver Connecticut Quality Improvement Innovation Award for its MyChinese 360 program. MyChinese 360 is a language program that is an online, for credit course in Mandarin. Both the U.S.- and China-based teachers use the program to connect the students for a virtual classroom experience in real time.

The original intention of this project had not been an international connection. But the project had a life of its own. In Rossman's words, "It just grew and grew from something small into something really grand." Staff believe that the grants were helpful, but they are convinced that it was not just the grants that made the program work. For these educators, this project shows the relevance of doing interdisciplinary work. To me, it seemed that it also was the philosophy, ingenuity, and commitment of the educators at Scofield and their Chinese counterparts that made a good idea into a great project. Now in the third year of the project, teachers intend to add an engineering component to the water quality testing unit through the eighth-grade art program. This will truly make Scofield a STEM-focused magnet middle school.

SHELBURNE COMMUNITY SCHOOL, SHELBURNE, VERMONT

The Alpha Program

http://www.scsvt.org/Page/415

The Alpha Program is multiage, grades 6 to 8 program that has been integrating curriculum since 1972. It is a nationally recognized program that has withstood the test of time and weathered many variations of curriculum reform. Based on the work of James Beane (1993, 1997), the curriculum begins with students' interests and their own questions about personal growth and social issues. This is a transdisciplinary approach, because it does not begin with the standards—but interestingly it evolves into a standards-based curriculum.

I visited the Alpha program when Cynthia Myers was one of the team leaders with Meg O'Donnell and Joan Cavallo. What I saw then astounded me. I was actually there the day that students presented their year-long curriculum and assessment plans based on policy documents and their own questions. They had spent some weeks with this task, and their conversations were spirited and thoughtful. Students eagerly showed me what they had learned and what they hoped to learn. Although that was several years ago, the program has kept its essence intact in spite of conservative trends across the country. In O'Donnell's words, the essence of the program is honoring student voice. It is a wonderful example of how an integrated approach can be both accountable and meaningful.

Today, the Alpha team teachers include Meg O'Donnell as a 10-year veteran, Gretchen Miller, and Leigh Petrucelli. Together they are certified in the four main disciplines. The team works in partnership with approximately 65 students. Alpha is one of four teams in the school, and students are randomly assigned to it—although it will be a different experience for these students than if they had been assigned to another, more traditional team. For these teachers, successful learning occurs when students are actively engaged in the process. Indeed these students are curriculum cocreators with their teachers and are given a high degree of responsibility. The philosophy of the teachers is exemplified in this program; their values and beliefs include the following:

- Create a safe space for every child to feel he or she belongs
- Value and teach self-assessment and reflection
- Expect academic excellence
- Develop a love of learning
- Encourage individuality and risk taking

The students are organized into three multiage groups. Each teacher primarily guides one of these groups and works with parents and mentors to support individual student progress. The three groups interact on a regular basis. Large blocks of time are scheduled with open physical spaces to provide for a variety of student groupings and learning experiences. Students who have been with the program for at least a year act as "goal partners" and lead the new students through the initiation into this unique program.

The students spend the first three or four weeks collaboratively designing the curriculum with their team leader. Originally the teachers modeled how to ask deep and meaningful questions, but now the older students do this and do it very well. Each student is responsible for developing 10 personally relevant questions for both the "self" and the "world." Students are then organized into multiage, mixed gender groups to share their questions and to find 8 to 10 common questions. The small group then shares with the class, and the students categorize all the questions to find general threads of commonality. At the same time they peruse the state standards for grades 6 to 8 and the curriculum guide for their school district, the Chittenden South Supervisory Union, to develop an understanding of what is required by the state of Vermont for student achievement. There are some clear connections to the standards, and often some new questions arise out of this process that are added to the mix.

The students, with the guidance of the teachers, sort the questions around common ideas and create themes for the year. They use a backward design approach to develop the assessments and activities that will demonstrate that they have met the state mandates. They gather resources and fine-tune the questions and then coordinate the calendar for the year to account for seasons and available resources. The end result is a standards-based curriculum that reflects the mandated middle school curriculum. Students feel validated when they discover that their questions are reflected in the standards, and it makes the learning more significant.

O'Donnell notes that the themes for each year are never exactly the same. The merging of authentic student questions with standards always brings fresh perspectives to the standards. A typical theme over the years, for example, has been "We the People," which includes government, careers, and conflict resolution. The self and world themes for 2011–2012 were these: becoming an expert (the individual seeks to become an expert in a chosen area), earth science, cultural studies, and ecology. Everything is integrated during the teaching of the theme except for a connected math class that is taught by grade level. Teachers play many roles, from lecturer to coach to facilitator and leader. Students also play many roles, from independent learner to collaborator with their peers to a participant in a large-group classroom setting.

Alpha's curriculum design process allows for differentiation. When students create the activities and assessments, all learning styles seem to be accounted for naturally. As well, technology is an integral part of the curriculum. For example, students create blogs and conduct research on the Internet. Since these students are digital natives, it makes sense that they are embedding technology into the curriculum in interesting and appropriate ways.

A goal of the program is that students develop a sense of community and leadership. Several required activities help students to develop this sense:

- Orientation activities and eighth-grade leadership retreat
- Annual play (required participation in afterschool practice and evening performances)
- A camping trip for which they raise funds by creating and selling quilts
- Eighth-grade finale
- Culminating events
- Daily morning meetings and student-led class meetings with class officers
- Student council

Parents are important partners in this endeavor. When I visited the school, many of the parents came out to talk to me and tell me how wonderful the school was. There is an active parent council. Parents commit to reading and assessing their child's portfolio each trimester. They will attend a two-hour portfolio conference each trimester led by their child. They are expected to support day and evening culminating events.

The teachers also keep up with their learning by attending a national learning lab for middle-level educators.

How do students do in this program?

Assessment plays a large role in the program. Each student has weekly academic goals (math, reading, writing, spelling, and theme expectations). The weekly goal setting, reflection, and self-assessment are done under the rubric of the Vermont Vital Results (Communication, Problem Solving, Functioning Independently, Personal Development, and Civic and Social Responsibility). Students keep portfolios organized by the Vital Results, and they assess their portfolios, set goals, and lead student-parent-teacher portfolio conferences every trimester. They select what evidence belongs in what category. For example, a piece of writing may go into the Communication category, or the Personal Development category, or the Civic and Social Responsibility category. Students see for themselves where their strengths and weaknesses are, given the hard evidence that they themselves have selected. This makes the learning very personalized and relevant.

Reporting includes student and teacher narratives about successes and challenges in each area of a Vital Result. These students are really aware of the KDB of the Vermont curriculum. (See Vermont's KDB Umbrella in Figure 2.2.) Local and standard assessment results are also reported. Alpha students do well on standardized tests—their results are comparable to, or better than, those of their peers in more traditional settings. More importantly, O'Donnell reports that students are well prepared for high school and beyond—they are active thinkers who are ask meaningful and deep questions about what they are learning.

MIAMI COUNTRY DAY SCHOOL, MIAMI, FLORIDA

Abess Center for Environmental Studies

http://www.miamicountryday.org/aces

iEARN (INTERNATIONAL EDUCATION AND RESOURCE NETWORK)

http://www.iearn.org

> *I like to think of our program as one of the best child-centered-solution-oriented-collaborative-authentic-inquiry based-creative-multiple intelligence-problem based-project based-21st century skills, STEM supportive curriculums out there. It happens every day for every child . . . making learning irresistible.*

These are the words of Rowena Gerber, the director of Abess Center for Environmental Studies (ACES) at Miami Country Day School in Miami, Florida. How could any program live up to that hype? But Gerber seems to have correctly identified most of the key elements of the solar cooking project and environmental studies program for students 4 to 12 years old. These students want to learn about the environment and are also working in a global collaborative context given Gerber's iEARN connection.

Miami County Day School is a private school with a holistic philosophy that is a college-preparatory learning community for preK–12 students. The 950 students come from a wide variety of backgrounds. Curriculum is integrated. ACES is an enrichment program situated within the school. At the center there are over 30 organic gardens and 150 animals. Clearly this is no ordinary classroom. Yet the solar cooking project is one in which students from across United States could engage—indeed students from across the world have been involved.

Students make solar ovens out of shoeboxes, pizza boxes, tires, lampshades, display boards, recycled binders, and sawed off garbage cans. At the end of this project-based study, the children actually cook food inside these foil-lined containers. They learn how to make the most efficient oven through discussions, videoconferences, webcasts, and trial and error. Students play the roles of scientists, journalists, scriptwriters, business executives, and botanists. How do they play these roles? These students have solar cooking partners in places as diverse as Australia, Japan, Haiti, Senegal, Dubai, Taiwan, Hong Kong, Ontario, and South Africa. There is much work to be done (https://media.iearn.org/projects/solarcooking).

Using the videoconferencing equipment right in their classroom, students have given live cooking demonstrations to students in Australia, Jordan, India, and Japan all at the same time. They have frequent Internet meetings with some of their partners. But it doesn't stop there. Realizing that 2 billion people are reliant on wood or charcoal, and many countries around the world could use solar cooking as an alternative to coal or wood, they wanted to share their technology.

The next step was to raise money to pay for solar ovens to be sent to Afghanistan, Sierra Leone, and Haiti. These ovens can cook 500 loaves of bread in an hour and 1200 meals twice a day. To raise money, students planted 35 edible gardens and maintained plants in an educational shade house. They coordinated plant sales and made herbal vinegar and oils, salsa, and other products. They have partnered with Rotary to match their fundraising. More recently, the students raised over $40,000 to send a village-sized oven and 20 family-sized ovens to Senegal. Students in Senegal and Miami Country Day School celebrated through a videoconference. Teachers from the National Science Teachers Association joined the students as they danced and played drums celebrating the arrival of the ovens in the Senegalese village. A touching brief documentary covering this event is at http://myhero.com/go/films/view.asp?film=Rowena.

Gerber reports the children are fascinated by the process and want deep learning. They pose many questions that indicate high-level thinking. Why? How come? How does the solar cooker work? What traps heat? What traps heat best? Why is that one working better than this one? What recycled items can we make one with? Do we need insulation? Which type of cooker heats up faster? Stays warm longest? Each question leads to another question. Using an inquiry model, students do experiments to find the answers to their questions.

How does this program fit accountability mandates? It is aligned with the Sunshine State Standards in science. Assessments include formative assessments such as drawing a diagram to explain a process. Portfolios, presentations, webcasts, PowerPoint presentations, and the actual effectiveness of the students' ovens are all ways that children demonstrate what they have learned. But, this program is about much more than scientific facts and environmental awareness. Ultimately it is about children learning to be humanitarians.

Teachers and students wanting to participate in this project can find more information on the iEARN project description page: https://media.iearn.org/projects/solarcooking. The iEARN (http://us.iearn .org/) connection in the United States is extremely valuable. iEARN is the world's largest nonprofit global education organization. It is also one of the oldest, having begun its first international collaborative online projects in 1988. There are over 130 countries involved in collaborative project-based learning that addresses curriculum subjects and encourages action on global issues. Participants connect through innovative technologies or the Internet. Over 100,000 teachers have been involved with iEARN since its inception.

Over 300 theme-based projects designed and facilitated by teachers are available. All projects align with educational standards. As well, every project addresses the question "How will this project improve the quality of life on the planet?" There is a curriculum integration toolkit and success stories of integrated project-based learning. Here are a few examples of ways American students have participated:

• *Global Art: A Sense of Caring* at the K–2 level integrates creative arts, language arts and social studies at Mill Creek Elementary School, Warrington, Pennsylvania. Students share artwork with other students around the world; the art shows ways they care for one another at school, in their families, and in the wider world. Students write a narrative in their own language. (http://media.iearn.org/projects/globalart)

• *One Day in the Life* for grades 6 to 8 at The Village Charter School, Trenton, New Jersey, integrates creative arts, language arts, and social studies. Students are partnered with students at three other schools— one in Idaho and two in Taiwan. (http://media.iearn.org/projects/onkedayinthelife)

- *Eradication of Malaria* for grades 9 to 12 is a science-based curriculum that involves students traveling to Africa and living with a host family. Students raise money for things like mosquito nets. A student at Alexander Dawson School in Boulder, Colorado, tells of his experience. (http://media.iearn.org/projects/malaria)

Or you can start your own project and look for partners in other countries that would like to participate. A list of ongoing projects includes the following:

- *YouthCaN* (Youth Communicating and Networking) is a youth-run initiative that uses technology to inspire, connect, and educate people worldwide about environmental issues. Through a network of conferences, activities, and events, they have united environmentally active youth to exchange ideas about the environment and empower others to make a difference in their own communities since 1992. (http://youthcanworld.org/)

- *The My Hero Project,* (an independent nonprofit organization) that partners with iEARN, is a project-based learning experience that integrates creative and language arts, humanities and social science, science, environmental studies, math, and technology. Students recognize the heroes around them and the heroic qualities that they themselves have. (http://myhero.com)

- *(OF)2—Our Footprints, Our Future* is an international initiative that encourages youth from around the world to use online tools and resources to measure their carbon footprint and develop ways to reduce their carbon usage. The goal is for one million students around the world to join together with their families, their schools, and their communities to reduce greenhouse gases by 100,000 tons and therefore reduce the size of their global carbon footprint. (http://media.iearn.org/projects/of2)

- In *The Teddy Bear Project,* students send a teddy bear to students in a partner class through postal mail. The students who receive a teddy bear send an email message each week to the students who sent them the bears. The emails are written in the voice of the bear describing itself in a new culture. Students also write in the teddy bear's journal from the perspective of the bear about experiences while living in another country and culture. (http://media.iearn.org/projects/teddybear)

- In the *Finding Solutions to Hunger Project,* participants research and discuss the root causes of hunger and poverty in the world and take meaningful actions to help create a more just and sustainable world. (http://media.iearn.org/projects/hunger)

- *Journalism 2.0: Empowering a New Generation of Civic Education Leaders in Ecuador, Pakistan, Tajikistan Thailand and the USA* is a two-year program funded by the Bureau of Education and Cultural Affairs of the U.S. Department of State. Students from these five countries examine the national elections to be held in 2012 and 2013, and develop journalism and media skills. U.S. students can take a World Youth News certification course developed by iEARN in collaboration with the *New York Times* and Columbia University Graduate School of Journalism. (http://www .worldyouthnews.org)

iEARN is an exciting option for teachers too. iEARN helps them meet professional development requirements by providing ongoing workshops, online courses, webinars, and consulting. The online courses connect educators around the world who are working on project integration, standards alignment, and assessment planning. Among the most exciting aspects of iEARN are the local, regional, and international face-to-face events. There is also an annual international conference attended by both students and educators. Conferences have been held in Argentina (1994), Australia (1995), Hungary (1996), Spain (1997), the United States (1998), Puerto Rico (1999), China (2000), South Africa (2001), Russia (2002), Japan (2003), Slovakia (2004), Senegal (2005), the Netherlands (2006), Egypt (2007), Morocco (2009), Canada (2010), and Taiwan (2011).

Take a look at http://www.iearn.org/events for information about upcoming events. Ed Gragert, Lisa Jobson, and Diane Midness have all been a huge part of IEARN's success and would be happy to give you any information you need.

HIGH TECH HIGH, SAN DIEGO, CALIFORNIA

http://www.hightechhigh.org/schools/HTH/

High Tech High (HTH) began as a charter school in California in 2000 supported by San Diego's business leaders and educators. It has evolved into an integrated network of schools from K to 12. It also includes its own comprehensive teacher certification program and an innovative Graduate School of Education. By 2010 it had three campuses and nine schools, approximately 3,500 students and 350 employees, and plans to expand further. The diverse group of students is chosen by a lottery by zip code. One hundred percent of students earn admittance to college, and 80% to four-year institutions.

Something is indeed different enough at this network of schools that they need their own teacher certification program. As new schools open, faculty who are experienced in the High Tech High philosophy work in each new school to ensure that the spirit is the HTH spirit. The material on their website talks about preserving the "soul" of the organization. What is this soul? What makes the difference? The goal of the original

High Tech High was to create a school where students were passionate about their learning and could learn the basic skills of work and citizenship.

The student body at every HTH school is selected to mirror the socio-economic and ethnic diversity of the community. Technology is integrated into academic subjects. Educationally disadvantaged students are encouraged to succeed in math and engineering. Graduating students are to be thoughtful, engaged citizens. HTH also wants to share its successes with other schools, so it is an open source organization that offers institutes, residencies, and free web-based material. Indeed a look at the website reveals a wide range of resources. The HTH facilities are equipped with the latest technology, ubiquitous wireless laptop access, and common areas in which artwork and prototypes can be displayed.

HTH has three design principles: personalization, adult world connections, and a common intellectual mission. Facilities are tailored to provide small group learning experiences. Each student has an advisor. Juniors complete a one-semester academic internship in an area of career interest. In other years students may do service learning or shadow an adult. The intellectual mission is to provide a rigorous curriculum so that all students can go on to higher education. Assessment is performance-based. All students do projects and present their work to the community. There is a rigorous senior project and digital portfolio.

Teachers work together in interdisciplinary teams to design the curriculum. Students are in teams of 50 to 70 students. The schedule allows for team teaching, common planning time, and project-based learning. Teachers in the schools publish their own online journal called *Unboxed: A Journal of Adult Learning in Schools.* The inaugural issue featured a project that integrated language arts and physics learning to meet standards in both subjects (Cornejo-Sanchez & Wakefield, 2008). Student pairs researched physics concepts such as entropy, magnetism, gravitation, and magnetism. Students used their imagination to develop short stories about these concepts and created comic books in which a superhero embodied each concept. Another article described an exhibition where students had developed a multimedia presentation to describe math-related topics. Students revised their presentations after extensive critique from peers (Stahnke, 2011).

The K to 12 projects explored in *Unboxed* are very creative and provide teacher's reflections. The Spring 2011 issue featured stories entitled "Canyon as Classroom," "Sunflowers and Math," "Going Against the Zeitgeist," "Exhibiting Student Writing," "Science Room as Drawing Room," "Experiencing Difference," "Illuminated Mathematics," "Bamboozled," and "Reading Art." "Cards" are also available in each issue. The cards are links to snapshots of different projects accompanied by student and teacher reflections. The huge variety of integrated projects is inspiring. The journal is an online journal, but you can ask to have a paper issue shipped directly to you.

Looking at the student digital portfolios on the school website also offers a glimpse into what happens at HTH. Viewing the portfolio of a student from the class of 2012 shows the kind of things that student has done over four years at HTH. Typically a portfolio includes projects done on such things as a United Nations Conference; renewable energy; an atomic timeline; sex, drugs, and rock and roll; the Latin America project; books; a chemistry world trade show; art; deconstruction icons; and the tragedy of war.

Portfolios have hyperlinks that lead you to other pieces of work such as research or position papers. Projects include such things as photos, audiotapes, short films, videos, and personal art work. A resume will often tell you what programs the student is proficient in, such as Adobe Photoshop, Dreamweaver, and Adobe After Effects. It is clear in viewing the portfolios that technology is an integral part of the work.

To really explore the soul of the school, I talked to Mark Aguirre. Mark is a veteran of the system, having been there since its second year. The second day of his first year of teaching was 9/11. Mark tells me that Larry Rosenstock, HTH's founding principal and CEO, describes the HTH philosophy as "We are building it as we fly," which is a lovely metaphor for growing success. In Aguirre's words, "We are plunging in. We are doing the best we can, and we do what we think is best for kids."

A hallmark of the school is projects and curriculum integration. The humanities are taught in an integrated class for all students. Aguirre describes the project that his Grade 9 humanities class is currently doing— Toga Night. He uses backward design to plan curriculum and integrates history and English. Among the students there is a wide range of skills levels, work ethics, and work habits. For him, it is important for students to learn deeply rather than cover a lot of material. He works collaboratively with his teaching partner, the physics teacher, and they plan for integration at times when it fits the curriculum being taught.

At the time I talked with Aguirre, his students were studying fifth-century BCE Athens, and the theme was "justice." The Toga Night was the culminating activity. Toga Night refers to a play that the students performed to an audience of about 200 people. Plays were very important in Athens in the fifth century, and there were actual competitions. Women, however, were not allowed to attend. Yet 80% of the roles in the Grecian plays were women's roles. In an effort to recreate the real-world context, students performed two different plays. The boys performed 350 lines of Homer's "Iliad" as it was written. The girls adapted Euripedes' play "The Trojan Women" in several ways to reflect social issues, including refugees and genocide. Then they acted out their adaptation. Students took on different tasks such as acting, lighting, sets, costumes, and directing.

In the weeks leading up to this play, students were wrestling with dilemmas such as, "Who is a better leader, Achilles or Agamemnon?"

"Religion or logic/reasoning?" Students worked on teams and did Internet research to create a timeline over seven centuries of ancient Greece. They also wrote essays. Aguirre taught them to be active readers. There was a lot of time spent critiquing each other's work for formative assessment. By their senior year, these students should be able to self-assess and self-critique.

Aguirre knows he is preparing his students for success for their next three years at HTH. He does not give tests (although students do very well on the California State Tests without his focusing on them). The skills that he and other teachers are teaching are organization, goal-setting, reflection, and critiquing. His personal goal is to encourage curiosity in his students, and he does this appropriately through the Socratic seminar. When asked how students do well on the large-scale test, Aguirre offers his own opinion, "Our kids care. They are really engaged in what they do. They are happy. We tell them to do their best on the tests and they do."

SCIENCE LEADERSHIP ACADEMY, PHILADELPHIA, PENNSYLVANIA

http://www.scienceleadership.org/

Science Leadership Academy (SLA) is a progressive science and technology high school in Philadelphia that opened in 2006. Developed in partnership with The Franklin Institute Science Museum, SLA provides a rigorous inquiry-based, project-driven curriculum focused on 21st century learning. SLA focuses on math, science, technology, and entrepreneurship.

SLA has received a lot of attention over its short history. It is considered a pioneer of the School 2.0 movement and was featured in *Ladies Home Journal* as one of the 10 most amazing schools in the United States (http://www.lhj.com/relationships/family/school/most-amazing-schools/?page=10). Chris Lehmann, the innovative principal, has also won his share of accolades. Examples from a long list of recognitions include being honored by the White House as a Champion of Change, named as one of the "40 under 40" by *Philadelphia Business Journal*, and named an honoree of the ASCD Outstanding Young Educator Award in 2009. He has spoken all over the world. He has written extensively and is the author of educational blog *Practical Theory* (http://practicaltheory .org). Clearly, Lehmann is a mover and shaker. When I talked to him about his school, he was very ill with walking pneumonia, but his enthusiasm and expertise were still strong.

Students are admitted to SLA through a project-based interview at the school. Students need to bring a paper or project that demonstrates their best work in Grade 7 or 8. As well, they need to have earned As or Bs at their previous school, with the possible exception of one C. They need to have scored Advanced or Proficient on the PSSA (Pennsylvania System of School Assessment). The students attending SLA are as diverse as Philadelphia itself and come from 74 different zip codes: 49% are African American, 36% are Caucasian, 7% are Asian, and 7% are Hispanic, with 1% from other ethnicities. Half are economically disadvantaged, and many will be the first in their families to attend college (Heller, 2011).

Why is this school so successful (beyond having a fine and energetic leader)? Visitor Lisa Heller (2011) describes it as a warm and welcoming place where students have happy faces. Students are polite and open, as is the principal's door; several students are usually hanging out in his office. Students in classrooms are clustered in groups around their laptops, presenting their learning to each other or debating different points of view. These students are not afraid to take risks; their skills and engagement were showcased in the 2011 PBS documentary called "Digital Media: New Learners for the 21st Century" (http://www.pbs.org/programs/digital-media/). Heller also describes the equally engaged and committed teachers, who act as guides and spend a lot of time collaborating to plan lessons and further innovations to the curriculum.

I was struck by the school vision or schoolwide ethos. Lehmann talks about the horizontal integration of the school. By this he means that all grades in all subject areas are on the same page. They have the same mission and a common language. They begin with the same three questions:

- How do we learn?
- How do we create?
- What does it mean to lead?

Across the school, there are common inputs, a common process, and common outputs. The common inputs are SLA's five core values:

- Inquiry: What is a worthwhile question?
- Research: What research needs to be done to find the answer?
- Collaboration: How can we work together to do the research?
- Presentation: What is the best modality to use to present my findings?
- Reflection: What have I learned? What would I do differently next time?

They use the common process of Understanding by Design (backward design, Wiggins & McTighe, 2005) to develop curriculum. The common outputs are shown in a rubric that all teachers use for their assessment. Figure 3.1 shows the common rubric.

This common vision gave SLA educators a common language to use to communicate with each other. It did not, however, allow for the

Figure 3.1   Science Leadership Academy Standard Rubric for All Assessments

	Design 20	Knowledge 20	Application 20	Presentation 20	Process 20
Exceeds Expectations					
Meets Expectations					
Approaches Expectations					
Does Not Meet Expectations					

SOURCE: http://www.scienceleadership.org/media/7376/. Used with permission of Science Leadership Academy.

unique language that teachers needed to talk with each other within each subject area. The next step was to collaborate on creating a standards-based report card in each distinct discipline for grades 9 to 12. This is vertical integration.

Curriculum integration comes in several forms at SLA. Technology is integrated across the school. One-to-one laptops are a feature of this school, but they serve to enhance student learning, not to dominate it. Chris Lehmann says that technology needs to be three things simultaneously: ubiquitous, necessary, and invisible. Students choose what technology they will use to demonstrate the learning in their projects; what is important is that projects are authentic and powerful and explore something that matters.

Laptops are used for research and accessing online resources, but students also use textbooks and books such as novels, poetry, plays, and nonfiction. There is rich blend of different sources. In history class, for example, students will look at primary sources, commentary, and first-generation reports from an immigrant or child of an immigrant, and will analyze websites. They will then create their own artifacts to demonstrate their learning.

Each year has a theme that is explored across subjects. Grade 9 looks at Identity, Grade 10 at Systems, Grade 11 at Change, and Grade 12 at Creation. The Grade 12 students are also preparing for their capstone experience, so there is less emphasis on the theme in Grade 12 than in other grades. In Grade 11, students have an individualized learning experience and go out to one of 150 community placements; these might involve service learning, a work placement, or taking a college-level course. While they are in these placements, students are looking at future career goals. At the end of the year, there is a structured reflective session to share experiences.

The museum component for Grade 9 involves four-week minicourses focusing on several areas of science from the Franklin Institute Science Museum. Examples of course titles are Identity, Galaxy Experience, and Computer Game Design. Students have access to the archives and exhibits. During the minicourse, they establish their particular interest. In Grade 10, they have an opportunity to apply for an internship in the area where they took the course. There are also leadership opportunities involved.

Students travel in cohorts to English, history, and science classes. These subjects are integrated when and how the teachers think best and are planned by the teachers. Organic integration happens because students see connections across subjects given the horizontal integration. Experiencing the five core values of inquiry, research, collaboration, presentation, and reflection in every venue brings a powerful message of the importance of these skills. These are the 21st Century Skills. The projects themselves are housed in distinct subject areas but are always evaluated for their design, knowledge, application, presentation, and process. These commonalities carry a powerful message about what is most important to learn.

The projects are posted on a public blog (http://www.scienceleader ship.org/blog). The day I looked at the blog, for example, students in a Spanish class had posted songs they had created to communicate who they were and where they came from. The words to students' songs were posted in Spanish, and there were one or two videos where the students sang their songs. Browsing through the thousands of blog entries, I found stories, photos, movies, and videos about subjects like the earthquake in Haiti and sustainable energy in Costa Rica. As well, there were a lot of blog entries exploring personal issues such as fear of success and procrastination. There is an opportunity for commenting on the individual blogs.

How does SLA maintain accountability? This is a college preparatory school. It is also a standards-based school—teachers consciously meet the standards Students take the same large-scale tests as students from other schools. When I asked Lehmann about the approach to the tests, he said that teachers spent some time preparing students for it, such as teaching them that knowing how to take a test is a life skill. The teachers do not teach to the tests but find that students are prepared through the project work that they do.

JALEN ROSE LEADERSHIP ACADEMY, DETROIT, MICHIGAN

http://www.jrladetroit.com

At Jalen Rose Leadership Academy (JRLA) all of the 120 students who enrolled in the first freshman class of 2011 must live and breathe ENACT over their four-year career (Figure 3.2). ENACT is an acronym for the characteristics of a research process:

Figure 3.2   ENACT Inquiry Cycle

ENACT

When you research think ENACT.

When you write a composition think ENACT.

When you answer a test question think ENACT.

When you want to demonstrate a deeper understanding think ENACT.

Exploring: Brainstorm, browse the web, hypothesize

Narrowing: Make a plan, predict what might happen, present a proposal, gather data

Analyzing: Display and compare data

Creating: Conclude, explain the significance of your findings (defend), make recommendations, declare the limitations, relay future questions for ongoing research

Teaching: Teach others, listen critically

SOURCE: Barbara Smith.

JRLA is an open-enrollment public charter high school on the northwest side of Detroit. In every succeeding year after 2011, a new class of 120 new freshmen begins. These students have the opportunity for an education that leads to college and a career—particularly in the area of sports and entertainment.

Jalen Rose, an ESPN/ABC analyst and 13-year NBA star, had a dream that students in Detroit, one of the communities hit hardest by the 2007–2009 recession in United States, could become leaders in the community. With cofounder Michael Carter, his dream became reality. Rose has been involved in education since establishing his philanthropic Jalen Rose Foundation in 2000. More than $1.2 million in grants have been awarded to underserved youths; according to a Fox news clip on the school website, drop-out rates in Detroit have decreased from 29.9% in 2007 to 19% in 2010; this change may be, in part, attributable to these grants.

JRLA is unique in many ways. There are high expectations for both students and teachers. The school day is longer than at traditional schools, and there are more school days a year. Classes are small. There is a ratio of 20 students to 1 teacher in most classes, but the ratio is 10/1 in math and English. Students must also attend six Super Saturdays, where they concentrate on one subject area for a whole day. The curriculum is leadership-focused, offering project-based experiences within the career context of sports and entertainment. As well, learning activities are set within a real-world context. For instance, 120 students visited and interviewed senior citizens on several occasions at Oakpoint Villa to learn about their lives as seniors and to write their biographies. Students also take part in a three-year novel writing project, where each novel is published.

Curriculum design begins with the Michigan State Standards and the Common Core State Standards. Students must take the following courses in order to graduate:

- A Leadership course each year (that includes a rigorous Health Education unit)
- A career-based elective for the first three years
- A Research and Technology course each year
- Four Science courses
- Four Mathematics courses
- A World Language Course for four years
- An Economics course
- Three Arts courses
- Three college courses over the course of Grade 11 and 12
- Participation in paid and unpaid Co-op experiences (Jalen Rose, n.d.)

Developed by the curriculum planning team led by Barbara Smith, Diane Manica, and school leader Chuck Muncatchy, this "break the mold" curriculum has been thoughtfully planned to build over four years. Curriculum integration occurs and in as many areas as possible in a variety of ways. There are several interwoven themes: leadership, sports and entertainment, global issues (in Grade 9), environment and social justice (in Grade 10), empowerment (in Grade 11), and "giving back" in Grade 12. Leadership, for example, is fused into the language arts through a writing course.

A unique part of this program is the E-labs. E-labs are electronic lab experiences that replace textbooks at JRLA. These online reference books and teaching guides have links to many varied digital sources, so students can engage in learning from many perspectives. The E-lab resources focus on multiple standards that are addressed in many project-based approaches to learning. To customize and differentiate curriculum at JRLA, E-labs have been developed for every subject. Math, for example, is integrated with technology through E-lab resources. Students can see how university professors or teachers at other schools solve math problems via PowerPoints or videos. Students can also view and use links that give them a chance to play games and take online quizzes to gain immediate feedback.

A good example of the philosophy of the school is the Research and Technology course, also developed within an E-lab context. This course is designed to teach action research and technology simultaneously. All research projects are archived in the school library. All projects must receive a grade of at least 80% or they will be turned back for revision. In addition to math being taught separately, it is also deliberately integrated into the Research and Technology course, as the data management and statistics units in grades 10, 11, and 12.

In Grade 9, the students are considered Novice researchers; in grades 10 and 11 they are Apprentices, and in the senior year they are Expert researchers. Each level is scaffolded so that students build on previous skills. Scaffolding is no doubt used in many schools (indeed it is a specific goal of the Common Core State Standards), but the method of scaffolding may not quite be as explicit elsewhere. At JRLA the research/inquiry skills are built on the research process ENACT (described above), which is used each year. The intent of this consistent use of ENACT is similar to the intent of the use of a common rubric at Scientific Leadership Academy, as described earlier in this chapter. The more students practice and use ENACT in a variety of contexts, the more proficient they become at inquiry, and the deeper the learning.

Looking directly at part of the curriculum description online offers a good glimpse of how students first learn to apply the ENACT model:

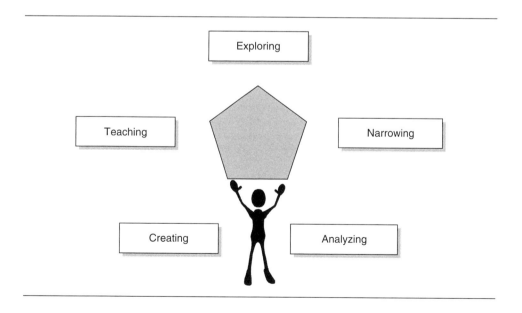

As **Novice Researchers . . .**

- You will work on an individual project with the help of a research advisor [who] is also working with 9 other student researchers.
- You will learn how to use technology [appropriate] to novice researcher.
- You will use a common language to learn how to develop reasoning skills so critical for university success.

The first topic, "**Nations United,**" links to Grade 9 History and Grade 10 Geography course. Both subjects must teach inquiry skills so the R & T [Research & Technology] course provides a place where you can "deeply understand" about a country in order to expand your worldview beyond that of the USA.

The Novice course is the first in a three-part course series that extends over four years. (Smith, 2011)

The differences between the ENACT inquiry model and a more typical one are summarized in Figure 3.3.

Figure 3.3   Differences Between the ENACT Inquiry Model and a Typical Inquiry Model

At JRLA, students will use the ENACT inquiry model and will . . .	In a typical inquiry program, students can . . .
• Complete 3 projects over 4 years from 1 semester to 2 years in length	• Can complete research units within a course within one school year
• Work collaboratively	• Participate as individuals in group work
• Participate in leveled research experiences (novice, apprentice, and expert)	• Repeat research experiences that are not necessarily graduated challenges from year to year
• Use a common language (explore, narrow, analyze, conclude, and teach)	• Learn a language for research each year that is dependent on the teacher's choice of model
• Begin with a hypothesis that will be revised by the end of the inquiry	• Develop and test a hypothesis to prove or disprove it
• Make predictions and learn how to estimate	• Think ahead to what might happen
• Learn how to use online catalogues and subscriptions to gather data as well as how to use spreadsheets and other software technology to organize data visually	• Use word processing to compile reports and use online cataloguing and online subscription sources

At JRLA, students will use the ENACT inquiry model and will . . .	In a typical inquiry program, students can . . .

• Gather secondary resources and document text sources:
  ○ Grade 9 students (novices) gather/document data from books and web sources.
  ○ Grade 10 and 11 students (apprentices) gather data from encyclopedias and e-mail as well as review with books and web sources.
  ○ Grade 12 students (experts) gather/document data from newspapers, magazines, and peer reviewed e-labs as well as review with books, encyclopedias, and web sources.
	• Gather data from a variety of text options

• Read responses from personalized e-mail letters from each researcher/expert	• Gather primary sources as an option
• Use criteria to determine the reliability and validity of each source	• Judge the reliability of sources
• Be assessed on quality of jot notes	• Summarize information from a variety of sources
• Write conclusions that reference summarized findings, recommendations, further questions, and suggestions for ongoing research	• Answer questions, solve problems, and make recommendations
• Work in a small group guided by a research advisor	• Work as part of a full class supported by a teacher
• Expect questions to improve at the end of immersion in study	• Answer questions at the beginning of the study
• Defend and teach their findings to others	• Present findings in essay, report, or oral presentation format
• Take part in self-evaluation	• May take part in self-evaluation

SOURCE: Adapted from the work of Barbara Smith at Jalen Rose Leadership Academy.

The curriculum is intriguing. In the spirit of the 21st century, the entire curriculum is online and available to anyone who visits the website. In fact, curriculum creators hope that other educators will explore their ideas and give feedback. To find the entire curriculum, browse the school's website at http://www.jrladetroit.com, click on Academics, and select a resource of your choice. You will be excited by what you find. Teachers can replicate the JRLA curriculum with all the websites intact or actually adapt the course to suit their own context.

In this chapter six contemporary programs that are both accountable and relevant to students were profiled. For me, these programs are an inspiration and show how imaginative both teachers and students can be.

DISCUSSION QUESTIONS

1. What is similar about these schools? What is different?

2. Discuss what aspects of these programs might work in your context.

SUGGESTED ACTIVITIES

1. Explore the websites for these schools, and find examples of their rich assessment tasks.

2. Read the description of each program, and determine what the Know, Do, and Be are. Create a KDB Umbrella for each program.

3. Look at the JRLA curriculum online. Adapt the ENACT cycle to your context.

Doing the Groundwork for Interdisciplinary Curriculum

The Integrated Curriculum Design Process. As you read this chapter, follow through the completed curriculum in Appendix A to see how the parts fit the whole.

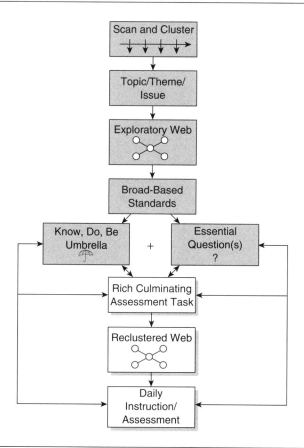

SOURCE: Adapted from Drake and Reid (2010).

Afirst time effort at designing an integrated curriculum can be challenging especially if one is working collaboratively with others. *Fortunately the process gets easier with practice until it is hard to conceive of a curriculum in any other way.* In this book you will find that a basic backward design process is used with several steps added to help connect the disciplines. A simplified version of this process can be found on page 75.

These steps have been put in a linear order so that they make sense when you read them, *but* the process itself is iterative. You will need to go back and forth between a Big Picture lens and a focused zoom lens. Before you can do a Scan and Cluster (the first step in the figure), you need to understand the concepts of Know, Do, and Be (KDB). Yet you will not actually choose the KDB until you create your KDB Umbrella. Before you get too committed to certain standards, you will want to create an exploratory web to brainstorm possible activities and assessments You may need to change the KDB Umbrella as you create your culminating activity, or change your culminating activity as you create your daily instructional plan. And so it goes.

In this chapter we will deal with the first six steps of the process. These steps address the first two questions of backward design: What do we most want students to know, do, and be? How can we connect the subject areas using the standards?

WHAT IS WORTH KNOWING?

Our modern world challenges us to reexamine the essential educational question: "What is worth knowing?" Schools have been charged not only with responsibility for their traditional subject areas but also with such cross-disciplinary topics as multiculturalism, nonviolence, cyberbullying, character education, gender equity issues, racism, AIDS education, and environmental issues. The list seems endless. The Common Core State Standards state that students need to learn both the classics such as Shakespeare and the genres of the popular culture. Media and technological literacies are embedded into these standards, as they reflect the 21st century world we live in. Living in a global world, students need to have a global perspective. Having an educated approach to contemporary issues seems essential for the productive citizen of the 21st century.

To really understand what is worth knowing, one needs to be familiar with the structure of knowledge (Figure 4.1). Based on Hilda Taba's work, Erickson (1995) suggests that knowledge moves up from facts at the base of the hierarchy to topics, disciplinary concepts (big disciplinary ideas), universal concepts (Big Ideas), and essential understandings (Enduring Understandings). At the top of the pyramid is theory.

Figure 4.1   The Structure of Knowledge and the Interaction of the Know and Do

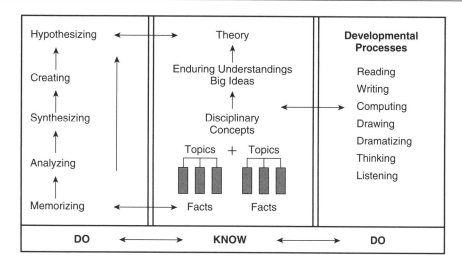

The Know is not independent from the Do. The Do skills are interdisciplinary processes that learners require to move up the hierarchy of knowledge. Reading, writing, computing, drawing, dramatizing, thinking, and listening are developmental processes that become more complex and sophisticated throughout an educational career and indeed throughout life. According to Erickson (1995), as we move higher on the structure of knowledge, we also move up from a lower to a higher level of skills, from memorizing to analyzing, synthesizing, creating, and hypothesizing. Thus, only when a student works in the conceptual realm can he or she be a critical thinker, one of the most desired but least defined goals of education.

Big Ideas

In interdisciplinary work, Big Ideas and Enduring Understandings are the most important thing to know. A universal concept is broad and abstract. It transcends the disciplines and cultures. It is represented by one or two words, and it is timeless and universal in application. Not all concepts are universal. Some are discipline-bound concepts. In the Common Core State Standards for Mathematics, conceptual categories are defined as Number and Quantity, Algebra, Functions, Modeling, Geometry, and Statistics and Probability. Although students will definitely be learning disciplinary concepts, it is the broader concepts that we are interested in to act as a KDB Umbrella across the disciplines. Generally, Statistics and Probability is the most frequently used conceptual category in interdisciplinary work, as it connects to the real world.

In *A Framework for K–12 Science Education: Practices, Crosscutting Concepts, and Core Ideas* (Committee on Conceptual Framework for the New K–12 Science Education Standard, 2012), for example, broad disciplinary concepts have been identified, such as *heredity*. Cross-cutting or interdisciplinary concepts are also identified. They are these:

1. Patterns

2. Cause and effect: mechanism and explanation

3. Scale, proportion, and quantity

4. Systems and system models

5. Energy and matter: flows, cycles, and conservation

6. Structure and function

7. Stability and change

Although these concepts are intended to cut across the different subdisciplines of science, such as life science, ecosystems, and earth and space science, they also are interdisciplinary and can apply to many different subject areas.

One of the most comprehensive lists of Big Ideas that I have seen can be found in the social studies curriculum document *The Ontario Curriculum: Social Studies, Grades 1–6; History and Geography Grades, 7–8* (Ontario Ministry of Education, 2004). This list (shown below) is also in the Ontario curriculum documents for grades 9–12, meaning that these Big Ideas are to be taught from K to 12. The Big Ideas are as follows:

- Systems and structures: human patterns, community, cooperation, governance, causation/cause and effect, natural patterns, environment
- Interactions and interdependence: causation/cause and effect, human and natural patterns, trade exchanges, globalization, community, relationships, civic rights and responsibilities, environment, ecology
- Environment: human and natural systems, human and natural patterns, exploitation and utilization of resources, regions, ecosystems, urbanization
- Change and continuity: causation/cause and effect, human and natural systems, human and natural patterns, time, sustainability, tradition, conflict and cooperation
- Culture: spirituality; ideology; economic, political, and legal systems; communication and language; familial and community structures; education; migration; diversity
- Power and governance: democracy, security, rights and responsibilities, conflict and cooperation, power relationships

Although these concepts have been associated with social studies, they are in fact universal concepts, as a quick glance reveals. Many of these concepts also appear in the cross-cutting concepts identified in the K–12 Science Framework.

Erickson's subject area concepts are a good starting place for identifying Big Ideas (Figure 4.2). The list shown above for Big Ideas for social studies is also helpful. Some concepts naturally fall into more than one subject area, such as "cause and effect" and "interaction." Others such as "time/space," "dynamics," or "ratio" appear in only one subject. Teachers, however, quickly see how most disciplinary concepts can apply to more than one discipline. Deciding whether a Big Idea is in the disciplinary or interdisciplinary realm leads to spirited discussion and a deeper understanding of universal concepts.

Figure 4.2   Examples of Subject-Specific Concepts

Science	Social Studies	Literature
Cause/effect	Cause/effect	Cause/effect
Order	Order	Order
Organism	Patterns	Patterns
Population	Populations	Characters
System	System	Interconnections
Change	Change/culture	Change
Evolution	Evolution	Evolution
Cycle	Cycle	Cycle
Interaction	Interaction	Interaction
Energy matter	Perception	Perception
Equilibrium	Civilization	Intrigue
Field	Migration/immigration	Passion
Force	Interdependence	Hate
Model	Diversity	Love
Time/space	Conflict/cooperation	Family
Theory	Innovation	Conflict/cooperation

(Continued)

Figure 4.2 (Continued)

Fundamental entities	Beliefs/values	
Replication		
Mathematics	**Visual Art**	**Music**
Number	Rhythm	Rhythm
Ratio	Line	Melody
Proportion	Color	Harmony
Scale	Value	Tone
Symmetry	Shape	Pitch
Probability	Texture	Texture
Pattern	Form	Form
Interaction	Space	Tempo
Cause/effect	Repetition	Dynamics
Order	Balance	Timbre
Quantification	Angle	Pattern
System	Perception	Perception
Theory	Position	
Field	Motion	
Gradient	Light	
Invariance		
Model		

SOURCE: From *Stirring the Head, Heart, and Soul: Redefining Curriculum and Instruction* (p. 71), by H. L. Erickson, 1995, Thousand Oaks: Corwin. Copyright 1995 by Corwin. Reprinted with permission.

Enduring Understandings

Beyond the Big Ideas is a still higher level of knowledge. Teachers need to teach to the Enduring Understandings. An Enduring Understanding is the knowledge that students will remember long past the lesson, for years to come (Wiggins & McTighe, 2005). Essential Learnings and Generalizations are other terms that are used (Erickson, 1995). Sometimes you will see the term Principles (Tomlinson et al., 2009). Enduring Understandings are similar to Big Ideas, because they are broad, abstract, universal in application, and timeless. However, usually an Enduring Understanding connects two concepts or Big Ideas. They can seem very superficial, but they are actually quite profound in that they express a relationship that is true in many different contexts or cultures.

Enduring Understandings are not always immediately apparent in curriculum documents. They are easiest to find in the more broad-based or abstract standards. Consider the following Enduring Understandings that emerged from disciplinary standards:

- The use, distribution, and significance of resources are affected by the interaction of humans with physical resources.
- Art reflects and shapes culture.
- Patterns are often revealed through statistical analysis, and they enable prediction.
- Diet affects health, appearance, and performance.

Enduring Understandings found in disciplines often reappear throughout grades K to 12. With a broader interpretation, these understandings are also interdisciplinary. Later in this chapter, we will see how Enduring Understandings can be interpreted using an interdisciplinary lens.

WHAT IS WORTH DOING?

As educators wrestle with vast amounts of content, there is a continuing shift to generic skills as most important to learn. Some worry that skills are taught at the expense of "important" content, but one needs the skills to process the content. Teaching these skills does not preclude teaching content; rather, the content is a vehicle for acquiring the skills and vice versa. In interdisciplinary work, "technology across the curriculum" and "language across the curriculum" are not hollow phrases but reflect complex performance skills that all teachers are mandated to teach in their areas with the new Common Core State Standards. Students might, for example, design, create, and market their own product using language arts, applied technology, and so on. Computers can be used to enhance critical thinking and for a variety of educational purposes such as experimentation, inquiry, problem solving, interactive learning, drawing, composing, and role-playing. Clearly, these uses are not subject- or content-specific.

The Do of the Common Core State Standards of Mathematics is clearly defined in the more generic Mathematical Practices interwoven through all conceptual categories such as Algebra and Modeling:

1. Make sense of problems and persevere in solving them.

2. Reason abstractly and quantitatively.

3. Construct viable arguments and critique the reasoning of others.

4. Model with mathematics.

5. Use appropriate tools strategically.

6. Attend to precision.

7. Look for and make sense of structure.

8. Look for and express regularity in repeated reasoning.

Many of these skills could also apply to other subject areas such as science. Indeed the narrative describing modeling in the mathematics document states, "Quantities and their relationships in physical, economic, public policy, social, and everyday situations can be modeled using mathematical and statistical procedures." In the real world, modeling really is important only when it is connected to a real-life application—which will ultimately be connected to at least one other subject area.

Inquiry and research skills belong in every discipline—albeit they may be slightly different in each subject area. The skills that compose the Do for science and engineering, for example, are defined in *A Framework for K–12 Science Education* and are a version of inquiry, or in this case the scientific method:

1. Asking questions (for science) and defining problems (for engineering)

2. Developing and using models

3. Planning and carrying out investigations

4. Analyzing and interpreting data

5. Using mathematics and computational thinking

6. Constructing explanations (for science) and designing solutions (for engineering)

7. Engaging in argument from evidence

8. Obtaining, evaluating, and communicating information

Similarly, literacy skills are embedded in every subject area. This is made explicit by the documents for literacy in history/social studies, science, and technical subjects. This interdisciplinary approach to literacy and new emphasis on informational texts means that there is shared responsibility for students' literacy development. Some teachers are inclined to think that they are to teach a single subject. "I teach science, not English" has often been the answer to previous attempts to get subject-area teachers to take responsibility for literacy skills. With the new emphasis on literacy, this disciplinary approach is harder, if not impossible, to accept. Some language skills that apply to all subjects are these:

- Reading between the lines (inference)
- Identifying the most and least important ideas in a text
- Drawing conclusions from a text
- Generating ideas for writing
- Writing a procedure, information report, business report, explanation
- Revising and editing
- Communication strategies (pairs, small groups, whole-class discussions, presentations)

What are the skills that North American graduates must acquire? There is much talk about the 21st Century Skills. One of the most influential organizations promoting complex interdisciplinary skills is the Partnership for 21st Century Skills or P21 (http://www.P21.org). P21 defines the 21st Century Skills as the following:

- Learning and innovation skills:
  - Creativity and innovation
  - Critical thinking and problem solving
  - Communication and collaboration
- Digital literacy skills:
  - Information literacy
  - Media literacy
  - ICT (information and communications technology) literacy

The criteria for each of these skills (or subsets of skills) are further defined for each skill's characteristics (Trilling & Fadel, 2009). Figure 4.3 shows you how P21 defines critical thinking and problem solving.

Looking at Figure 4.3, it is clear that there are many parallels between the mathematical practices in the *Framework* and the scientific and engineering inquiry skills discussed above. Indeed critical thinking and problem solving might very well cut across all disciplines. The Partnership for 21st Century Skills offers a "P21 Common Core Toolkit" (available at their website) that helps districts to align the Common Core State Standards with the *Framework.* The toolkit offers a comprehensive guide to alignment of the P21 skills with the new standards, sample lesson vignettes that use the P21 skills and the Common Core State Standards, resources for those implementing the standards, and assessment resources.

Figure 4.3   Critical Thinking and Problem-Solving Skills as Defined by the Partnership for 21st Century Skills

Students should be able to:

Reason effectively

- Use various types of reasoning (inductive, deductive, etc.) as appropriate to the situation

Use systems thinking

- Analyze how parts of a whole interact with each other to produce overall outcomes in complex systems

Make judgments and decisions

- Effectively analyze and evaluate evidence, arguments, claims and beliefs
- Analyze and evaluate major alternative points of view
- Synthesize and make connections between information and arguments
- Interpret information and draw conclusions based on the best analysis
- Reflect critically on learning experiences and processes

Solve problems

- Solve different kinds of non-familiar problems in both conventional and innovative ways
- Identify and ask significant questions that clarify various points of view and lead to better solutions

SOURCE: Copyright © Partnership for 21st Century Skills. Reprinted by permission of the Partnership for 21st Century Skills, http://www.p21.org.

HOW DO WE WANT OUR STUDENTS TO BE?

Inevitably, the Do blurs into the Be. We cannot do something without it being grounded in a value system. We read, write, listen, and speak from an often-unrecognized value-laden perspective. Our Doings are based on a set of values. To further complicate the picture, our students today need to be global citizens. They need sophisticated skills for this role, such as the ability to understand and consider different cultural perspectives and the ability to address issues in different languages. What is worth knowing is not content bound but does involve complex performance skills and is concerned with how we want people to be in the world.

Rarely is Being identified in the curriculum, although it is usually implicit in the standards. The Being layer has been problematic because it was difficult to measure and it fell into the territory of values. The controversy revolved around whose values should be taught. Some parents believe that teaching values does not belong in the schools. The reality is that values are taught in the school every day whether we acknowledge it or not. If, for example, the teacher negotiates the curriculum, students experience democratic values. Teaching citizenship is value-laden. Teachers have expectations of students that are also value laden such as good work habits and respect for others. Many classrooms develop a code of conduct that students follow. Character education and service education both teach the Be aspect of the curriculum.

The Partnership for 21st Century Skills has a cluster of "skills" that actually represent the Be. They are under the label of Career and Life Skills and include flexibility and adaptability, initiative and self-direction, social and cross-cultural skills, productivity and accountability, leadership and responsibility.

The Know, Do, and Be are interwoven. The Common Core State Standards want students to Be college and career ready. English language arts Common Core State Standards want students to Know (strong content background), Do (respond to varying demands of audience, task, and purpose; comprehend as well as critique; use technology and digital media strategically and capably) and Be (independent learners who value evidence and appreciate other perspectives and cultures). The Common Core State Standards for mathematics want students to be numerate—to Know (mathematical concepts) and Do (problem solve applying mathematical concepts/procedures in a real-world context) and Be (persistent, precise problem solvers). The framework for science wants students to be scientifically literate. Students need to Know (the content—disciplinary and cross-cutting concepts) and Do (apply cross-cutting concepts to deepen understanding of core ideas by using scientific inquiry and engineering design projects in a real-world context). For the Be, by the end of Grade 12 the science standards require that students be able

> to be critical consumers of scientific information related to their everyday lives, and to continue to learn about science throughout their lives. They should come to appreciate that science and the current scientific understanding of the world are the result of many hundreds of years of creative human endeavor. (Committee on Conceptual Framework, 2012, p. 19)

At the same time, the standards want the student to Be in awe and wonder for the beauty of the natural world.

Service learning is another route to both interdisciplinary work and the Be. Research on service learning from 1990 to 1999 done by the

National Service Learning Partnership indicates that students who engage in service learning demonstrate an increase in the following areas (Billig, 2000):

- Altruism and caring for others
- Concern about their community
- Social competence
- Personal and social responsibility
- Trustworthiness and reliability

Clearly, these characteristics are in the Being realm. Interestingly, the research also indicated some associated gains in academic skills and knowledge for those who participated in the service learning as well as fewer discipline problems and improved attendance (Billig, 2000).

It is impossible to teach a value-free curriculum unless learning remains at the lowest level of regurgitation of facts. As soon as higher levels of thinking are demanded, students have to apply values. How does one evaluate, process information, problem solve, and apply life skills without some value base? For many teachers, the Be is actually the most important thing that they teach, and it gives them the greatest rewards.

The Big Picture Learning (http://www.bigpicture.org) is an educational reform group that helps design public charter high schools. It began with one school—the Metropolitan Regional Career and Technical Center in Providence, Rhode Island—and today there six such "Met" schools among the 67 Big Picture schools around the United States, 23 in Australia, 27 in Israel, 13 in the Netherlands, and one in Canada. The network's philosophy stresses that the schools must be personalized and each student must have an equal opportunity to learn. These schools are changing the face of U.S. education under the Big Picture Learning umbrella. Dennis Littky (2004) is codirector of Big Picture Learning, and it was his vision that has guided curriculum planning based on a unique perspective on the real goals of education. He wants students to be

- Lifelong learners
- Passionate
- Risk takers
- Problem solvers and critical thinkers
- Ingenious thinkers
- Self-directed
- Willing to give back to society
- Creative
- Persevering
- Morally courageous
- Self-respecting
- Able to use the world around them well

- Literate and be able to work with numbers
- Able to truly enjoy life and work

Using a curriculum based on this interpretation of the KDB, students have individualized learning plans that emphasize their unique needs and passions. The curriculum is based on five learning goals that the teachers believe are necessary for success at college and work (Littky, 2004):

- Communication: How do I take in and express information?
- Social reasoning: What do other people have to say about this?
- Quantitative reasoning: How do I measure or represent it?
- Empirical reasoning: How do I prove it?
- Personal qualities: What do I bring to this process (e.g., respect, honesty, empathy, self-responsibility, perseverance, organization, self-awareness, time management, cooperation, community involvement)?

The Big Picture schools do not teach subjects. These five learning goals are interdisciplinary. They also show how the Know, Do, and Be are truly interdependent.

THE SCAN AND CLUSTER: USING THE ZOOM LENS TO IDENTIFY THE KDB

The first question of backward design is how to determine what is worth knowing, doing, and being. So far, we have looked at this question with a wide-angle lens. In other words, we looked at what we expected a student to know, do, and be at the end of his or her career as a student. Now we will look at knowing, doing, and being when creating a curriculum at a certain grade level. At this point, we will use a zoom lens to zero in on the mandated standards.

When we are creating a curriculum for a specific level, we need to decide on the Know, Do, and Be based on the mandated standards for that level. The process begins at the disciplinary level. The KDB Umbrella is the focus for all planning. To identify the KDB at the specific grade level, the standards of each discipline need to be scanned through the Scan and Cluster process mentioned at the beginning of the chapter.

I have developed many curricula with teams of teachers, both as a teacher and as a curriculum professor. In each case, the number of standards we needed to address across selected subject areas overwhelmed us. We found that if we selected broad-based standards representing Enduring Understandings or Ideas and 21st Century Skills and developed curricula around them, we were actually covering many of the more concrete standards at the same time. This did not mean that we simply checked off a standard when it was peripheral to the core teaching. Rather, we had to teach the smaller standard to authentically cover the broad-based standard.

A Scan and Cluster is done both horizontally and vertically. It is done horizontally to identify patterns across the disciplines. It is also done vertically to identify what the students have learned in the grades before and what is expected in the next grade. If teachers create a curriculum map, a Scan and Cluster is a natural next step. (See Chapter 1 for curriculum mapping.) This process will take an hour or two but is invaluable for seeing the Big Picture. Once teachers do a Scan and Cluster, they have a new way of thinking about standards. Thereafter, they can easily sweep through the standards to do a Scan and Cluster whenever they need to.

Educators often resist this step as too labor intensive, but it is really necessary to get to know standards in an "intimate" enough way that one can cluster them into meaningful chunks. The Common Core State Standards in Mathematics offer a good example of this process, as they have clustered connected standards together into meaningful chunks at every grade level. They are organized in a hierarchal order with Domain (concept) at the top, Cluster Heading and a cluster of related standards. See Figure 4.4.

Figure 4.4   Example of a Cluster in Geometry: One Set of Related Standards Chunked Together Under the Cluster Title "Circles"

Domain: High School Geometry

Cluster: Circles

Related Standards

Understand and apply theorems about circles

- G-C.1. Prove all circles are similar.
- G-C.2. Identify and describe relationships among inscribed angles, radii, and chords. *Include the relationship between central, inscribed, and circumscribed angles; inscribed angles on a diameter are right angles; the radius of a circle is perpendicular to the tangent where the radius intersects the circle.*
- G-C.3. Construct the inscribed and circumscribed circles of a triangle, and prove properties of angles for a quadrilateral inscribed in a circle.
- G-C.4. (+) Construct a tangent line from a point outside a given circle to the circle.

Find arc lengths and areas of sectors of circles

- G-C.5. Derive using similarity the fact that the length of the arc intercepted by an angle is proportional to the radius, and define the radian measure of the angle as the constant of proportionality; derive the formula for the area of a sector.

SOURCE: http://www.corestandards.org/the-standards/mathematics/high-school -geometry/circles/.

Teachers need an organizer to Scan and Cluster the standards in a relevant manner. A good organizer is framework of the Know, Do, and Be categories (Drake & Burns, 2004). With this framework in mind, the first step is the scan. Scanning means skimming all the standards for a general sense of what is required. This gives an overview of the way the KDB Umbrella might be created. The horizontal scan involves scanning across the disciplinary standards for the grade in question. This can be done for the standards of all the disciplines or just the ones that are scheduled for integration. The vertical scan is to look at the standards vertically for two grades below and one grade above the specific grade level under consideration (Figure 4.5). This gives a sense of what the students will be expected to know and do and where they are headed in the future.

The process of scanning and clustering can be done using a template similar to a curriculum map, but the map specifically looks at clustering standards from across the curriculum. There are many different ways to do the process. Using colored markers to differentiate between 21st Century Skills and Big Ideas is a very good way to begin. Figure 4.6 offers a horizontal Scan and Cluster, and Figure 4.7 illustrates a vertical Scan and Cluster from the context of the Grade 4 curriculum design on habitats. In Chapter 2, Figure 2.11 also illustrates a vertical Scan and Cluster. A more detailed explanation of scanning and clustering can be found in *Meeting Standards Through Integrated Curriculum* (Drake & Burns, 2004).

CREATING THE KDB UMBRELLA

At this point you probably have a good idea of what is an age-appropriate topic that is relevant and is also connected to a set of standards. Your goal is to create a KDB Umbrella that will guide all your subsequent planning (Figure 4.8). It is good that this KDB Umbrella is as broad-based as is practical, because you will need to ensure that you actually teach and assess whatever appears on the Umbrella. Choose only one or two Big Ideas and

Figure 4.5   A Diagram to Show the Process of a Scan and Cluster for Grade 7

Grade	Math	Science	Arts	Language Arts
5				
6				
7				
8				

Figure 4.6   A Horizontal Scan and Cluster

Broad-Based Standard	Clusters
Investigate the dependency of plants and animals on their habitat and the interrelationships of the plants and animals living in a specific habitat (science).	*Science* • Classify organisms according to their role in the food chain. • Demonstrate the understanding of the food chain as a system in which energy from the sun. • Formulate questions about and identify needs of animals and plants in specific habitat. • Use appropriate vocabulary. • Compile data through investigation. • Construct food chains that include different plant and animal species.
	Math • Collect and organize data and identify their use. • Predict the results of data collected. Interpret displays of data and present information using mathematical items. • Solve simple problems using the concept of probability.
Begin to develop research skills (English).	*Social Science* • Ask pertinent questions. • Locate relevant information. • Sort and classify information to identify issues, solve problems, and make decisions. • Construct and read a variety of graphs, charts, diagrams, maps, and models. • Communicate information using media works, oral presentations, written notes, descriptions, and drawings. • Use appropriate vocabulary.
	Language Arts • Use vocabulary learned in other subject areas. • Use effective openings and closings in oral presentations.
	Visual Art • Identify monochromatic color schemes. • Demonstrate awareness that overlapping shapes creates the illusion of depth. • Plan a work of art. • Solve artistic problems in their art work.
Produce two- or three-dimensional works of art that communicate ideas for specific purposes and to specific audiences (Visual Art)	• Identify strengths and areas of improvement in their own work and others.
	Language Arts • Use some vocabulary learned in other subject areas. • Use appropriate tone of voice and gestures in social and classroom activities.

SOURCE: Tom Martin, Phil Teeuwsen, and John Molnar.

Figure 4.7   A Vertical Scan and Cluster

	Science	Language Arts	Visual Art	Drama and Dance
Grade 2	Topic: Growth and change in animals. Investigate physical and behavioral characteristics and the process of growth of different types of animals.	Determine the meaning of words and phrases in a text relevant to a Grade 2 topic or subject. Write informative/explanatory texts in which they introduce a topic, use facts and definitions to develop points, and provide a concluding statement or section.	Produce two- and three-dimensional works of art that communicate ideas or specific purposes.	Communicate understanding of works in drama through discussion, writing, movement, and visual artwork.
Grade 3	Topic: Growth and change in plants. Investigate the requirements of plants and the effects of changes in the environmental conditions on plants.	Determine the meaning of words and phrases in a text relevant to a Grade 3 topic or subject. Write informative/explanatory texts to examine a topic and convey ideas and information clearly.	Produce two- and three-dimensional works of art that communicate ideas or specific purposes.	Compare own work with work of others in drama and dance through discussion, writing, movement, and visual artwork.
Grade 4	Topic: Habitats and communities. Investigate the dependency of plants and animals on their habitat and the interrelationships of the plants and animals within habitats.	Determine the meaning of words and phrases in a text relevant to a Grade 4 topic or subject. Write informative/explanatory texts to examine a topic and convey ideas and information clearly.	Produce two- and three-dimensional works of art that communicate ideas or specific purposes.	Communicate orally and in writing response to own and others' work and compare responses.

(Continued)

Figure 4.7 (Continued)

	Science	Language Arts	Visual Art	Drama and Dance
Grade 5	Topic: Human organ systems. Investigate the structure and function of the five major organ systems.	Determine the meaning of words and phrases in a text relevant to a Grade 5 topic or subject. Write informative/ explanatory texts to examine a topic and convey ideas and information clearly.	Produce two- and three-dimensional works of art that communicate ideas or specific purposes.	Describe orally and in writing response to own and others' work in drama and dance.

SOURCE: Tom Martin, Phil Teeuwsen, and John Molnar.

Enduring Understandings and only a few 21st Century Skills (there are not that many of these), and make sure the Be is embedded in the standards *or* that you will actually require students to demonstrate this in the culminating activity and the daily activities and assessments.

Figure 4.8   The KDB Umbrella

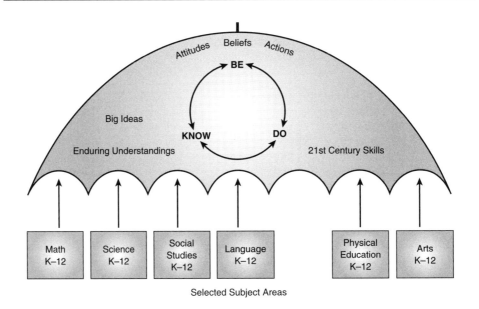

FINDING THE KNOW

To find the Know in the documents, scan the different disciplinary documents to identify the Big Ideas or universal concepts. Often, such concepts are poorly identified in the documents. Although this weakness is being addressed in more recent versions of curriculum documents, it is still often up to the educator to determine a conceptual focus to tie the disciplines together. Using interdisciplinary concepts as a lens, educators may scan the grade-level documents and decide that a concept such as "interdependence" is relevant to the standards in more than one subject area. A Grade 4 curriculum, for example, that is integrating content on ecosystems and geographical regions can focus on "interdependence" as a conceptual lens. This allows for a natural connection across the subject areas.

When scanning for the Know, it is helpful to keep the structure of knowledge in mind. What are the facts, disciplinary concepts, Big Ideas, and broad-based standards that could serve as Enduring Understandings?

Big Ideas

Teachers can identify Big Ideas in curriculum documents by circling or highlighting the nouns that express universal concepts. At this point, teachers can identify the Big Ideas that can act as an umbrella for the disciplines. If there are no Big Ideas embedded into the standards, teachers can add a conceptual focus to bridge the disciplines. Adding a conceptual focus is rarely a false fit; rather, it tends to focus an integrated unit in manageable ways. A conceptual focus that is a natural fit usually is obvious even if it is not stated directly in the documents—since most documents are not yet written from an interdisciplinary perspective.

Anne Foley and Marjorie Condon (2005) offer an effective process to determine the Big Ideas. This works for science and social studies or history and geography. Language arts or math standards often represent the process skills needed throughout the teaching of science and social studies. To begin, photocopy all the standards for one subject at a given grade level. Then, cut up the photocopied standards into individual statements, removing any identifying information such as code number or strand (e.g., earth and space science or life systems). Mix up the individual pieces of paper. Sort the standards into piles according to a Big Idea that unites them. There will usually be only three or four piles. Identify an umbrella Big Idea for each pile.

I did this with a group for Grade 1 science, and we found that almost every standard fell under the concepts of reproduction, survival, or patterns. These ideas are much bigger than topics such as "bears" or "pioneers." The umbrella for all of our selected three Big Ideas was "interdependence."

Similarly, other groups at other grade levels easily completed this process to identify the Big Ideas. Amazingly, the teachers had identified possible themes for a full year.

In Figure 2.12 in Chapter 2, there is a sample of a yearlong conceptual map. This is an interesting way to do long-term planning with concepts. It is not far, then, to connect the Big Ideas across subject area to create the KDB Umbrella.

Enduring Understandings

One way to create good Enduring Understandings is to connect two Big Ideas with a verb (Erickson, 1995). Here are some examples:

- Cultures define conflict.
- Patterns occur in all systems.
- Individual values influence decision making.

Typically, the Enduring Understanding is connected to the Essential Questions. Chapter 5 deals with how to create Essential Questions in detail. The same process that is outlined in that chapter can be used for creating Enduring Understandings.

A logical and common way to identify the Enduring Understandings is to begin with the disciplinary documents. Are there any standards that stand out as most important for students to meet? Enduring Understandings are not necessarily immediately apparent in curriculum documents. They are easiest to find in the more broad-based standards. Sometimes documents identify the standards that are most important to learn in a topic area. Usually the Enduring Understandings emerge from these standards.

Enduring Understandings found in single disciplines are often spiraled throughout K to 12. With a broader interpretation, these understandings are also interdisciplinary. Figure 4.9 indicates how an understanding that originates from disciplinary standards can be interpreted from an interdisciplinary perspective.

FINDING THE DO

It is important to cluster standards into meaningful chunks to identify the Do. To find the Do in disciplinary standards, we need to know (a) what complex performance skills we are looking for, (b) the subset of skills embedded in those complex performance skills, and (c) the criteria necessary to demonstrate the subskills. Most complex skills are found in every disciplinary document. It is very important to have an idea of the skill subset involved in a complex performance skill to be able to cluster skills

Figure 4.9   Interdisciplinary Enduring Understandings

Enduring Understanding	Discipline of Origin	Related Disciplines
The use, distribution, and significance of resources are affected by the interaction of humans with physical resources.	Geography	Science Mathematics History
Art reflects and shapes culture.	Art	History Geography
Patterns are often revealed through statistical analysis and enable prediction.	Mathematics	History Geography English Science
Diet affects health, appearance, and performance.	Health	Mathematics Science History Geography Physical Education

appropriately. Some of the complex skills one might look for are communication, problem solving, inquiry, design and construction, research and information management, prediction, critical thinking, and presentation skills. These are 21st Century Skills that have many parts—all of which may need to be taught. For example, look back at Figure 4.3 to see how the Partnership for 21st Century Skills identifies the subset of skills necessary for critical thinking.

One helpful method is to use different-colored highlighters to identify the potential standards to chunk together. If, for example, teachers choose research as the skill to be emphasized in an interdisciplinary approach, they would highlight each standard that is related to research in the subject areas. This would include the subset of skills such as asking a question, collecting relevant data, and analyzing the data. We may wish to search for communication skills in a disciplinary document. This is a huge area encompassing reading, writing, listening, and oral language skills. Each set of skills has many subskills within it. Unpacking the standards by noting the verbs will reveal which communication skills are required for each standard. This unpacking has, in part, been done for you in the Common Core State Standards for Literacy in History/Social Studies, Science, and Technical Subjects. In these documents, communication skills are named for the subject areas.

Within the standards, there is often room for interpretation. When the word *describe* is in a standard, a student must use a communication skill. The description may be demonstrated through writing or speaking. This interpretation is up to the teacher. The student, however, is expected, to use standard language conventions regardless of the method of communication. "Language: Conventions, effective use and vocabulary" is a separate strand of the Common Core State Standards as are Reading, Writing, and Speaking and Listening. The four strands are not meant to be implemented in isolation; rather, they are intended to be an integrated model of literacy.

Another way to approach the Do is to look for a smaller skill or subset of skills in the disciplinary guidelines. We may look for "presentation skills" rather than for the larger umbrella of communication skills. Presentation skills will have their own set of criteria that students may need to learn before they can present well. These criteria are now explicit in the Common Cores State Standards College and Career Readiness Standards for Speaking and Listening. As soon as students are doing a presentation in any subject area other than English language arts, they are doing an interdisciplinary task.

To scan the documents and cluster them into the Do, we select a complex skill, identify the subset of skills embedded in it, and recognize the necessary criteria to master the subskills. This sounds very complicated, but once one has done this type of Scan and Cluster, it becomes fairly easy. What makes this task harder is that disciplinary documents generally do not identify the complex skills and the criteria for their sets of subskills explicitly. What makes it vitally important, however, is that the identification of criteria directly aligns with the assessment of interdisciplinary work. These criteria become the performance indicators in the rubrics designed to assess the skills.

DISCOVERING THE BE

In many standards, the Be does not exist, because the standards were constructed deliberately to be value free, in an effort to avoid the contentious issue of whose values are correct and therefore teachable. Nevertheless, the standards do have implicit values within them. This is particularly true when the standards are broad-based.

When doing a Scan and Cluster, teachers can identify the Be element that is inherent in existing standards. They can analyze the standards to discover implicit values (see Figures 2.5 and 2.6). Also, there is a way to discover the Be that is implicit in an Enduring Understanding. The formula is this: "When you understand that (fill in the Enduring Understanding here), then. . . ." This resulting statement identifies the "so what" implicit in a standard and informs us how we want students to Be in the world.

Figure 4.10 shows how this might look using the Enduring Understandings that previously may have seemed value free. I am indebted to Nina Schlikin, who was superintendent of School Union 29, Poland, Maine, when she shared this valuable idea with me.

Figure 4.10   Finding the Be in the Enduring Understandings

When you understand that . . . (Enduring Understanding)	then you understand that . . . (BE)
WYUT . . . the earth's water systems influence the climate and weather of the region where they are located,	TYUT . . . we must use water in a responsible way.
WYUT . . . different geographical regions are interdependent (e.g., economically, culturally, governmentally),	TYUT . . . we must consider many different aspects of a region and how it affects other regions when making decisions.
WYUT . . . medieval society influenced modern society,	TYUT . . . we need to study history to understand how the past affects the present so that we can make wise decisions about the future.
WYUT . . . the proper knowledge and use of vocabulary and language conventions affects effective communication,	TYUT . . . we need to know and use proper language conventions so that we can communicate effectively with others and so that we can succeed in life.
WYUT . . . the human use of technology has an impact on ecosystems and that humans are responsible to preserve ecosystems.	TYUT . . . we must use technology in a way that sustains ecosystems.

NOTE: WYUT = When you understand that . . . TYUT = Then you understand that . . . .

CREATING AN EXPLORATORY WEB

At some point in this process, educators need to work with more than the abstract. They need to know that it is possible to connect subject areas through standards. At this point they can brainstorm for possible ways to connect selected subject areas and still be aligned with the standards. Usually this is done through a multidisciplinary lens when the standards and their possibilities are fresh in one's mind. Figure 4.11 shows you a typical exploratory web.

CREATING ESSENTIAL QUESTIONS TO GUIDE CURRICULUM PLANNING

Essential Questions and Unit Questions

Essential Questions align the KDB with a Rich Culminating Assessment Task. They also act as a focus for planning the unit. The Essential

Figure 4.11   An Exploratory Web

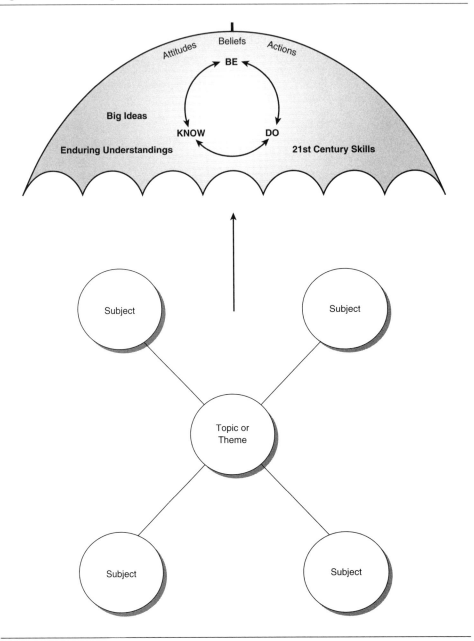

Question is a question that you decide upon as you think about your KDB Umbrella and what you unit might look like. In addition, there are usually unit questions that zoom in on the specific content to be covered if it is a long unit. These questions might act as guiding questions for a miniunit when you are planning for daily activities and assessments.

Essential Questions are different from unit questions. They are written in "kid speak," pose a problem or reveal a controversy, or ask students to prove a point. Unit questions help the students answer the Essential Question and address the Enduring Understanding. Unit questions are subject specific. In Figure 4.12 shows examples of Essential Questions and unit questions from Schmied (2005a).

Essential Questions cut across the disciplines and relate to the real world. Because they are open-ended, they require an interdisciplinary approach to answer them. They lead to other questions and are engaging to students. Like Enduring Understandings, Essential Questions are timeless, cross-cultural, universal, and written at the conceptual level.

Essential Questions are meaty questions that require higher order thinking. Some experts suggest that to ensure higher order thinking, it is best to begin an essential question with a *why* or *how* rather than a *what, when,* or *where.*

- How does a community work together effectively?
- How do cultures affect one another?
- How can you measure freedom?
- Why do different cultures use land differently?
- How do religious conflicts from the past affect us today?
- Why is *x* heroic?

Figure 4.12   Essential Questions and Unit Questions

Essential Questions	Unit Questions
How does culture define conflict?	What is conflict? How did culture influence the way Americans reacted to English laws in 1776? How do differing cultures express conflict?
How are patterns seen in systems?	What is a variable? What is a system of equations? How do you solve a system of linear equations with two variables?
How do values influence decision making?	What is the role of values in your life? How does Tom Sawyer's decision show/demonstrate what he thinks is important? How are decisions related to core values?

SOURCE: Reprinted with permission from "A view that matters: Understanding essential questions," presented by Kathy Schmied © 2005. Performance Learning Systems, Inc®, Allentown, PA. www.plsweb.com. All rights reserved.

Wiggins and McTighe (2005) argue that Essential Questions do not have to begin with *why* or *how*. Instead, these questions can begin with any adverb as long as they are wide-open questions that lead to a rich inquiry:

- What is love?
- What is the purpose of life?
- Who is the master of the universe?
- Where is your real home?

CREATING ESSENTIAL QUESTIONS ACROSS THE CURRICULUM

I attended a workshop in which Kathy Schmied (2005b) introduced me to an intriguing process to create Essential Questions. Participants in her workshop formed groups of four. Each group was given play dough and a card that said either "A bird has a beak" or "Life forms are equipped with the tools needed to survive." We were asked to keep what was on our card a secret from the other groups and to make a representation with the play dough of the statement on our card. No one realized that Kathy had given out equal numbers of only these two statements.

Kathy asked us to share our representations and asked these questions:

- Why did you choose this item to represent your creation?
- Did you have an image in your mind prior to your creation?
- What type of discussion did your group have prior to creating your representation?
- How were the different creations connected to the statements given to the groups?
- How do the statements differ?
- How did the differences in the statements affect the outcomes?

It was fascinating to see the different creations that were produced. Each group that had received the bird statement created a representation that was clearly a bird with a beak. The groups that had received the statement "Life forms are equipped with the tools needed to survive" created a wide variety of representations for the statement. Kathy pointed out that the bird statement was a "fact statement" and that the life forms statement was a "conceptual statement."

Kathy emphasized that the difference between a fact statement and a conceptual statement meant a difference not only in the end product but also in the approach and planning for the representation. Those of us who received the conceptual statement spent time in rich discussion about what the statement meant and how to best represent it. In contrast, the participants with the factual card did not have to spend time deciding what a bird was. Kathy noted that this is true in teaching situations as well. When we work at the factual level, we do not need to challenge our thinking. When we work at the conceptual level, we need to engage in higher order thinking.

My experience in the workshop illustrated to me how difficult it may be for some teachers to accept the ambiguity around forming Essential Questions. When my group received the "Life forms are equipped with the tools needed to survive" statement, one person in the group offered her answer. When each of the other three group members offered a different interpretation, the first person angrily argued that hers was the "right answer" and that we should create our representation based on it. While the rest of us entered a rich discussion about the various things the statement could mean, the first person physically withdrew from the group.

A Formula for Essential Questions

Schmied (2005a) offers a simple, but effective, formula:

CONCEPT + VERB + CONCEPT = A GOOD ESSENTIAL QUESTION

This could be interpreted as:

BIG IDEA + VERB + BIG IDEA = A GOOD ESSENTIAL QUESTION

She had us develop a word bank that was filled with verbs that work well in creating Essential Questions. Here are some examples of good verbs:

- Guide
- Relate
- Promote
- Influence
- Provoke
- Change
- Affect
- Perpetuate
- Diminish
- Help
- Transform

To create good questions, teachers connect interdisciplinary Big Ideas with a verb to create a question that begins with *how* or *why.* The following questions are further examples:

- How do resources promote conflict?
- How do social inequities provoke civil war?

- Why does culture perpetuate conflict?
- How do values influence decision making?

Connecting Essential Questions to Enduring Understandings

Using Schmied's system, teachers can create their own Essential Questions and thus will potentially create Enduring Understandings. Alternatively, they can use this same process to create Enduring Understandings and then move to Essential Questions (Figure 4.13). Once more, the curriculum designer must recognize that this will not be a linear process; the designer may return more than once to places he or she has passed before.

Figure 4.13   Creating Enduring Understandings and Essential Questions

Enduring Understandings	↔	Essential Questions
Cultures define conflict.	↔	How does culture define conflict?
Patterns occur in all systems.	↔	How are patterns seen in systems?
Individual values influence decision making.	↔	How do values influence decision making?
The use, distribution, and significance of resources are affected by the interaction of humans with physical resources.	↔	How are the use, distribution, and significance of resources affected by the interaction of humans with physical resources?
Art reflects and shapes culture.	↔	Why does art reflect and shape culture?
Patterns are often revealed through statistical analysis, and how do they enable prediction.	↔	What patterns are often revealed through statistical analysis, and they enable prediction?
Diet affects health, appearance, and performance.	↔	Why does diet affect health, appearance, and performance?

Developing Essential Questions From Enduring Understandings

Sometimes an Essential Question is developed from the standards themselves. Usually such a question involves a broad-based standard found in one discipline, often from a science or social studies document. Mary Anne McDowell developed Essential Questions from the overall expectations in her province's Grade 4 science curriculum guidelines for a unit on life systems. These broad-based standards also acted as their Enduring Understandings. Figure 4.14 illustrates this connection.

Figure 4.14   Creating Enduring Understandings and Essential Questions From Broad-Based Standards

Broad-Based Standards $\longrightarrow$	Enduring Understandings $\longrightarrow$	Essential Questions Topic Questions
Investigate the dependency of plants and animals on their habitat and the interrelationships of the plants and the animals living in a specific habitat. $\longrightarrow$	Plants and animals in a specific habitat are interdependent. $\longrightarrow$	How are plants and animals in a specific environment interdependent?
Describe ways in which humans can change habitats and the effects of these changes on the plants and animals within the habitat. $\longrightarrow$	Humans are a part of the natural environment and have an impact on it. $\longrightarrow$	How are humans a part of the natural environment, and what impact to they have on it? What potential impact do humans have on their environment for better or worse?

SOURCE: Mary Anne McDowell.

In this chapter, how to do the groundwork to create an integrated curriculum was explored. Importantly it is an iterative process where the most important step is to get to know the relevant standards very well. After completing these steps, curriculum designers are ready to put the meat on the bones. In the chapters that follow, we will see how to put this meat on the bones in a way that aligns the standards, content, instructional activities, and assessment in a purposeful way.

DISCUSSION QUESTIONS

1. Explain what the structure of knowledge means to you.

2. How are the Know, Do, and Be connected? Give an example in your own context of this relationship.

3. Read about Big Ideas and Enduring Understandings (Know) and 21st Century Skills (Do). Discuss how this view of what is most important to learn shifts how you design curriculum.

4. For many teachers, the Be is most important. What do you think? How might you teach the Be? Assess it?

5. Recall a unit that you experienced as a student or a teacher. If there were Essential Questions, did they enhance the lessons? If not, what Essential Questions might have improved the unit?

SUGGESTED ACTIVITIES

1. Select standards in three or four subject areas. Include social studies (history/geography) and science. Identify the Big Ideas and Enduring Understandings, recognizing that the curriculum may or may not do it for you. Figure 4.2 should be useful to you.

2. Read about the Do. Using the same standards as in the previous question, identify the 21st Century Skills. Remember that the 21st Century Skills are not necessarily identified for you. You need to scan the standards to see what 21st Century Skills are embedded in the standards. Some 21st Century Skills would be communication (e.g., writing, presentation), problem solving, critical thinking, and design and construction. Look for the subset of skills for one 21st Century Skill. For example, some of the subset skills for critical thinking are found in Figure 4.3.

3. Choose several broad-based standards (from different subject areas). Using the formula from Figure 4.10, extrapolate to discover the Be in the standards.

4. Perform a Scan and Cluster of the standards for your desired grade level. See Figure 4.6 for an example of a horizontal scan, and Figures 4.7, 2.8 and 2.9, to see examples of a vertical scan. Begin with a horizontal scan (across the desired grade level) of the standards in the desired subject areas. Using different-colored highlighters, scan one curriculum document at a time to identify the Know, Do, and Be. When you have completed that task, do a vertical scan (two grades below and one grade above). What patterns do you see?

How Do Teachers Know When Students Have Met Expectations?

The Integrated Curriculum Design Process. As you read this chapter, follow through the completed curriculum in Appendix A to see how the parts fit the whole.

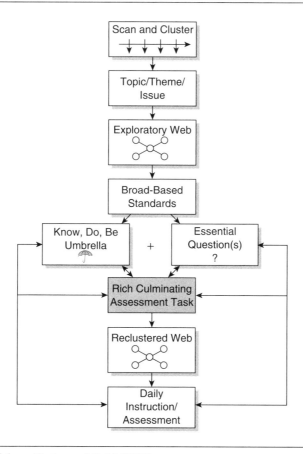

SOURCE: Adapted from Drake and Reid (2010).

The previous chapter presented the groundwork that one needs to explore before designing an integrated curriculum as well as some of the preliminary steps in this process. We looked in depth at the first question of backward mapping: What should students know, do, and be? Then we explored ways to connect disciplines with a Know/Do/Be (KDB) Umbrella, an exploratory web, and the creation of Essential Questions. This chapter examines the next question of backward mapping: How do we, as teachers, know when students know it? What evidence do we have of their knowledge and understanding? What criteria will determine levels of performance? It is helpful to remember that this is rarely a linear process. As you address the Rich Culminating Assessment Task, you will need to revisit the previous steps and perhaps make some changes there in order to ensure alignment.

Before addressing this next step, this chapter explores interdisciplinary assessment: What is it? How do you do it? Who does it? What is assessed? This is followed by an exploration of ways to create substantive Rich Culminating Assessment Tasks (interdisciplinary core assessment tasks) that are aligned with the KDB Umbrella. Finally, we look at appropriate assessment tools to measure levels of student performance on the Rich Culminating Assessment Task.

INTERDISCIPLINARY ASSESSMENT

What Is It?

The term *interdisciplinary assessment* describes the assessment of concepts and skills that cut across the curriculum—the Know (Enduring Understandings and Big Ideas), the Do (21st Century Skills), and the Be. The teacher can assess more than one subject at a time. To think about assessment from an interdisciplinary perspective, one must view the curriculum from the Big Picture perspective.

Although a test is fine as one type of evaluation tool, interdisciplinary assessment tasks require much more. Students must show what they know through what they do. Assessment tasks are performance-based and, as a result, look much like a rich instructional activity. However, the assessment is embedded in the instructional strategy and needs to be aligned with the KDB. Appropriate assessment tools need to accompany the Rich Culminating Assessment Tasks; these tools measure the level of student accomplishment on the learning goals during that activity.

Integrated assessment raises some confusing issues. Usually, teachers must report student achievement in a specific discipline. Indeed, students need to attain disciplinary standards. Naturally, then, teachers tend to think in disciplinary blocks. However, when they shift from the disciplinary focus to the Big Picture, they can work differently. In fact, many teachers say the only way they can assess everything is to integrate the curriculum!

Interdisciplinary assessment is not a term that is frequently used. Yet much of the assessment done in the disciplines can be used in an interdisciplinary way. Enduring Understandings and Big Ideas are universal and timeless, cutting across the disciplines. (A review of Figure 4.9 shows how a seemingly disciplinary understanding can be truly interdisciplinary.) Thus, in each subject, students are studying Enduring Understandings and Big Ideas that could also be explored in other subject areas.

The 21st Century Skills are also interdisciplinary. They are complex, require the acquisition of a subset of skills, and are embedded in the standards. For example, every discipline requires some communication skills. Communication skills should not fall simply into the realm of English or language arts. They rightfully belong in every subject. They are life skills that everyone needs to be successful. This has been addressed in the *Common Core State Standards for English Arts & Literacy in Science, History/Social Studies, and Technological Studies* document. Similarly, research skills are also found in every subject. They may have a slightly different slant, but basically, research is research. This is the same with most of the 21st Century Skills.

The Be is always interdisciplinary. It is about how a student undertakes a task—what he or she does with the Know and Do. The Be is not always assessed. Many districts include the Be in an anecdotal report or as a checklist. Teaches may choose, for example, to assess the effort a student has put into a project or how he or she cooperated in a group; however, current thinking in assessment is that this should not be a part of an actual grade. The Be is often a separate category on the rubric and, in turn, on the report card, where it is shown as "learning skills" or is given a similar name. The Be is generally not as highly valued as the grades in subject areas, although many teachers believe it should be.

To state the most obvious, the Know (content) of interdisciplinary assessment tasks comes from more than one subject area. The Do of most assessment tasks, even when they are subject-based, is already interdisciplinary. We see this in cross-curricular skills such as writing or research skills. When a student gives a PowerPoint presentation about American foreign policy in his history class, he is using a skill set that is equally applicable to his success in a presentation on Jane Austen's social criticism in his English class. It is just as important for academic success to learn the interdisciplinary skills as it is to acquire the mandated knowledge of a subject. It is the interpretation of the assessment task, not the task itself, that determines whether it is disciplinary or interdisciplinary.

From the Big Picture perspective, all assessment tasks are generic. The teacher has a wide range of choices—but it is not an infinite list. Some tasks are more complex than others, and thus different tasks are more appropriate in different situations. Some assessment tasks are listed in Figure 5.1.

Assessment *Of*, *For*, and *As* Learning

Teachers also need to think of the purpose for the assessment. Earl (2003) differentiates among assessment *of* learning (summative), assessment *for* learning (diagnostic and formative), and assessment *as* learning

Figure 5.1   A Sampling of Assessment Tasks

Sample Assessment Tasks			
Big Book	Survey	Videotape	Song
Blog	Podcast	Webpage	Graphic Novel
Crafts	Test	Report	Interviews
Flow Chart	Election	Brochure	Editorial
Electronic Portfolio	WebQuest	Comic Book	YouTube Video
Create a Musical Instrument	Participation in Discussion	Play an Instrument	Persuasive / Argument Writing
Voluntary Responses	Research Project/ Paper	Architectural Design	Computer Program
Puppets	Sculpture	Menu	Eulogy
Map	Family Tree	Mobile	Painting
Recipe	Timeline	Scale Model	Flag
Fiction	Panel Discussion	Costume	Collage
Coordinate an Event	Advertisement, Commercial	Design and Build a Model	Musical Composition
Invention	Constitution	Pantomime	Play Set
Multimedia Presentation	Newspaper, Magazine	Film—Movie Documentary	Instructions, Guidebook
Slide Show	News Story	Diorama	Mock Trial
Jewelry	Teamwork	Debates	Dance
Poetry	Experiments	Visual Display	Photo Essay

Summative evaluation is given at the end point of an instructional segment and is intended to sum up what a student has learned. Traditionally, summative assessment is a test, and it has its place in any educational system. However, a summative assessment can also be a performance assessment that can be interdisciplinary and include the KDB.

The student projects at High Tech High illustrate how students demonstrate their learning. They have created everything from photo essays to an interactive museum-quality exhibit that fits in a window frame to illustrations of the principles of math and physics (http://www.hightechhigh.org/projects/). At the Met schools, students create exhibitions as their summative evaluation (Littky, 2004). These exhibitions are conversations in which the students talk about the process of their learning (Do), and they emphasize both personal growth (Be) and the depth of their learning (Know). Also, students set high standards for themselves (Be) and develop action plans for what comes next (assessment as learning).

Perhaps the most powerful shift in assessment practices is the shift to assessment *for* learning and assessment *as* learning. Shifting to these types of assessments results in significant increases in student test scores and in student learning (Black, Harrison, Lee, Marshall, & Wiliam, 2003). It also requires a dramatic shift in most teachers' practices. Assessment *for* learning includes diagnostic assessment that allows the teacher to make decisions on the direction the teaching should go. Often, this type of assessment is given at the beginning of a unit. Assessment *for* learning is mostly about regular ongoing feedback that enables the students to improve at the same time as it informs the teacher what to do next. This is similar to formative assessment but requires that the students act on the assessment to improve their work. This kind of feedback is not graded. Students act as active assessors in the assessment *as* learning process. Students assess their own work, set goals, and can articulate their own metacognition. Assessment as learning may include journaling, self-assessment, peer assessment, portfolios, and student/teacher/parent conferencing. All tasks require that the learner be reflective about his or her learning. Assessment as learning is never graded.

What Are Interdisciplinary Assessment Tools?

Interdisciplinary assessment tools accompany an interdisciplinary assessment task and are used to measure levels of achievement. They, too, are generic. Again, it is the use of the tool that determines if it is interdisciplinary or not. These are some interdisciplinary assessment tools:

Checklists

Rubrics

Classroom tests

Maps

Self-assessments

Peer assessments

Graphic organizers

Concept maps

Portfolios

Conferences

Both the task and the tool can be adapted to certain circumstances. A generic assessment tool can be applied to each generic product. An advertisement is an advertisement, for example, regardless of the nature of the subject. This is true for any number of generic products such as newspaper articles, a developed argument, persuasive writing, and a brochure. Each product meets certain criteria to be acceptable. One can create an assessment tool based on these criteria, rather than on the characteristics of a discipline.

Who Is Responsible for Teaching the Cross-Curricular Skills?

The "Big Picture teacher" needs to accept responsibility for teaching the procedural skills or making sure students learn the skills necessary to perform the assessment task he or she is asking for. For example, if the students are required to create a computer-generated brochure, they will need to be taught how to manipulate the software to do so. Thus, the teacher needs to have an understanding of the skill to both teach and assess it effectively. This may mean a willingness to learn a new skill or to share the teaching of this skill with a teacher who is able and willing to do this. When a teacher brings technology into the mix, it will often be the student who is the expert and not the teacher, so there may be reversal of roles. Still the teacher and students can collaboratively create a rubric or another assessment tool that accurately assesses what students must know, do, and be to demonstrate that they have mastered the required learning.

Students can't be expected to demonstrate what they do not know how to do. I learned this lesson many years ago. Bruce Hemphill, Ron Chappell, and I were teaching a Grade 9 integrated curriculum. Our students had developed final presentations for their culminating activity. We were thrilled with the students' learning. Confident that others would also be impressed, and hoping to convert our audience to interdisciplinary approaches, we had asked other teachers and parents to attend the presentations. But at the event, the students' presentations were dreadful. The students mumbled into their cheat sheets. Our last hope of redemption lay with a young woman who came to the stage with an audiotape. Alas, she simply turned on the tape recorder and sat there while it played, her barely audible voice whispering her words. After that, we always taught presentation skills before we asked students to perform. Also, we assessed these skills to show the students that we believed they were very important.

Who Assesses What?

Judy Sara is an interdisciplinary curriculum coordinator who spent time studying interdisciplinary assessment as a research project for her master's of education degree. She teaches at the Australian Science and Mathematics School in Adelaide, Australia. This school was set up in 2002 to lead the reform in science and mathematics. It offers an innovative program designed to integrate technology across the curriculum. Although Judy's examples are in the area of nanotechnology, they are really informative for anyone doing interdisciplinary work with any subjects at any level.

Under the title "Toward Nanotechnology," Judy and a group of eight other teachers implemented an 18-week program of 500 minutes weekly for Grade 11 in nanotechnology. There are 12 summative assessments in her program. Judy and her team discovered that they were confronted with assessment tasks outside their areas of expertise. For Judy, coping with this reality is often a question of attitude and willingness to learn new things. What is the purpose of teaching students the skills to be a lifelong learner if teachers believe that the only things they can do are ones they learned while studying to be teachers at a university? In her experience— and she attended a faculty of education 35 years ago—teachers can learn new things and are more than capable of teaching and assessing in areas other than the specializations they were trained in at a university.

Judy and her colleagues came to recognize that there were many ways to assess interdisciplinary work effectively. One way is to have different teachers from different subject areas each evaluate her or his subject-specific part of an assessment task. In Judy's unit called "Technological World," the teachers assessed more than one subject in a number of tasks. For example, students worked in groups of three on the fertile question: "What technology has had the most significant impact on society?" This task was assessed as a science or history task as well as an English task. The groups selected a particular technology and researched it. Then, students wrote essays on the impact on society of their chosen technologies, based on either the science behind the chosen technology or the history of it. This task had English, technology, science, and history rubrics attached to it. The English teacher marked all the essays; the science teacher marked the science and technology essays; a history specialist marked the history essays. In this way, each teacher had a "grade" for reporting in his or her respective discipline.

In another approach, teachers may focus the assessment on only one subject area, although they rely on other subject areas to complete the task. In "Toward Nanotechnology," the Australian team made the decision to concentrate the assessment tasks on only one subject area—even though they were using information that came from a number of areas. The Rich Culminating Assessment Task that serves as an example later in this chapter follows this tradition. This particular assessment task was used to assess English but relied on knowledge from one of the main Rich Culminating Assessment Tasks during the year—a Nano Innovation Expo. An English and a science specialist jointly designed the task. All the teachers assessed the results of this task. A number of the teachers on the team had not taught English before. The English specialist enlightened them on terminology such as "register" and "form." She gave them examples of what to look for and tips for teaching. Also, she showed them examples of the types of comments she would put on different papers and gave feedback on their comments. The English teachers also taught and assessed this task. They relied on the science teacher's expertise to judge the validity of the science and technology that the students were bringing to the "town meeting" in the Rich Culminating Assessment Task described later. This is an excellent example of how literacy across the curriculum can be implemented.

In yet another approach, teachers, peers, invited students, and invited guests were asked to contribute to the evaluation of the Rich Culminating Assessment Task for the Nano Innovation Expo. Students designed nano-products and displayed their ideas, such as stopping the spread of cancer, portable thin TV screens, paints to make planes fly faster, and medicine delivered on contact lenses. The nanoproduct was assessed primarily as a science task, but it also brought in skills from English and philosophy. Visitors received a comprehensive assessment tool that included a description of the task and several rubrics to assess the level of achievement for presentation of the product. The criteria included a rationale for developing the product, the ability to explain the science behind the rubric, a detailed explanation of how the product would be manufactured, and their confidence in this product as a good financial investment.

For Judy Sara and her team, there are many similarities regardless of what approach is chosen to evaluate interdisciplinary work. Teachers decide what they want the students to know and do for each assessment task. Then they spend time developing, reviewing, and revising rubrics according to teacher and student responses. For example, the team has revised the rubrics to have five levels of performance rather than the traditional four. Many students perform very well but do not meet the extremely high criteria that the teachers tend to set for the highest level. The teachers found they could measure a truly exemplary performance if five categories were available.

How do teachers assign disciplinary grades from interdisciplinary tasks? Often this is straightforward once a teacher has selected certain standards from different disciplines. The task may result in different grades for different subject areas. Melissa Rubocki of District School Board of Niagara has developed her own method (Drake & Burns, 2004). She keeps a record of each standard in each subject area. When a student completes a standard in one subject area, she assigns a level on that standard and records it in her mark book. In this way, she can actually assess standards from any number of subject areas at one time. When she needs to grade the students, she takes into consideration both the levels they acquired for each standard across one subject area and the difficulty or complexity of the standard. She then translates this into a letter grade as required in Ontario for elementary students.

A SAMPLE OF A RICH CULMINATING ASSESSMENT TASK

Creating a Rich Culminating Assessment Task requires thoughtful reflection. Here are some guidelines:

- Students should be given a written copy of the task early—perhaps on the first day of the unit.
- The task should be written in the active voice and in the present tense.
- The KDB, the context, the students' role, and the audience need to be clearly stated.
- The product or performance should be described fully.
- Rubrics or assessment tools should be given to students at the beginning with detailed criteria for assessment.
- Students can help to create the assessment tools for deeper understanding of the criteria.

The following interdisciplinary core assessment task from Judy Sara's team in its "Toward Nanotechnology" unit serves as a good example. I have created the KDB Umbrella in Figure 5.2 below on the basis of their work. The goal of the unit was to demonstrate both knowledge of (Know) and the ability to use (Do) the function and power of language. The English component was the only subject assessed, as the team already had enough assessments for science.

Students used their knowledge of nanotechnology to demonstrate the language skills of choosing words and language for specific purposes; they were required to reflect on a previous assessment task—the Nano Innovation Expo. Students also had to demonstrate a good grasp of the science content to fulfill the language expectations. Also, they were expected to be innovative problem solvers, good team members, and good role players during this time (Be). Figure 5.3 shows the Rich Culminating Assessment Task, and Figure 5.4 show the rubric that accompanies the task.

Figure 5.2   A KDB Umbrella for "Toward Nanotechnology"

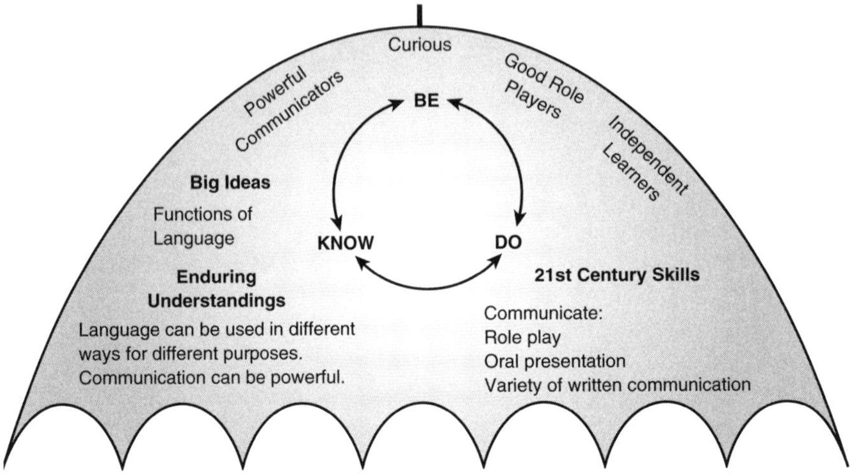

SOURCE: Based on the work of the Australian Science and Mathematics School curriculum writers.

Figure 5.3   A Rich Culminating Assessment Task for "Toward Nanotechnology"

Rich Culminating Assessment Task

The Scenario

There are plans to build a nanotech factory at Point Cimota, a town that is undergoing economic decline and needs new industry. Several problematic issues have emerged, including the safety of the new technology. The goal of the town council meeting is to reach an agreement about how to solve the problems and to produce a signed statement committing every member to a specific action in response to the issues. The nano products that you created for the Nano Innovation Expo should be considered as a possible product the new factory might produce. Include an acceptance or rejection of the proposal to build the nanofactory backed by solid reasons.

The Context

You are a member of the town council who has been assigned a specific role to play. Your role will be decided by a "lucky dip" from a container. There will be several of you playing the same role, because there are a number of town councils within the class. This group of members playing the same role will constitute your planning group. You will meet in your planning group to discuss how you might play your character and what issues the character might raise. As well, you need to decide what types of words the character may use and how he or she might act.

Now you will join your town council. The members of the council are as follows:

1. Dr. Serious, the mayor of Point Cimota

2. A scientific advisor from Madlab University

3. A member of the Point Cimota EnviroCare group

4. The manager of the Gizmo & Co. Productions factory

5. An unemployed person

6. A local window cleaner/supermarket employee

7. A local shopkeeper

Under the chairpersonship of Dr. Serious, the town council

- Uses a tape recorder to tape the meeting.
- Selects a scribe to record group discussions and recommendations.
- Conducts the meeting with the mayor as chairperson for the group discussion.
- Selects a spokesperson for a debriefing session.

The mayor also needs to be prepared to open the town council meeting with a speech.

The Activity

1. You play your role at the town council meeting and address the issues that arise.

2. At a debriefing session, the selected member of your town council presents your council's recommendations to the whole class.

3. You will write a number of newspaper articles for the local paper about the Point Cimota nanoplant. Your articles will cover the main points of discussion from your council meeting, the final agreed-upon statement about Point Cimota, and a description of how the different council members acted at the meeting.

Assessment Task

Prepare a section of the newspaper. It will contain at least three articles and at least two visuals. The emphasis in this assignment is on the function and power of language.

Article 1: Provide an outline of your town council discussions on building the nanofactory. This may include the following:

- Worthwhile information from any town council group at the debriefing session
- The recommendations that came out of the debriefing session in your town council
- Your opinion of the recommendations as a journalist

Article 2: Describe how different individuals communicated at the meeting.

Article 3: Include the following in this article:

- A reflection on the nanoproduct you developed for the Nano Innovation Expo.
- How the town council members worked together
- Why the town council decided on a certain nanoproduct
- How you found out about science and fabrication
- Feedback from the assessors

Two visuals: The newspaper section you are preparing must include two visuals; they may be associated with any of the three articles.

You will be assessed on the function and power of the language you use, the drafting process, and your use of language conventions. The power of your communication will depend on your accurate knowledge of nanotechnology.

SOURCE: Australian Science and Mathematics School Curriculum.

Figure 5.4   The Rubric for a "Toward Nanotechnology" Rich Culminating
Assessment Task

Your Name				
Toward Nanotechnology, The Function and Power of Language				
Awareness of *features and functions* of language. Accuracy and fluency of expression in an appropriate *form and register.*				
Beginning 1	**Developing 2**	**Proficient 3**	**Accomplished 4**	**Exemplary 5**
Draft of one article handed in.	Drafts of some articles presented and some feedback acted upon.	Drafts of all three articles and newspaper pages presented and some feedback acted upon.	Drafts of all three articles and newspaper pages presented a number of times and some feedback acted upon.	Drafts of all three articles and newspaper pages presented a number of times. Each draft shows considerable improvement.
Writer struggles with a limited vocabulary, groping for words to convey meaning.	Often language is vague and abstract or does not contain enough detail. Some incorrect concepts.	Words are chosen adequately to describe activities and show reflection.	Sense of writing flair with challenging use of words. Imagery identified.	Words convey the intended message in an interesting, precise, and natural way. The writing is full and rich, yet concise.
Sequence is difficult to follow. Lacking a central idea or focus.	Ideas are haphazard and mechanical; occasional awkward construction.	An easy flow where ideas are easy to follow.	Information in logical sequence. Sentences well built with consistently strong and varied structure.	Information is in logical, interesting sequence with sections built around sound topic sentences.
No clear understanding is evident.	Need to look at ways to change language to suit the audience.	Clear understanding of the appropriate choices of language for a presentation.	Multiple examples and references used or explained. Evidence of a variety of registers to suit audience and purpose.	Language used is innovative, and register is most appropriate for the audience.

SOURCE: Australian Science and Mathematics School curriculum writers.

PLANNING RICH CULMINATING ASSESSMENT TASKS

When curriculum designers plan backward, they need to "think like assessors" (Wiggins & McTighe, 2005). Similarly, when planning integrated curriculum, educators need to think like "interdisciplinary assessors." This means that educators are not simply designing engaging activities for students. They design with assessment as a priority. The key to a relevant interdisciplinary curriculum is a relevant and challenging Rich Culminating Assessment Task. *The learning activities leading to this task will need to be relevant and challenging.* It is not enough to experience a field trip, for example. The field trip is a part of a Rich Culminating Assessment Task, because it contributes to the students' learning of content and skills that, in turn, result in a complex assessment task that aligns with the KDB.

As interdisciplinary assessors, the teachers need to address three questions as they create their assessment tasks. At all times, they are focusing on the KDB Umbrella. These steps are summarized here and then explained at greater length in the remainder of this section.

Step 1: What do I need to know before I can create a Rich Culminating Assessment Task?

    a. What is the KDB? What are the generic criteria necessary to demonstrate the KDB?

    b. What are the broad-based standards that the KDB represents?

    c. What are the possible activities and assessments embedded in the standards?

    d. What is (are) the Essential Question(s) to guide curriculum planning?

Step 2: What kind of assessment task (evidence) do we need to demonstrate the KDB?

Step 3: What assessment tools can we use to measure the evidence and provide specific criteria to distinguish levels of performance?

Step 1: What Do I Need to Know Before I Can Create a Rich Culminating Assessment Task?

(a) What Is the KDB? What Are the Generic Criteria Necessary to Demonstrate the KDB?

This may look like two separate questions, but they are actually two sides of the same coin. When teachers work with interdisciplinary assessment, they need to have an idea of the fundamental makeup of the Enduring Understandings, Big Ideas, and 21st Century Skills first. Recognizing these fundamentals in the existing documents is the only way that they will be able to identify the KDB and create the KDB Umbrella.

The basic assumption is that the Know and the Do are embedded into every curriculum document from K to 12. These Enduring Understandings, Big Ideas, and 21st Century Skills reappear throughout the curriculum, so students meet them again and again in an increasingly sophisticated way. I saw this as I selected examples for this book. In several grades, teachers were expected to teach "systems" and "interdependence" and that "humans have an impact on the environment." At every grade level, teachers were expected to teach problem solving, literacy, and research skills, among other things. Yet every curriculum was very different, particularly when it was set in its local context. Similarly, the same type of assessment tasks and accompanying tools appeared at every grade level. Armed with this understanding, teachers can Scan and Cluster for these interdisciplinary criteria (subskills) in the documents. They can create effective curriculum maps looking for natural connections as described in Chapter 2 (see Figure 2.14).

Given that the Know and Do are embedded in the documents, the teachers need to be able to find them. They may not find the Know or Do in their entirety, but they may, for example, find some of the subskills of a 21st Century Skill embedded in the standards. The subskills are the criteria for the 21st Century Skill. For example, teachers will recognize that when a standard requires a student to develop a good question, this is the first step in research. Asking a good question is a subskill for the 21st Century Skill of research, as well as a skill in its own right. Asking a good question does not belong to one discipline. On the contrary, it is necessary for all subject areas. Research, for example, is embedded into the Common Core State Standards for English language arts.

This means that a prerequisite for thinking like an interdisciplinary assessor is to have a working familiarity with the characteristics of the Enduring Understandings, Big Ideas, and 21st Century Skills. It is a bit of a chicken-and-egg dilemma. How do teachers learn the criteria for the KDB? Do teachers need to learn them before they start curriculum mapping or before they do a Scan and Cluster? Will teachers learn the criteria naturally as they work with generic assessment tools and those curriculum documents that show the spiraling of concepts and skills for each strand in a subject? Or are descriptions of the criteria in a state of ongoing development as a group of teachers make sense of them in their context?

I think it is a bit of each. As with anything else, teachers' knowledge of criteria for the KDB will deepen as they get more experience and reflect on this experience.

(b) What Are the Broad-Based Standards That the KDB Represents?

A good way to connect the mandated curriculum and the assessment to the KDB Umbrella is to choose two or three broad-based standards to represent the desired learning. These standards may come from all the subjects involved in the integration, or they may represent just one subject. This often happens when the standards are very similar in two subject areas such as science and geography, or when the integrating subjects such as English or math are being used as process skills. A broad-based standard is one that is global in nature, and many examples may sit under its umbrella. In this sense, it is similar to Enduring Understandings and Big Ideas. In fact, as we have already seen, Enduring Understandings sometimes come directly from the broad-based standards.

An important characteristic of a broad-based standard is that many more concrete standards fall under it. This is how teachers can incorporate many standards when they cover a broad-based one. Examples of broad-based standards are the following:

Students will

Understand the three states of matter and of changes in those states.

Use a variety of strategies to help them read.

Apply numeracy skills in everyday situations using concrete objects.

Use multiple approaches to exploring and inquiring.

Demonstrate responsible emotional and cognitive behaviors.

(c) What Are the Possible Activities and Assessments Embedded in the Standards?

In the act of creating the KDB, teachers also need to have some idea of the kind of activities and assessments that are suggested by the standards. This requires two-dimensional thinking again. To do this, it is helpful to develop an exploratory web. In this way, teachers can look at the standards in the different subject areas and see what kinds of activities are suggested by the standards in each area. Often this leads to activities and assessments that are interdisciplinary. It is important that this web is exploratory, because it may change drastically as the curriculum designers move forward. A template for an exploratory web is in Figure 4.11.

(d) What Is (Are) the Essential Question(s) to Guide Curriculum Planning?

Essential Questions are the questions that have emerged from the Big Ideas and Enduring Understandings. When a unit is driven by an

Essential Question, it will ensure higher order thinking and the demonstration of 21st Century Skills. In Chapter 4 there is a detailed section on how to create effective Essential Questions.

Step 2: What Kind of Rich Culminating Assessment Task (Evidence) Do We Need to Demonstrate the KDB?

What Rich Culminating Assessment Task will offer the best evidence to show student achievement of the KDB? In backward mapping, Wiggins and McTighe (2005) refer to *core assessment tasks*. These are complex assessment tasks that get at the heart of the learning. A Rich Culminating Assessment Task is a core assessment task. It may be a culminating activity that ends the unit and acts as a summative evaluation. In a longer unit, there may be more than one Culminating Assessment Task. Also, a unit may include some core assessment tasks that are disciplinary but set in the context of the broader KDB Umbrella.

The Rich Culminating Assessment Task must be comprehensive, multidimensional, and interdisciplinary. The Know and the Do in the task are embedded in the standards across the disciplines. Thus, the student is reaching the standards in more than one discipline through one assessment task. The Know is often derived from science and social studies. English and math offer process skills. Also, the arts often act as process skills. Students can demonstrate what they know through the creation of a piece of art. It is important again to ensure that the process skills are taught! A visual arts teacher, for example, needs to know that the integrity of his or her discipline is intact when students create an art piece to demonstrate their knowledge in science.

A review of Figure 5.1 shows a variety of potential assessment tasks. A Rich Culminating Assessment Task may include one or more of them. This depends on the complexity of the task and the KDB Umbrella.

Step 3: What Assessment Tools Can We Use to Measure the Evidence and Provide Specific Criteria to Distinguish Levels of Performance?

Once the Rich Culminating Assessment Task is determined, an appropriate tool is selected or created to measure student success at the task. Because a Rich Culminating Assessment Task is complex, more than one assessment tool may be needed to articulate expectations of success in various components. For example, an assessment tool for a Rich Culminating Assessment Task may include the teacher's observations, a checklist for participation in a class discussion, and a rubric that outlines the criteria for the task and measures levels of performance.

Regardless of its sophistication, any assessment tool needs to articulate the criteria for success. If it is a checklist for participation, for example, the teacher needs to consider not only how often a student participates but also the quality of the participation. If it is a dance that is being evaluated, a rubric can outline the criteria for an effective performance, including a carefully defined subset of skills. Also, there will be levels of success for each subset of skills. Traditionally four levels are used, ranging from a poor performance to an excellent one.

It is also important that whatever tool is used, it is of high quality—one that has validity (measures what it is supposed to measure) and reliability (consistency). This is murky territory, and teachers need a lot of training to create high-quality assessments. Although there are some fine examples of assessment tools available on the Internet, many are poorly constructed. Discussion among teachers about the quality of assessment tools builds assessment literacy. As well, the process of doing a Scan and Cluster and developing the KDB Umbrella helps build a better understanding of assessment.

ASSESSING THE DEVELOPMENT OF BIG IDEAS AND ENDURING UNDERSTANDINGS: AN EXAMPLE FROM A FIFTH-GRADE UNIT

In this section, we will follow my interpretation of Lydia Janis's curriculum development on the Civil War for the fifth grade. Lydia was a teacher whose teaching practice was described in a book called *The Parallel Curriculum* (Tomlinson et al., 2009). Lydia followed the principles advocated in this book. She integrated history, government, geography, and economics. The learning principles were always at the forefront of the thinking.

Lydia's first challenge was whether to follow the objectives from her textbook or the state standards. As she read the state standards, she found that they did capture key understandings that students needed in order to understand this period in history but also allowed her to develop Big Ideas, Enduring Understandings, and 21st Century Skills. The broadbased standard that guided her curriculum design was the following: "Demonstrate an in-depth understanding of major events and trends in U.S. history."

The Civil War provided the specific content for doing this. She could use parts of her text for the content. Also, many of the state standards in social studies could fall under this broad-based standard and allow for the creation of a relevant curriculum.

Lydia developed her own set of the KDB as follows:

Know:

Enduring Understandings:

All conflicts have causes.

The key to resolving conflicts is a comprehensive understanding of related causes and effects.

Big Ideas:

Cause and effect

Conflict resolution

Do:

Develop an argument

Research

Be:

Able to resolve conflict

Lydia decided that a good Essential Question would be "How is a comprehensive understanding of related causes and effects key to resolving conflict during times of war?"

At this point, Lydia could develop her Rich Culminating Assessment Task (Figure 5.5).

Lydia began her unit with a preassessment that focused on the conceptual learning of the unit. She provided an initial word bank of Big Ideas revolving around the Civil War. Students created a concept map using the word bank and provided concrete examples of the Big Ideas. In the concept map, the students drew lines to connecting Big Ideas and Enduring Understandings. To measure student growth in concept attainment during

Figure 5.5   A Rich Culminating Assessment Task for the Civil War

Rich Culminating Assessment Task

You will create a Civil War quilt that demonstrates the important Enduring Understandings and Big Ideas of the time. You will work individually, or in groups of two, three, or four.

Develop a visual plan for the Civil War quilt. Your quilt must depict the following:

- Key people and events of the Civil War period
- Cultures, economies, and livelihoods of various groups in the North and South
- The roots and consequences of slavery
- Varied viewpoints and perspectives and the resulting conflicts
- How conflict resolution and compromise mediated these conflicts
- Other important conclusions about this period

Individually, you will write a reflective piece to interpret your quilt and how it demonstrates the six requirements. Support your conclusions with evidence.

the unit, she used the rubric in Figure 5.6; she used the one in Figure 5.7 for measuring development in acquisition of the Enduring Understanding.

She also used a generic checklist to teach the 21st Century Skills for developing a strong argument. This checklist is in Figure 5.8.

Now Lydia could fully prepare her daily lessons. For an introductory activity, Lydia prepared a flowchart to show the major concepts of the Civil War in history, economics, geography, and government. She used open-ended discussion questions to generate student interest and to facilitate making connections with previous experiences and student interests. She used Civil War photographs that depicted a pattern and a relationship. She used these photos to demonstrate the kind of analysis she wanted students to make.

During the unit, Lydia used teaching methods that were inductive. All activities and assessments were related to the Rich Culminating Assessment Task and her KDB Umbrella. Students were given a wide range of materials such as data tables, graphs, photographs, actual newspaper

Figure 5.6   Lydia's Rubric for Concept Development

	Beginning	**Developing**	**Competent**	**Proficient**	**Expert**
Level of Understanding	The learner can communicate the term associated with an abstract concept.	The learner can paraphrase the definition of a concept.	The learner can provide examples and non-examples of the concept.	The learner can provide key attributes that distinguish the concept category.	The learner can link the concept with other related concepts.
Example	"Civil"	"Civil means something to do with citizens of a place. A civil war is a war fought inside a country and among its citizens."	Examples: "I am a citizen of the United States." "I am not a citizen of Russia." "World War II was not a civil war." "The recent war in Ireland was a civil war."	Citizens Members State Nation Law Rights Public	"People have civil wars when they can't resolve their conflicts or achieve their rights peacefully."

SOURCE: From *The Parallel Curriculum* (2nd ed., p. 104), by C. A. Tomlinson et al., 2009, Thousand Oaks: Corwin. Copyright by Corwin. Reprinted with permission.

Figure 5.7   A Rubric for Measuring the Acquisition of Enduring Understandings

	Beginning	Developing	Competent	Proficient	Expert
Levels of Understanding	The learner can define and provide examples of a synthesis if the essential information upon which an Enduring Understanding is based.	The learner can identify a topical or temporal relationship among concepts and essential information.	The learner can extend the principle or rule to novel examples within the disciplines or field of study.	The learner can articulate a general conceptual relationship as conditional if/then, cause/ effect, part/ whole, etc.	The learner can extend the Enduring Understanding across disciplines or fields of study.
Example	"The civil war was a war between the northern and southern states in the United States in the 1860s."	"The civil war was fought because of disagreements about slavery and economics, and states' rights."	"There have been recent civil wars going on Yugoslavia. Ireland, and Mexico. They were caused by some of the same kinds of things that caused our civil war."	"Civil wars are caused by citizens' inability to find a way to resolve their differences about rights and laws peacefully."	"Empathy, compromise, and consensus can be used to resolve conflicts peacefully because they honor the individual perspectives and values."

SOURCE: From *The Parallel Curriculum* (2nd ed., p. 106), by C. A. Tomlinson et al., 2009, Thousand Oaks: Corwin. Copyright by Corwin. Reprinted with permission.

Figure 5.8   Checklist: Developing a Strong Argument

- Clearly states the claim or argument
- Provides sufficient evidence related to the claim or argument
- Selects credible evidence sources
- Consults multiple sources
- Selects relevant evidence
- Clearly explains all assumptions
- Provides a logical argument
- Refutes alternative claims or arguments

SOURCE: From *The Parallel Curriculum* (2nd ed., p. 106), by C. A. Tomlinson et al., 2009, Thousand Oaks: Corwin. Copyright by Corwin. Reprinted with permission.

articles, and journals of women, slaves, and soldiers. She asked open-ended questions and used Socratic questioning. During the activities, students constantly searched for patterns, relationships, causes, and effects. She used large- and small-group strategies to support student analysis and concept attainment through discussion, shared inquiry, think-pair-share activities, and debriefings. Ongoing assessment was provided through the products created during daily activities such as document analysis, reflective journals, and concept maps.

Lydia also had students role-play a re-creation of the Lincoln/Douglas debates and the Dred Scott decisions. Her students examined varying perspectives on the rights of people versus the rights of the state, and they had to prove their points of view with legitimate evidence. Small-group reflections followed as well as a large-group debriefing. Here, students articulated the Big Ideas and Enduring Understandings.

At the same time, Lydia modified activities to account for different learning styles. For students with learning difficulties, she provided different print documents to support analytical reading. She worked with students needing individual help and held conferences with some to scaffold their concept-based learning. Students with writing difficulties could tape-record their reflective analysis for the Rich Culminating Assessment Task. For the more advanced students, she provided more challenging questions and more sophisticated print documents. At all times, Lydia was conscious of aligning the standards, activities, and assessments.

PLANNING FOR THE RICH CULMINATING ASSESSMENT TASK: AN EXAMPLE FROM A FOURTH-GRADE UNIT

It is tempting to just begin by creating a Rich Culminating Assessment Task. But there are many things to think about before you do this. Tom Martin, John Molnar, and Phil Teeuwsen developed an interdisciplinary "Habitat" unit for Grade 4 students. We will follow them through their process.

Step 1: What Do I Need to Know Before I Can Create a Rich Culminating Assessment Task?

(a) What Is the KDB? What Are the Generic Criteria Necessary to Demonstrate the KDB?

What are the criteria that demonstrate the KDB? Armed with some knowledge of what Enduring Understandings, Big Ideas, and 21st Century Skills look like, these teachers did a Scan and Cluster of the standards in science, language arts, visual arts, and drama and dance. They created a horizontal Scan and Cluster and a vertical Scan and Cluster. (Please refer back to Figures 4.6 and 4.7.) With this information, they proceeded to create the KDB Umbrella

(b) What Are the Broad-Based Standards That the KDB Represents?

These are the standards that Tom, Phil, and John used:

Demonstrate an understanding of the concepts of habitats and community, and identify factors that affect habitats and communities of plants and animals.

Investigate the dependency of plants and animals on their habitat and the interrelationships of the plants and animals living in a specific habitat.

Describe ways in which humans can change habitats and the effects of these habitats on the plants and animals within the habitat.

Although the core content was science-based, this was an interdisciplinary unit that included math, language arts, drama, social studies, science, and visual arts. The Do skills cut across the disciplines. The problem solving revolved around an experiment required in the science curriculum. The research belonged in language arts. Different methods of communication were involved in all subject areas. Drama was derived from the arts. Mapping came from social sciences. Above all, they wanted students to be cooperative, responsible for their own behavior, creative, and inquisitive. Once they had identified the broad-based standards, they created their KDB Umbrella as seen in Figure 5.9.

(c) What Are the Possible Activities and Assessments Embedded in the Standards?

Before Tom, Phil, and John did their Scan and Cluster, they discussed the Grade 4 curriculum. They were experienced teachers who had the advantage of knowing the curriculum, and each had a good sense of what was important to teach. They had a good understanding of the fundamental makeup of the 21st Century Skills and were familiar with the concepts they needed to teach in Grade 4. This allowed them to go through the Scan and Cluster process relatively quickly to find the Big Ideas and 21st Century Skills. They used broad-based standards as Enduring Understandings. They found the criteria for the skills embedded in the standards.

To explore possibilities for their curriculum unit, they created an exploratory web. This web looked at standards in different subject areas that could

Figure 5.9   A KDB Umbrella for "Habitats"

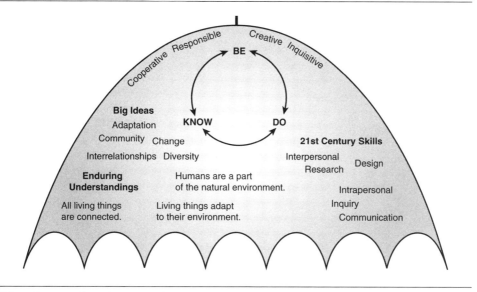

SOURCE: Based on the work of Tom Martin, Phil Teeuwsen, and John Molnar.

be included in the unit and as integrated activities assessments. This exploration also gave them a good sense of what type of Rich Culminating Assessment Task could be aligned with the discipline-specific standards. Their web is in Figure 5.10.

(d) What Is (Are) the Essential Question(s) to Guide Curriculum Planning?

After much discussion, these teachers chose the question:

If all living things are interconnected, how does human activity affect the habitats of plants and animals?

Step 2: What Kind of Big Assessment Task (Evidence) Do We Need to Demonstrate the KDB?

Now they were ready to develop a Rich Culminating Assessment Task that would act as a culminating activity (Figure 5.11).

This was a straightforward interdisciplinary core assessment task directly connected to the broad-based standards. The authors needed to constantly check that the task was aligned with their KDB Umbrella. It focused directly on the Enduring Understandings and Big Ideas. The 21st Century Skills were interdisciplinary. The Be would be evident while the students prepared for the task and completed it.

Figure 5.10   An Exploratory Web

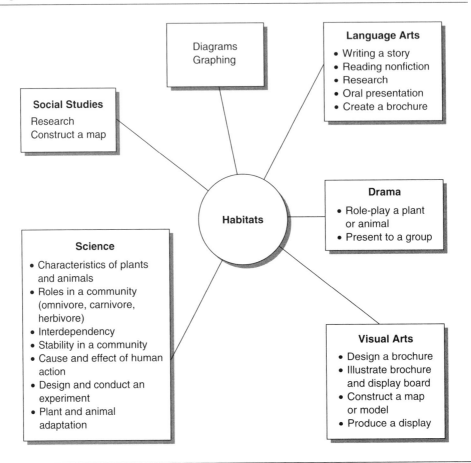

SOURCE: Based on the work of Tom Martin, Phil Teeuwsen, and John Molnar.

Figure 5.11   A Rich Culminating Assessment Task for "Habitats"

In a group of three, you will decide on a role of a plant or animal in a natural community. Consider choosing an endangered species. In your role, you will present your knowledge of your plant/animal and its habitat to the class in a storefront-style display. This presentation must include a visual display on a cardboard structure no larger than two student desks. Be as creative as possible with this display board. The information you need to display will be generated from the following activities:

1. Research to identify the distinguishing characteristics of your plant or animal and its habitat. Create a cross-classification chart that includes data on its life cycle, needs, food, and enemies. (Research skills)

2. Brainstorm for factors that may affect your plant/animal. Develop a hypothesis and conduct an experiment to test for one or more of these factors. (Hint: This experiment may revolve around testing variables affecting plant growth.) Write a lab report. (Problem-solving skills)

3. Construct a model or map of your habitat indicating significant information. (Design and construction)

4. Produce a brochure on the computer outlining the status of your plant or animal (endangered, threatened, extinct) and the effects of human activity on it. Include what steps can be taken to protect the species and possible future outcomes. (Technological skills)

Your responsibilities include observing and listening to your classmates' presentations and evaluating them using a rubric created by the class. You will also be using the rubric and checklist to evaluate your own presentation. There will be a teacher evaluation of your research, lab report, brochure, map or model, and presentation (both for content and role-playing).

SOURCE: Based on the work of Tom Martin, Phil Teeuwsen, and John Molnar.

Step 3: What Assessment Tools Can We Use to Measure the Evidence and Provide Specific Criteria to Distinguish Levels of Performance?

The next step was to determine appropriate assessment tools. Again, the teachers had to put on their interdisciplinary assessor hats. What 21st Century Skills and subskills had the students been exposed to as they spiraled through the curriculum? How could the teachers build on this? Were there any new skills that needed to be taught before the students could devise a rubric?

The students had already done some research in other units and had used a research rubric. They knew the subskills involved. The rubric for this 21st Century Skill and its subskills would be reviewed. The criteria to distinguish levels of performance would be discussed. Students could look at exemplars the teacher had collected from previous years as well as assignments that represented lower quality work. Modifications to the rubric could be made if necessary. This process was similar for the inquiry skills, as the students had conducted some experiments already. They had also been exposed to mapping skills and accompanying rubrics, so they could review these and make any necessary modifications.

Although the students had used presentation rubrics before, they needed to learn role-playing skills. This would be a good place for students to learn the role-playing skills and to modify the presentation rubric they had already used to assess the role-playing. Finally, they were asked to produce a simple brochure using computer technology. They needed to learn the software and the computer skills to produce such an item. Students would receive a generic product guideline that outlined the criteria for producing an effective brochure, and the teachers would teach the skills that were necessary. Together, they could develop the indicators to distinguish levels of performance.

They developed one rubric for the Rich Culminating Assessment Task that included all the areas that they had considered (Figure 5.12). Concerned with the Be, these teachers focused on a peer and self-evaluation rubric for teamwork, attitude, and participation (Figure 5.13).

Figure 5.12   A Rubric for a Rich Culminating Assessment Task for "Habitats"

Exploring Plant and Animal Habitats				
	Level 4	**Level 3**	**Level 2**	**Level 1**
Research	Information was very well researched and of appropriate length.	Information was well researched and approximately of appropriate length.	Information was satisfactorily researched and half of the desired length.	Information was not well researched and under half of the desired length.
Visual Presentation	Unique, creative, colorful, and neat.	Creative, colorful, and neat.	Somewhat creative, colorful, and neat.	Lacks creativity, color, and neatness.
Oral Presentation	Presenters were knowledgeable about their topic. Audience was interested. Tone of voice, posture, and eye contact were excellent. All areas were covered.	Presenters were knowledgeable about their topic. Audience was interested. Tone of voice, posture, and eye contact were good. Most areas were covered.	Presenters read the research related to their topic. Audience was somewhat interested. Tone of voice, posture, and eye contact were satisfactory. Some ideas were covered.	Presenters were unprepared and were not able to offer much information. Audience was disinterested. Tone of voice was low. Poor posture. Very little eye contact with audience.
Conventions, Grammar, Spelling, Et Cetera	There are practically no errors or omissions.	There are only a few minor errors and/or omissions.	There are several minor errors and/or omissions.	There are several major and/or consistent errors and/or omissions.

SOURCE: Based on the work of Tom Martin, Phil Teeuwsen, and John Molnar.

Figure 5.13   Peer and Self-Evaluation Rubric for "Habitats"

Peer and Self-Evaluation Rubric				
	Level 4	**Level 3**	**Level 2**	**Level 1**
Teamwork	Helped to decide what the goals of the group were and worked hard to meet these goals.	Accepted and respected the goals of the group and worked hard to meet these goals.	Did not always respect the goals of the group but still worked hard to meet these goals.	Consistently complained about group goals and failed to try as hard as possible to meet the goals.
Attitude	Encouraged others to get involved. Was cooperative and helpful. Expressed opinions in a respectful way. Performed tasks with a positive attitude.	Was cooperative and helpful. Expressed opinions in a respectful way. Performed tasks with a positive attitude.	Was usually cooperative and helpful. Did not always express opinions in a respectful way. Performed tasks with a positive attitude.	Was not very cooperative or helpful. Was not always respectful when expressing opinions. Did not always have a positive attitude.
Participation	Was willing and able to do a number of different tasks within the group.	Was willing and able to do different tasks within the group.	Was willing and able to do a few tasks within the group.	Was not always willing and able to do different tasks within the group.

SOURCE: Tom Martin, Phil Teeuwsen, and John Molnar.

In this chapter we have explored the concept of interdisciplinary assessment. The first example comes from an Australian team who are deeply involved in this type of assessment. The second example looks at how we assess interdisciplinary Big Ideas and Enduring Understandings. Finally we looked at the steps one team negotiated in order to plan for their Rich Culminating Assessment Task and the assessment tools that they created.

DISCUSSION QUESTIONS

1. Consider some of the assessments that you have experienced as a student or teacher. Were there any interdisciplinary aspects to these assessments? If not, could there have been?

2. What benefits can you see from assessing more than one subject at a time?

3. What problems can you envision when assessing more than one subject at a time? Are there any clear ways to solve these problems?

4. Differentiate between assessment tasks and assessment tools. When can these be considered interdisciplinary?

5. Who do you believe is responsible for teaching cross-disciplinary skills? Why? How might this happen in your own context?

6. Review the three steps to creating a Rich Culminating Assessment Task. The first step has three parts:

   a. What is the KDB? What are the generic criteria necessary to demonstrate the KDB?

   b. What are the broad-based standards that the KDB represents?

   c. What are the possible activities and assessments embedded in the standards?

   Step 2 is to decide what assessment tasks could act as evidence to demonstrate the KDB. Step 3 is to select assessment tools to provide specific criteria and measure the levels of performance. This sounds like a very complex process, but it is easier when you actually do it. Can you describe this process in your own words? Why are all the parts necessary?

7. "The key to a relevant curriculum is a relevant and challenging Rich Culminating Assessment Task." Do you believe this? What does this statement mean to you?

SUGGESTED ACTIVITIES

1. Analyze the Toward Nanotechnology Rich Culminating Assessment Task. What makes this a good assessment task? The assessment tool measures language skills because the teachers already had a lot of data on science. How could they have made this task interdisciplinary?

2. Do a preliminary Scan and Cluster to identify a set of broad-based standards from more than one subject area. (You might want to begin with the Scan and Cluster in Chapter 4). Create an exploratory web (you can use the template in Figure 4.11) to see possible activities embedded in the standards. Create the KDB Umbrella.

3. Once the KDB Umbrella is created, you have enough information to create a Rich Culminating Assessment Task. After you have selected the task, write an assessment task description in a way that you would present it to students. Be sure to follow the criteria for a well-written assessment task.

4. Select good assessment tools to measure success. Do these tools really measure what you want to measure? Why? Do they connect back to the KDB Umbrella?

6

Putting the Pieces Together

The Integrated Curriculum Design Process. As you read this chapter, follow through the completed curriculum in Appendix A to see how the parts fit the whole.

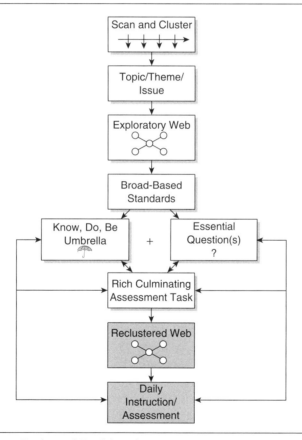

SOURCE: Adapted from Drake and Reid (2010).

In this chapter, we explore how to create integrated learning experiences that enable students to attain the required standards. The example walks through the teachers' thought process for creating the daily instructional activities/assessments aligned with standards. The rest of the chapter is devoted to exploring an integrated approach to implementing the daily instructional activities/assessments. A full example of this type of curriculum design can be found in Appendix A.

DESIGNING DAILY ACTIVITIES AND ASSESSMENTS

Using Two-Dimensional Thinking

Curriculum designers must use their two-dimensional thinking to create day-to-day activities. The daily activities must be aligned with the Big Picture (the KDB and the Rich Culminating Assessment Tasks). At the same time, each activity must address a standard and have an accompanying assessment strategy. Thus, the instructional activities are aligned in two dimensions: A constant double-check is necessary to make sure that daily activities/assessments indeed both lead to the Rich Culminating Assessment Task and are aligned with the KDB. In fact, at this stage curriculum planners usually can see the fruits of their work and that alignment works. It is a bit like finding the completing parts to a complex jigsaw puzzle. It is an energizing and exciting experience.

Figure 6.1 shows how one works in two dimensions.

A Reclustered Web

One trap that people can find themselves in is to shift back to the first exploratory web to design daily activities/assessments. The end result is a multidisciplinary curriculum; this is fine if this is what you want. But if you want to think in new ways, brainstorming around the Essential Question(s) usually brings forward new ideas a more integrated activities/assessments. Once you have decided on the Rich Culminating Assessment Task, you can brainstorm to create a new web—the reclustered web (Figure 6.2). Now you are not brainstorming around subject areas but rather around what types of learning the students need to address the Essential Question, complete the Rich Culminating Assessment Task, and demonstrate the KDB. If there is only one Essential Question, then the brainstorming should be around this question. If there is more than one Essential Question, each question can be used to create a miniunit.

Figure 6.1   Two-Dimensional Thinking to Create Daily Activities

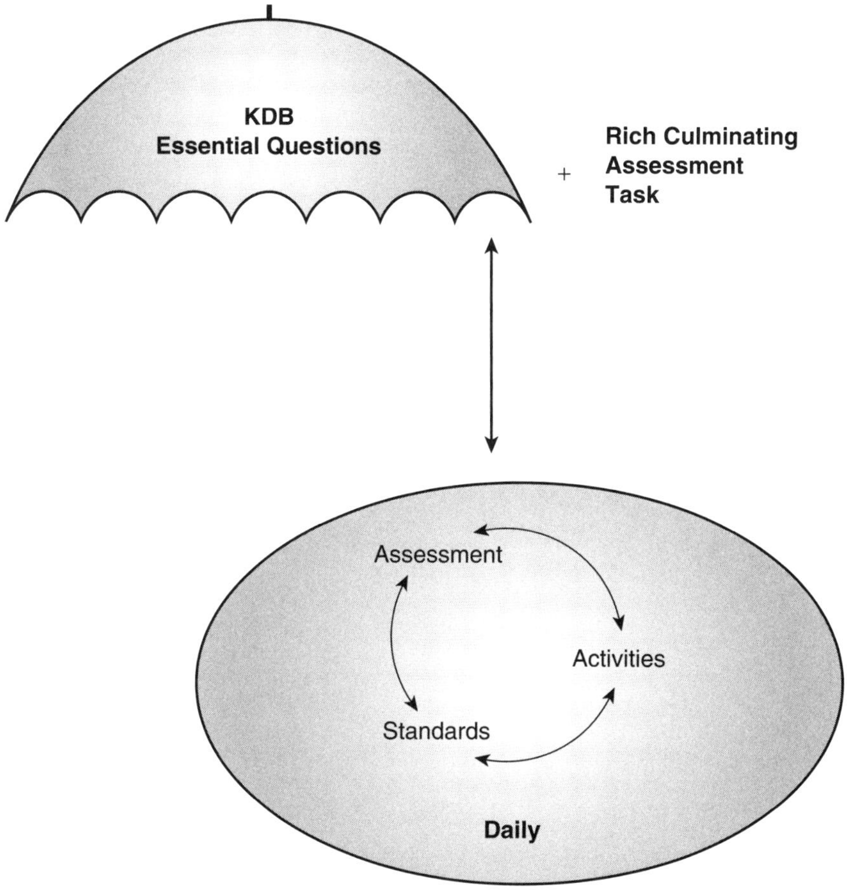

A Template for Planning Daily Instructional Activities/ Assessments Connected to Standards

When we teach for assessment *for* learning and assessment *as* learning, it is important to build in time for feedback. It is good to remember that instructional activities should be seamlessly interwoven with assessment. Often the instructional task is also the assessment tool. Finally, we look at the task of internal alignment of the day-by-day instructional activities with appropriate assessment tools and standards. Creating the daily instructional/assessment activities requires thinking like an interdisciplinary assessor. Figure 6.3 is a chart that curriculum designers can use to think out the curriculum and ensure that it is aligned and that assessment is interwoven with instructional activities and aligned with standards.

Figure 6.2   A Reclustered Web

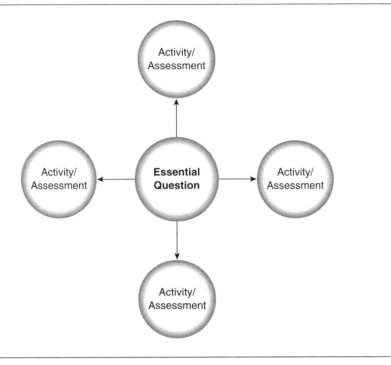

Figure 6.3   A Template for Planning Daily Instruction/Assessment

Instructional Activity	Assessment	Standards	Connection to the KDB/Rich Culminating Assessment Task
Instructional Activity 1	Assessment Task: Assessment Tool:	Connected standards	How it connects
Instructional Activity 2			

CREATING THE DAILY ACTIVITIES/ ASSESSMENTS FOR A SEVENTH-GRADE UNIT

Let's look at the thinking behind Vladia Jusko McBrain, Rumeeza Salim, and Susan McLachlin's Grade 7 unit called the Red Hill unit. They integrated science, geography, and English. Interestingly, this unit is quite similar to both the one developed by John, Phil, and Tom for Grade 4 (Chapter 4). They both developed units for strands under the rubric of life systems in science. For Grade 4, the topic was "habitats and communities." For Grade 7, it was "interactions within the ecosystem." Clearly, these units will build on the same Enduring Understandings and Big Ideas. In the Red Hill case, the students used an immediate and significant environmental issue in their area: A proposed highway in Red Hill would cut through a sensitive environmental area and a culturally significant site and would arguably violate aboriginal rights.

Step 1: Doing the Groundwork

Vladia, Rumeeza, and Susan started with a Scan and Cluster of the science, English, and social sciences documents. They found a natural fit for geography (themes of geography) and science (life systems: interactions within ecosystems). They selected four broad-based factors to guide their work:

Geography standard:

1. Produce a report on current environmental events in the news.
2. Use the five themes of geography (location/place, environment, region, interaction, and movement) to focus your inquiry.

Science standard:

3. Investigate the interactions in an ecosystem, and identify factors that affect the balance among components of an ecosystem.
4. Demonstrate an understanding of the effects of human activities and technological innovations as well as the effects of changes that take place naturally on the sustainability of ecosystems.

A broad-based English standard would also guide the planning:

- Produce pieces of writing using a variety of forms, techniques, and resources appropriate to the form and purpose.

They also brainstormed around an exploratory web (Figure 6.4), and they created their KDB Umbrella (Figure 6.5)

Once the Grade 7 team had created the KDB Umbrella, they reviewed the standards for suggestions and created an exploratory concept web to think about the kind of activities to include in the unit. As they moved along in this process, they decided on two Essential Questions.

- How are plants and animals interdependent?
- How are humans a part of the natural environment, and what potential impacts can humans have on their environment (for better or worse)?

Figure 6.4   An Exploratory Web for the Red Hill Unit

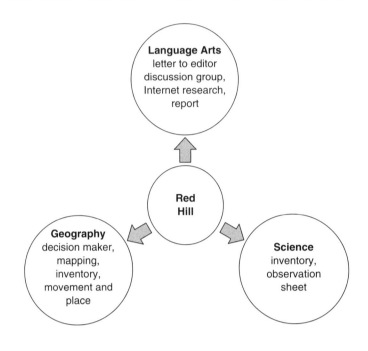

Figure 6.5   The KDB Umbrella for Red Hill

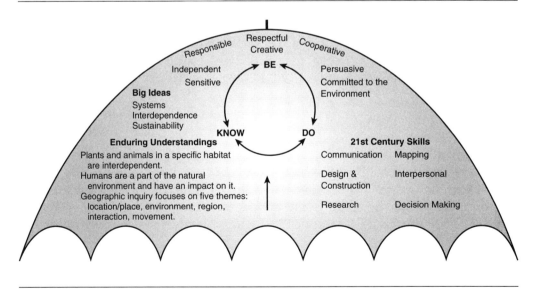

SOURCE: Based on the work of Vladia Jusko McBrian, Rumeeza Salim, and Susan McLachlin.

Step 2: Creating the Rich Culminating Assessment Task

To create the Rich Culminating Assessment Task, Vladia, Rumeeza, and Susan needed to continually check that the task aligned to the KDB Umbrella. Indeed, the task needed to provide evidence that the students had achieved the KDB. An adapted version of their task follows:

> You have been invited to present at an environmental forum. Research a specific environmental issue. Locate the area where the issue is occurring on a map. In groups of three, prepare a seminar presentation on this issue. One person should represent the viewpoint of an environmentalist. One should be a representative who opposes environmental protection (perhaps a representative of big business who is lobbying for the change to the natural environment). The third person should play a government official who is looking for a compromise that will satisfy both groups. Present the three sides to the audience. Use data to support your opinions. Be sure to think about the five themes of geography in your analysis. Bring in visuals such as maps, graphs, notes, reports, and decision-making charts to strengthen your position. You will be assessed for your presentation style and the strength of your argument. It is important that there are three distinct points of view. There will be peer assessment and teacher assessment.

Rumeeza, Vladia, and Susan believed that this Rich Culminating Assessment Task connected directly to the Know. To demonstrate what they knew, students had to Do basic research (researching); produce a map (mapping); analyze, synthesize, and evaluate data by applying a decision-making model (decision making); write a persuasive letter (writing); and present orally to an audience (oral communication). Finally, they needed to demonstrate interpersonal skills such as cooperation in their groups. The Be would be evident in the way the students did the task. Were they cooperative? Independent?

Step 3: Creating the Daily Instructional Activities/ Assessments Connected to Standards

How did Rumeeza, Vladia, and Susan plan for the daily activities? First they created a reclustered web around their two Essential Questions. This allowed them to create integrated activities rather than multidisciplinary ones. See Figure 6.6.

Creating the Daily Activities/Assessments

With the reclustered web done, they could now approach the last step, organizing the daily activities/assessments so that they led back to the

Figure 6.6   A Reclustered Web With Two Essential Questions

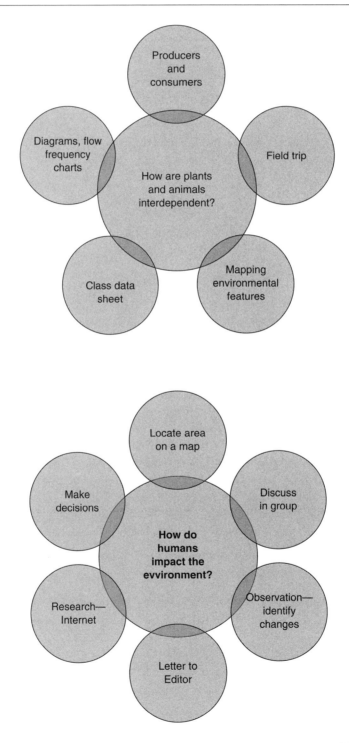

KDB and the Rich Culminating Assessment Task and answered the Essential Questions. The standards guided their process. Figure 6.7 shows the template that they used. The last column shows how each activity connected to the KDB and Rich Culminating Assessment Task. They also created appropriate assessment tools.

THE SEAMLESS INTEGRATION OF CURRICULUM, INSTRUCTION, AND ASSESSMENT

Education is a complex endeavor. The goal is to enhance student achievement. Yet this goal is set within a complex web of interconnected aspects that include the following:

- Curriculum, instruction, and classroom assessment
- Learning, teaching, and assessment
- Assessment *of, for,* and *as* learning
- Know, Do, and Be
- The head and the heart
- Disciplinary boundaries

When looked at as a complex system, the traditional defining boundaries of such aspects blur, overlap, interconnect, and may even disappear.

In this last section about putting the pieces together, I will focus on how some of these interconnections play out in the classroom as teachers go about the business of meeting mandated standards in a way that works best for students. To do this, educators constantly need to be aware of using the two-dimensional lens to see the Big Picture at the same time as they teach their daily lessons. In other words, they need to approach daily lessons from a systems perspective.

Learning Principles as an Instruction/Assessment Guide

Perhaps the most essential ingredient to guide any curriculum planning is how people learn best. We know a lot about how people learn through research on the brain, learning styles, and multiple intelligences. By tapping into our own experiences and applying research findings, we can construct a list of learning principles. For many years I asked people to tell a story about their best learning experience. Listening to the stories, the group would discuss what principles of learning emerged from their collective experiences. From there, there was a group discussion on what instructional strategies made sense given the learning principles. Finally, the discussion revolved around the best match of assessment, learning strategies, and instructional activities.

Figure 6.7   Daily Activities/Assessments of the Red Hill Unit

Instructional Activity	Standards	Assessment Tasks/ Tools	KDB Rich Culminating Assessment Task
Essential Question: How are plants and animals interdependent?			
You will go on a field trip to Red Hill Creek (where a new highway is proposed). In groups, you will map one section of Red Hill Creek. Pictorial symbols will be used to represent major environmental features such as trees, weeds, birds, and insects. The sections will be used to create a class overview of the area. Using the community Data Sheet, compile a list of species in the area you mapped.	Compile quantitative and qualitative data gathered through investigation. Use diagrams, flow charts, and frequency tables. For example, use a chart to record numbers of producers and consumers in a particular habitat. (S, G) Identify living (biotic) and nonliving (abiotic) elements in an ecosystem. (S) Identify populations of organisms within an ecosystem and factors that contribute to their survival. (S)	Tasks: Make charts, diagrams, maps Tool: Teacher marks for accuracy	This field trip shows students that real environmental issues are in their own community. This task integrates geography and science. Enduring Understandings: Plants and animals in a specific habitat are interdependent. Humans are a part of the natural environment and have an impact on it. Big Ideas: Systems Interdependence Sustainability
Essential Question: How are humans a part of the natural environment and what potential impacts can humans have on their environment (for better or worse)?			
Use the list to join a discussion on how community members provide food and shelter for one another. Use the observation sheet to identify the changes made to the natural environment. Be ready to discuss in class	Use appropriate vocabulary. (S, G, E) Demonstrate an understanding of the themes of geography, particularly movement and place. (G)	Task: Discussion Tool: Teacher observation	Research skills Interpersonal skills Mapping Systems thinking

Instructional Activity	Standards	Assessment Tasks/ Tools	KDB Rich Culminating Assessment Task
In a group, research a current environmental issue using the Internet and other sources. On a map, locate the area where your issue is occurring.

Summarize important facts about this issue. Use a decision-making organizer to organize your ideas and help you to move toward a solution. (Think about the organizer from the Environmental Explorer as a starting place.) | Communicate an understanding that various individuals and groups have different opinions on this issue. (G) Analyze, synthesize, and evaluate data by applying a decision-making model to an environmental issue. (G) Produce maps for a variety of purposes. (G) Use the five themes of geography. (G) | Task: Research Tool: Teacher assessment of summary Task: Decision-making organizer Tools: Rubric, teacher and peer evaluation | This task builds on the last two by asking students now to locate an environmental issue anywhere in the world. The observations in the last two exercises should help to keep them aligned with the Enduring Understandings/ Big Ideas. |
| Individually, write a one-page letter to the editor of the local paper where your issue is located. Use the five themes from geography to express your opinion about this issue. Use a direct and persuasive style to try to get readers to agree with you. Edit your work individually and then in pairs. | Produce a report on a current environmental event. (G) Use knowledge of a variety of written forms to produce a piece of writing appropriate for the purpose and the audience. (E) Revise and edit work focusing on content and style, independently and in collaboration with others. (E) | Task: Letter Tool: Rubric; partner evaluation, revision, and editing; teacher evaluation of final letter | Students will need to express the relationships in the Enduring Understandings and show understanding of Big Ideas. Students will need to show cooperation for the editing process. |

SOURCE: Adapted by Vladia Jusko McBrian, Rumeeza Salim, and Susan McLachlin from Biodiversity Performs (http://worldwildlife.org/fun/games/performs/biod-performs.pdf) and Environmental Explorer (http://www.nationalgeographic.com).

Figure 6.8 offers a chart of these principles in no particular order. A close look at this chart shows that these principles also match the constructivist theory of learning and assessment *of, for,* and *as* learning. Education is student-centered; students are actively involved in their own learning. The learning material is relevant to students and connected to prior experiences. Assessment is an inherent part of the learning system.

Figure 6.8   Alignment of Learning Principles With Instructional Activities and Embedded Assessments

Learning Principles	Instructional Strategies	Embedded Assessments
Learn by doing	Active learning	Assess the doing—performance assessment
Material is relevant	Activities are personally relevant	Meaningful assessment that students can learn from
Making connections	Connects to real life, to previous personal experiences, and across disciplines (as well as curriculum mandates)	Embedded assessment connected to instruction
Fun, enjoyable	Enjoyable, fun	Enjoyable element
Challenging	High standards	Assessment embodies high standards.
Clear expectations	Teacher is explicit about criteria for success and gives these criteria to students at beginning of the learning experience. No surprises.	Students are assessed on stated criteria.
Ongoing feedback	Includes ongoing feedback	Assessment is ongoing descriptive feedback that is not graded
Learn in different ways at different rates	Choices. Allow for different ways to reach standards to allow for different learning styles and multiple intelligences.	Choice of assessments related to different activities
Reflection	Build in time for reflection	Journals, discussion, quiet time, self-assessment, peer assessment

Learning Principles	Instructional Strategies	Embedded Assessments
Metacognition	Metacognition strategies	Provide feedback on metacognition—but actual metacognition is not graded
Positive reinforcement	Variety of positive reinforcements built into activity. Supportive environment.	Ongoing assessment includes constructive criticism and opportunity to redo.
Variety	Use variety in teaching strategies	Use variety in assessment strategies
Learn by teaching	Teach others—jigsaw puzzle, tutoring, demonstration	Self-assessment, peer assessment
Modeling	Teacher walks the talk.	Teacher self-assessment, student assessment of teacher

Interweaving Curriculum, Instruction, and Assessment

We have now explored the pieces of integrated curriculum model using a backward design. When a teacher actually teaches the curriculum unit, such a plan will act as a guideline for what to do each day. But what will it look like in practice? The written plan may deal with meeting standards and be perfectly aligned throughout, but it will take on a life of its own when students are added to the equation. Who are the students in the class? What prior learning do they bring to the classroom? What are their learning styles, interests, and special needs?

Given that there are many, many excellent books on teaching and learning and differentiation that teachers can use as a resource, I am not going explore specific teaching or differentiation strategies here. Most teachers are excellent at deciding on interesting activities that students like to do. And teachers who are attracted to integrated models are often wonderful educators open to new ways of doing things. The end result of open and innovative teachers working with backward design is that all the instructional activities that students complete work toward enabling them to demonstrate that they have achieved the KDB.

This book has largely been about connecting the mandated curriculum with the Know, Do, and Be with assessment *of, for,* and *as* learning at the curriculum design level. In this next section, I will explore how assessment *of, for,* and *as* learning can be implemented in the classroom as a dynamic system, blurring the lines between instruction and assessment. The data for this information came from sources similar to those for Figure 6.8.

My colleagues, Joanne Reid and Danielle Beckett, and I collected stories of best assessment experiences. The Canadian Social Science Humanities and Research Council, in part, funded this research. We asked over 300 practicing educators and administrators and students in teacher education and graduate education to write stories about their best assessment experiences. The instructions were as follows: Please tell us a story of your best assessment experience—a time that excited or energized you. Why were you excited or energized?

The stories were fascinating to read, informative, and aligned with previous theory (Assessment Reform Group, 2002; Black & Wiliam, 1998). These stories provided us with "living examples" of assessment as an integral part of learning. We analyzed the stories, and 10 themes emerged (Drake, Reid, & Beckett, 2010). Like the assessments recommended above in a systems approach, most stories exemplified more than one theme. Some stories were seen from the student point of view, some from the role a teacher or administrator. Some stories were recent, but often they had taken place many, many years ago—stretching back into the primary grades. Many took place in a context outside of school. The themes that emerged from the stories are presented below with some suggestions for implementation.

Demystification/Transparency

Students found that they were successful when they knew exactly what was expected from them. Students were taught what they needed to know in order to succeed and did not feel like they were constantly guessing what the teacher wanted. In these stories, the end goal was clear, and the teacher was actively helping students to understand what the expectations for success looked like. Precise performance criteria were available—either through an assessment tool as a rubric offered at the beginning of instruction or as criteria posted in class in a highly visible site. The KDB was made explicit and also posted. Students also had the opportunity to analyze samples of work at different levels of proficiency so they could understand what quality looked like. As well, they often worked with the teacher to create the assessment tool—ensuring that they understood the criteria.

Feedback That Can Be Acted Upon

Feedback is central to assessment *for* learning. But not all feedback is helpful. Certain factors ensure better feedback. Helpful feedback needs to be selective, descriptive, and given immediately. The feedback should focus on only one or two things that improve the work and are not too daunting for the student—a paper covered in red is not helpful. Importantly, the feedback needs to be a catalyst for action—too often feedback is ignored. For feedback to be a catalyst, students must be given the opportunity to revise the work and resubmit. Another key strategy is to give feedback only—no grades—because students are distracted by grades and think that the mark is the only important thing. Implementing a no grades policy often meets resistance from students (and parents), but once they understand the purpose, it is possible to build a true culture of learning.

Feedback can be oral or written, but it needs to be specific enough to act upon. Feedback needs to go beyond "nice work" to, "Your use of metaphor works well, but you need to make sure that the language conventions are used properly to convey your ideas clearly." Students can be taught how to give useful feedback to others—which in turn will help their own work. Brookhart's (2010) *Formative Assessment Strategies for Every Classroom* is a good resource.

Diagnostic feedback. An equally important side to feedback is how teachers use it to inform their practice. What are the next steps for students? Diagnostic feedback—a subset of assessment *for* learning—is often given before a unit starts. This type of assessment determines such things as learning styles, special needs, multiple intelligences, and/or what students already know and can do. This diagnostic "attitude" carries on throughout teaching. The teacher needs to know each student's current understanding and where to go next.

In my own experience, for example, I had always used a traditional questioning strategy, allowing for a certain number of hands to go up, choosing a student to answer the question and perhaps another to elaborate on or correct the first answer. If the resulting answer was correct, I assumed that all the students had heard the answer and understood it. I moved on without really knowing which students understood and which ones did not. But with a shift to diagnosis and feedback as a philosophy/practice, it is the responsibility of the teacher to find ways to know who does "get it" and who does not. It is also the teacher's responsibility to find ways to reach every student and ensure that everyone does "get it." Correspondingly, it is the responsibility of the student to actively engage in learning.

There are strategies to help teachers know where students are at, and my use of them transformed my instructional practice. Today, I use high-tech devices such as clickers and cell phones, low-tech strategies such as thumbs up–thumbs down, and individual whiteboards and dry erase markers to check for understanding after teaching a specific thing. I have students write one-minute essays to find out what concepts and misconceptions they hold. Most useful for me are the exit cards. After each class, I give students index cards on which they write down one thing that they learned and one thing they still need to learn. Students sign their names on the index cards. Thus, I can approach an individual student regarding a misunderstanding or find a new way to teach a missed concept to the whole class.

Flexibility with respect to the curriculum. An unintended consequence of listening to student feedback was that I discovered I needed to shift away from my written curriculum plan in order to address the needs of the students. Once I was comfortable with this, I was able to be flexible and still true to the original curriculum. Since I was working with the Big Picture as my guide, I was able to redesign the daily activities when I needed to and still arrive at the same place at the end of the unit—students were able to demonstrate the KDB of the Rich Culminating Assessment Task.

I find that implementing this philosophy can dramatically change the role of a teacher. By really listening to student feedback and acting upon it, I was much more of the constructivist teacher than I had been in the past. And I was much more accountable to both my students and my curriculum.

Rich Culminating Assessment Task

We were surprised at the number of times a Rich Culminating Assessment Task was described. These project-based learning tasks were remembered years later. Interesting to us was the fact that the storytellers often described how the teacher prepared them to complete the tasks through daily activities/assessments and how they received ongoing feedback that they had acted upon. This type of task has been described often in the school-based examples scattered throughout the book and is an example of assessment *of* learning.

Fun, Creativity, and Choice

Again and again, the storytellers told us that they remembered a particular assessment experience because it had been fun as well as challenging. These characteristics were often attributed to the richness of the assessment task. As well, students remembered games that tested their skills or knowledge, such as Jeopardy or Deal or No Deal. They appreciated having the opportunity to be creative through projects such as scrapbooks, posters, and writing an artist's sketchbook or activities such as role-playing. In particular, they liked to be able to choose the format in which to demonstrate their learning.

Personal Involvement

Both students and educators appreciated being involved in the instruction/assessment process. Students talked enthusiastically about cocreating rubrics with their teachers. They valued peer and self-assessment because both types helped them learn—but also they needed to learn how to do both types of assessment (connecting back to clear expectations and transparency about the task at hand). It is important to note that such assessment is for feedback only—not for grades.

For the teachers, collaboration with their colleagues helped build professional learning communities and increased the validity and reliability of their assessments. They worked with others through a strategy called *moderated marking.* In moderated marking, a group of teachers actually mark student papers. First they do this as individuals, and then they compare their evaluations. Rich professional dialogue can follow that increases the teachers' assessment literacy and is an enjoyable experience.

Grading and Learning Skills

These stories were not about taking a test and getting a good grade. The few stories about testing described how a teacher had created a situation where the student could learn how to do well on a test. In one, for example, each student created a test on class material and administered the test to one other student in the class who evaluated it for how well the test captured the KDB. Most stories about grading reflected achievement on a relevant assessment task that students had worked hard on. The grade mattered to them because it acted as an external affirmation of how they had assessed their own work—assessment *as* learning.

Learning Skills—The Be

Current assessment theory suggests that such things as effort and attitude not be included in a grade, as this distorts the picture of what a student actually knows and can do. Yet, some stories revolved around appreciating the inclusion of the Be in grading. Theses stories were usually in a skill-related subject area such as physical education, art, or music. In these stories, teachers had found ways for students to succeed in their classes even if they did not have innate talents in that area.

Emotional and Relational

Teaching, learning, and assessment are highly emotional and relational enterprises. Everyone can think of times when they have had negative learning experiences—and this is particularly true of assessment. Our stories were about caring teachers who went the extra mile to ensure that the student was able to learn in an optimal way. In some cases, the teacher went out of his or her way to go to offer the student alternative paths to learning. There was a strong element of trust between student and teacher.

Identity Shapers

Many of our stories described "aha!" moments. The student, for example, suddenly had an insight that he or she was actually smart. The aha! did not come from a high grade but from a teacher's comment and steady belief in the student. Educators also experienced aha! moments. These stories revolved around times when their assumptions about learning and assessment were turned upside down. A teacher who insisted on a math exam for his Grade 10 students recognized that some students could demonstrate what they knew better in an individual interview. This set in motion his interest in new ways of assessing and learning. As a result his Grade 10 students had an interview with the teacher as the assessment. Another teacher who had assumed that certain students were incapable of succeeding at complex performance tasks shifted his expectations when he saw that these very students did better on the task than their more academic peers who were afraid to explore new ways of problem solving in case they did not do it "right" or as the teacher expected. Again this led to new ways of teaching, learning, and assessing.

Evidence-Based Practice

Educators told stories about how they had followed recent policy mandates and that this had led to increased student achievement. According to the policy they followed, instruction and assessment are seamless and must be connected to curriculum mandates. Evidence-based practice meant paying attention to data to target their instruction. Data could be obtained by standardized tests, but it was more likely gleaned through teacher observation through questioning and conversations. Indeed, listening to the students was a powerful way for teachers to practice assessment *for* learning. These educators were now more confident in using their professional judgment in making decisions about curriculum and assessment.

Some Implications of These Principles

These stories shed a new light on effective classroom assessment that goes far beyond traditional conceptions of evaluation as a separate entity disconnected from the curriculum and instruction. These 10 principles reflect a dynamic interplay that balances assessment *of, for,* and *as* learning. They also demonstrate that learners' experiences of curriculum, instruction, and assessment are deeply interconnected in effective learning experiences.

For the educator, really implementing this system of assessment can profoundly change how one teaches. I, for one, found that implementing this philosophy dramatically changed my practice as a teacher. I thought that I was a pretty good teacher. As mentioned in the Preface, I carefully strove to make the learning relevant. But I left out the assessment-*as*-learning piece—not understanding that it was an integral part of the puzzle. As I go deeper and deeper into this new territory, I understand that the real way to ensure accountability and relevance is to seamlessly connect curriculum, instruction, and assessment—just as the books tell me. I also learn that you can teach on old dog to do new tricks and that it definitely is worth it—for both the student and the "old dog."

In this chapter, we explored how to create daily activities/assessments. We followed Vladia, Rumeeza, Susan, as they made their daily decisions on instructional activities and embedded assessments that led to the KDB and the Rich Culminating Assessment Task. Following these steps ensured the curriculum was aligned. Then we explored principles of assessment for teachers to consider as they create the daily instructional activities/assessments and actually implement their units with the students in their classrooms.

DISCUSSION QUESTIONS

1. Discuss two-dimensional thinking. How is this different from traditional planning? What benefits can you see?

2. Why are two-dimensional thinking and principles of learning offered together as a way to plan the daily activities? What is the relationship between the two for you?

3. How do the KDB and assessment *of, for,* and *as* interconnect in the Red Hill unit?

4. Think back to positive learning experiences in your life. What principles of learning were involved? Similarly, think of negative learning experiences. Can you extrapolate any learning principles from these experiences?

5. Explore Figure 6.8. How does this fit your previous learning experiences? How might these experiences have been different if this chart had been considered?

6. Review assessment *of, for,* and *as* learning in Chapter 5 and at the end of Chapter 6. How does this fit with Figure 6.8?

7. Review Cathy Griffin's completed Grade 5 unit in Appendix A. How has she followed the concept in this book?

SUGGESTED ACTIVITIES

1. Using Figure 6.8, consider how assessment and instruction can be integrated with the standards to create some daily learning activities. Make sure that the activities and assessments align with the KDB and the Rich Culminating Assessment Task.

2. You have created several different assessments and activities. How well have you included assessment *of, for,* and *as* learning? To include these three types of assessment, what do you need to add or omit?

3. Create you own curriculum using backwards design. Use Cathy Griffin's curriculum unit in Appendix A as a model.

Epilogue

Curriculum Integration in the 21st Century

Well into the 21st century, the original rationale for an integrated curriculum is more valid than ever. It is a time of ever-escalating change. A number of popular videos illustrate how different the 21st century really is and suggests why educators need to pay attention. We need to prepare our students for the future they will live in. Take a look at the series of YouTube videos called *Did You Know?* that you can find by googling "did you know?" A 2011 video in this series, designed to inspire educators in Iowa to change, is available at http://www.youtube.com/watch?v=dMsNct4X_GU,but you may find a more recent version. Another popular video on changing education paradigms by Sir Ken Robinson is at http://www.youtube.com/watch?v=zDZFcDGpL4U.

The global changes on our planet touch all aspects of living, from economy to education. Arguably it is technology and the Internet that acted as the catalyst for these changes. Even the Internet has evolved over time. Web 1.0 was primarily a place where one could get information. Web 2.0 evolved so that it is interactive and the user produces content. Social networks such as Facebook and Twitter provide the platform for interactions. Blogging and tagging are commonplace skills for students in schools today. On the horizon is Web 3.0; this version is predicted to be intelligent and omniscient. Web 3.0 will link information together from many different places, such as your car, television, and washing machine. Gone will be the computer, and every person will be connected at a personal level 24/7. The Web will be personalized and respond to the individual's needs (http://www.youtube.com/watch?v=bsNcjya56v8).

Although we are not yet at Web 3.0, we can see already how the Internet has changed the possibilities for classroom teaching. The range of options is mindboggling. Webinars, WebQuests, iPads, iPods, e-books, videoconferencing, gaming, smartphones, whiteboards, clickers, Ning, and Skype, to name a few, are only some of the things that educators are exploring. Textbooks and blackboards may soon be something of the past. Many districts are experimenting with online material rather than textbooks. A laptop or iPad for every student is not uncommon. There is a proliferation of educational applications that can enhance learning.

The problem of lack of resources is less problematic when one considers developments like the Aaskash tablet that is available in India and cost about $35 (Watters, 2011a).

Research on the Internet is not discipline-bound—yet students today do research on the Internet. Doing the research for the 2007 edition of this book, I used primarily print sources and attended hands-on conferences. For this edition, most of my research was done on the web. My contacts have connected like a semantic web, some originating through Twitter (my own PLN). Then, I had actual conversational interviews with educators on the phone or on Skype. Although my focus has remained interdisciplinary programs, I have not used the multiple binders, still sitting on my shelves, of articles and examples collected over 22 years. Indeed I use Live Binders (http://www.livebinders.com) to store my research online. I have used new tools to access information.

The personalization of the Internet can already be seen as Google and Facebook struggle with capturing market share. As I write today, Google +1 announced that its trial period with selected users is complete, and it is now open to any user. Google +1 will make note of all one's personal interests and customize one's Internet use to them. Facebook also announced Hoot Me as a site where students can search for other students who are working on the same problem and talk to them in real time face to face. Although social networking sites are banned in many locations, advocates suggest there are many reasons to use Facebook in the classroom—the most powerful reason being that this is website that students use (Watters, 2011b). The day after Watters's article was published, YouTube announced a site specifically for teachers—a guide for using videos in class (Barseghian, 2011). By the time you read this book, the battle for supremacy with educators may be old news. Yet the fact that these three announcements came out within two days of one another demonstrates the high level of competition to capture the minds and hearts of educators.

Education in this context can't go by the rules of the traditional factory model. The success of the Khan Academy (http://www.khanacademy.org) shows that people want to learn on their own time and in their own way. The Khan Academy offers over 2,400 free videos that break down complex concepts and skills into easy to understand instruction, from simple equations to squared error of regression lines. Although the short videos are largely in math and science, there are also some that encompass the humanities. Practice exercises are offered, and participants can get immediate, ongoing, and comprehensive feedback on how well they are doing. Teachers can use these videos for "flip lessons" that flip traditional teaching: Students read about the lesson at home or watch a video, and then they can be involved in hands-on application in class. Students can also work at their own rate and at any time of day or night—allowing them to catch up or to move ahead of grade level skills (Thompson, 2011).

Another approach to personalization is the math curriculum at the School of One in New York City (http://schoolofone.org/concept.html). Here, students learn 400 math skills from grades 4 through 9. (These will be aligned with the Common Core State Standards.) Each student has a different customized learning plan called a "playlist" to learn these skills. Students can learn in different modalities such as large group instruction, small group instruction, small group collaboration, virtual instruction, and with a live remote tutor on a whiteboard. Each day, students are told where to attend the day's lesson. At the end of the lesson they must answer five questions correctly in order to move onto the next lesson. Regular unit quizzes are given. An algorithm determines where the student goes each day determined by academic records, diagnostic tests, feedback on student learning, and available spaces (Dubner, 2010). The Spring 2010 pilot indicated that students who participated in the afterschool program and the in-school program "learned at a rate 50–60% higher" than their counterparts at traditional schools (http://schoolofone.org/research.html).

In *A New Culture of Learning*, Thomas and Brown (2011) explore how technological possibilities are changing the nature of teaching and learning. They see people as being intrinsically motivated and learning in "collectives." A collective is an online group where people of like minds gather to share ideas and to learn from each other. Thus a student who is interested in a particular topic would do his or her research online and find a group that is interested in the same thing. Joining the group, students can participate as much or as little as they wish and can belong to the collective as long as they wish. Thomas and Brown offer the example of nine-year-old Sam, who uses programs like Scratch to learn the fundamentals of computer programming. He joined a programming community online, where he posted a game he created. Thousands of kids working with Scratch also posted their games, and they could modify each other's games. As well, Sam got feedback when the students who had played his games clicked the Love It button to show what they liked about his work. The Love It button is similar to clicking "Like" in Facebook or "Favorites" in Twitter. It can be interpreted as a measure of public approval. Through remixing each other's programs and communicating with his programmer friends, Sam is learning through a collective.

The nature of the collective is dynamic and fluid. Individuals create personal learning networks (PLNs). Learning is very personalized, but knowledge creation is collaborative. People can share their learning either, for example, through blogs or by contributing to knowledge through Wikipedia. The learning can occur 24/7, and there is not a "teacher" who is acting as an expert; instead the teacher coaches and finds nonhierarchal ways to for all students to contribute to the knowledge base. There are no tests or examinations.

People are intrinsically motivated to participate—not for money but for satisfaction and pleasure (Pink, 2009). Volunteers offer advice on Firefox for problem solving. People can add to Google Maps. Contributors to Wikipedia give their time for free. You or I could add or delete an entry on this digital encyclopedia as you now can also do for Britannica's online encyclopedia. This is a surprising shift, as many educators still insist students use Britannica because it is written by experts, while Wikipedia can be written by anyone. Educators are sharing their curriculum and "secrets" online. For example, the entire Grade 9 curriculum of Jalen Rose Leadership Academy is online for the purpose of sharing; educators can download and adapt the lessons if they are appropriate. Many journals, Flickr, and Creative Commons are open sources—available to anyone with Internet access.

One important example of learning in the collective is the creation of a PLN. Many teachers are creating their own PLNs and learning within them. Consider John Burk, a physics teacher who is teaching the laws of physics in Grade 9 by using the video game "Angry Birds" (Dukes, 2011). The students use a software program to see if the birds' movements match physics in the real world. Burk is a blogger who belongs to a PLN of about 100 physics teachers from around the world. Members of this community help each other out. They gather every week for the "global physics department" meeting. Every Wednesday, 20 or 30 teachers go online to listen to a presentation. If Burk has a problem he can't solve, he submits a query to readers of his blog, called Quantum Progress (http://quantum progress.wordpress.com), and he knows that he will get feedback from his community in short order. By openly sharing with others and getting ongoing feedback, he discovered "the feedback I get by letting people in to see these earliest moments of creation have made the product so much better than I could have imagined" (Dukes, 2011). Experts indeed predict that there will be a proliferation of online professional development for the Common Core State Standards. This proliferation will probably encourage educators learning through PLNs.

New research on the brain indicates that we need to think very carefully about personalization and intrinsic motivation. Early research suggests that working with digital texts is actually changing the pathways of young people's brains (Small & Vorgan, 2008). The brain itself is plastic in nature and capable of changing through learning—refuting the concept that we are born with a fixed intelligence (Willis, 2006). The plasticity of the brain provides hope for change and improvement for youngsters with learning disabilities (Doidge, 2007).

Willis (2009) teaches her students about their brains and how they can "grow" them. Basically, they need to get a good sleep and be in a safe environment. Students need to have their curiosity aroused with new experiences and to apply what they learn to something different. The principles of videogaming are helpful. Students can enter at their own level and use practice and rehearsal until they reach the next level. They get the pleasure rush of a dopamine release and are motivated to go on. Their brains are changing at the same time, as they are intrinsically motivated to continue learning.

Even assessment is different in the 21st century context. Group projects can be done through social networking, and students "evaluate" which social networks are good and which ones are not by how much they use them. In fact, there is some suggestion that peer evaluation is becoming the most valued type of evaluation—as members of a social network can "like" or "unlike" something (Davidson, 2011). This is assessment by the collective, as seen above in the example of Sam, who got feedback for the game he created on Scratch. The more schools rely on online learning as a base for research, the more students may be involved in this collective learning that is outside the bricks and mortar of a school. Collective and personalized learning transcends the boundaries of disciplines.

Big Picture schools provide a good example of personalized learning. Students at a Big Picture school follow a radically nontraditional path, but their graduation rate is 92% (http://bigpicture.org/schools/). One third of the 70 schools are charter schools, and two thirds are public. Each student develops a plan that grows out of unique needs or a personal passion. Theirer (2010) offers an example: A student with an interest in skateboarding might take an internship with a skateboarding manufacturer, with a city engineer designing a skateboard park, or at a skateboard shop. In the course of the internship, the student may learn design, business, and/or technological skills. People in the community act as mentors, teachers, and advisors, and parents are involved as a part of the philosophy that education is everyone's business.

Given the real-world context it is not hard to see how students at the Big Picture schools are engaged in a transdisciplinary program. The students' abilities at Big Picture schools are authentically measured by the quality of their work. The perform tasks in their internships. They also give exhibitions every quarter of the school year.

An important aspect of this learning is its appeal to the particular interests of students and to their intrinsic motivation. Continuing along the line of the Big Picture schools, a recent movement has been passion-based learning—particularly popular among those who are technology innovators. Maiers (2011) offers several principles of passion-based learning:

- Reach out to the at-risk students who are not motivated in school.
- Make what happens in school relevant to the real world.
- Develop personal talents and multiple intelligences.
- Let students follow their passion through a school enrichment model.
- Become digital citizens and learn side-by-side with students.
- Create a PLN (personal learning network), and help students to create their own PLNs.
- Be passionate about your teaching.
- Connect with parents.

Maiers (2011) offers two examples of passion-based schools. The Island School in New York City, Public School 188, is one (http://techbrarian .com/home/). At the school's website, one can see samples of student work and the emphasis on technology in the form of blogging, filmmaking, animating, graphic design, robotic engineering, and programming. One teacher's blog for Grade 6 to 8 classes has a graphic of one fish swimming in the opposite direction of all the other fish with the caption, "Follow your own path." His blog tells students that the most important things that students should know about class are these:

1. Choose your own way to solve problems.

2. Take risks.

3. Overcome obstacles. Find what you love. (http://techbrarian.com/ home/)

As we move further into the 21st century and the technological age, it is easy to see that curriculum integration fits into the trends that are explored above. It seems to me that the way we do business will be an integrated one. As well, as I work with the Common Core State Standards, I can see how they are made for curriculum integration. If one follows the seeming logic and reason professed in the documents, then interdisciplinary work will become the norm rather than the exception. The interpretation of these documents and the way they are assessed will ultimately determine this. In any event, you will be able to apply this type of thinking in your own context, and your practice will be richer for it. Good luck!

Appendix A

A Completed Unit

Conservation Clubhouse by Cathy Griffin

The Integrated Curriculum Design Process

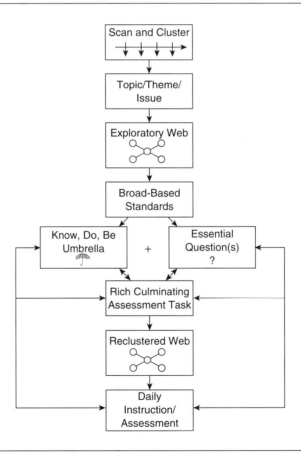

SOURCE: Adapted from Drake and Reid (2010).

In this appendix is an example of a unit that uses the curriculum process offered in this book. It would be helpful to follow this curriculum as you read through Chapters 4 to 6. In this way you can see how each individual step fits into the Big Picture. There is also a secondary example in Appendix B and a checklist to guide your work in Appendix C.

This unit is called Conservation Clubhouse for Grade 5 and is slightly adapted from the work of Cathy Griffin. It offers a very good example of the process. Although it appears as if Cathy followed a linear process, it actually always seems to be an iterative one. Cathy had to go back and forth between steps to ensure alignment, as you will likely find yourselves doing.

The process is the same for any standards-based curriculum regardless of grade level. This particular curriculum is based on Ontario curriculum expectations (Ontario Ministry of Education, 2000, 2004, 2005a, 2005b). Cathy, as an experienced teacher, knew that she did not have to reinvent the wheel and that there would be helpful resources available to build on. Indeed, she found the previous work of Atkinson et al. (2001) to be useful.

This version of Conservation Clubhouse represents a revision of her first unit plan—completed after she taught the unit once following the initial plan. The primary goal for her revisions was to incorporate student voice into the planning procedures. Throughout the unit, you will artifacts and activities that reflect the coconstruction with students.

At the end of the unit, Cathy offers her own reflections on her experiences.

CONSERVATION CLUBHOUSE: A GRADE 5 INTEGRATED UNIT

Scan and Cluster

Not included here is the actual scan that Cathy did with relevant curriculum documents to identify clusters of connected standards. She used different colored highlighters to differentiate connected groups of standards on relevant pages from math, science, arts, and language arts curriculum documents for grades 3, 4, 5, and 6. For the vertical scan, she looked at these curriculum guidelines for repeated patterns over the years. Figure A.1 is an example of her vertical cluster in science.

For her horizontal scan, Cathy looked across Grade 5 science, math, arts, and language arts documents and chunked together standards that fit into meaningful clusters. Cathy selected broad-based standards—two standards from science and one from language arts to act as the headings for her clusters. (See Figure 4.4 for an example of a Common Core math standards cluster.) She created clusters of related standards for each broad-based standard. In these clusters, you will find standards from subject areas other than the one the broad-based standard originated in as well as the subject area itself. Figure A.2 is a summary of her horizontal scan.

Figure A.1　Vertical Cluster

	Science
Grade 3	**Focus: Assess impact of soils on society and the environment and vice versa.** *Do*—identify, investigate, assess, demonstrate, explain, communicate *Know*—composition, characteristics and types of soils. • ways in which humans can have a harmful or positive effect • the process of composting, advantages and disadvantages • interdependence between living and nonliving things that make up soil
Grade 4	**Focus: Assess social and environmental impacts of human uses of rocks and minerals.** *Do*—identify, investigate, assess, test, compare, classify, analyze, demonstrate, explain, communicate *Know*—physical properties of rocks and minerals • testing procedures for above • scientific inquiry/research skills • origin of rock types
Grade 5	**Focus: Analyze the immediate and long-term effects of energy and resource use on society and the environment, and evaluate options for conserving energy and resources.** *Do*—identify, investigate, assess, test, design, build, test, compare, classify, analyze, evaluate, demonstrate, explain, communicate *Know*—forms of energy and sources including renewable and non-renewable • how energy is transformed and conserved • impacts of resource use and conservation • design process, technological problem solving skills
Grade 6	**Focus: Assess the impact of space exploration on society and the environment.** *Do*—identify, investigate, assess, test, design, build, test, compare, classify, analyze, evaluate, demonstrate, explain, communicate, taking different points of view into account. *Know*—characteristics and components of our solar system, relationships among earth, sun, and moon • Canadian contributions to space exploration and scientific understanding • How humans meet their biological needs in space

You may find this process works nicely using broad-based standards. Others find that they chunk according to 21st Century Skills and Big Ideas/Enduring Understandings. This is interpretive work, and the point is to make meaningful connections among the standards in a way that makes sense to you. If you choose not to use broad-based standards here, please be sure to identify three or four of the general standards to represent your unit. It is these standards that you can point to when discussing with others how your unit is focused and standards-based.

Figure A.2   Horizontal Scan

Broad-Based Standard	Clusters
Analyze the immediate and long-term effects of energy and resource use on society and the environment and evaluate options for conserving energy and resources. (Science)	*Reading* • Make judgments and draw conclusions about the ideas and information in texts and cite stated or implied evidence from the text to support their views. • Identify the point of view presented in texts, ask questions to identify missing or possible alternative points of view, and suggest some possible alternative perspectives. *Media Literacy* • Use overt and implied messages to draw inferences and construct meaning in media texts. • Express opinions about ideas, issues, and/or experiences presented in media texts, and give evidence from the texts to support their opinions. • Identify whose point of view is presented or reflected in a media text, ask questions to identify missing or alternative points of view, and, where appropriate, suggest how a more balanced view might be represented. *Math* • Read, represent, compare, and order whole numbers to 100,000, and decimal numbers to hundredths.
Use technological problem-solving skills to design, build, and test a device that transforms one form of energy into another. (Science)	*Science* • Use technical vocabulary. *Visual Art* • Use a variety of materials, tools, and techniques to determine solutions to design. *Math* • Estimate and measure the perimeter and area of regular and irregular polygons, using a variety of tools and strategies.

(Continued)

Figure A.2 (Continued)

Broad-Based Standard	Clusters
	• Select and justify the most appropriate standard unit (i.e., millimeter, centimeter, decimeter, meter, or kilometer) to measure length, height, width, and distance, and to measure the perimeter of various polygons. • Represent, compare, and order whole numbers and decimal numbers from 0.01 to 100,000, using a variety of tools.
Use a variety of forms to communicate with different audiences and for variety of purposes. (Language Arts)	*Science* • Use a variety of forms to communicate with different audiences and for variety of purposes—use technical vocabulary. *Music* • Apply the creative process to create and perform music for a variety of purposes, using the elements and techniques of music. *Visual Arts* • Apply the creative process to produce a variety of two- and three-dimensional art works, using elements, principles, and techniques of visual arts to communicate feelings, ideas, and understandings. • Use elements of design in art works to communicate ideas, messages, and understandings. *Media Literacy* • Create a variety of media texts for different purposes and audiences, using appropriate forms, conventions, and techniques.

Exploratory Web

Once Cathy completed her Scan and Cluster she had a good idea of how the different subject areas connected in meaningful ways that were true to curriculum standards. She completed an Exploratory Web by brainstorming for possible instructional activities that would meet the standards and be relevant to students. She did this through a multidisciplinary lens. What activities fit each of her selected subject areas? She needed to sure that the instructional activities led to her broad-based standards.

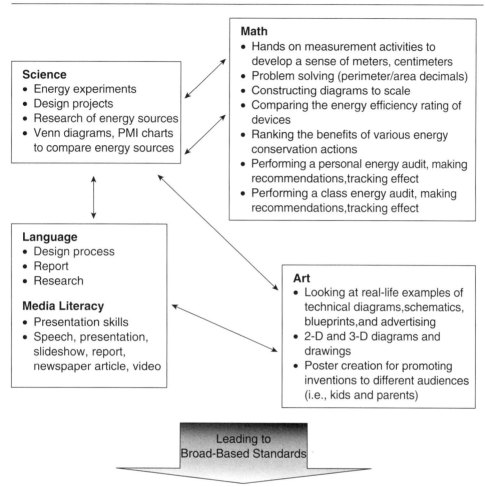

Use technological problem-solving skills to design, build, and test a device that transforms one form of energy into another. (Science)

Analyze the immediate and long-term effects of energy and resource use on society and the environment, and evaluate options for conserving energy and resources. (Science)

Use a variety of forms to communicate with different audiences and for variety of purposes. (Language)

Broad-Based Standards

Cathy selected three broad-based standards to represent the unit. These were the standards that she would plan to meet through instructional activities and assessments:

1. Analyze the immediate and long-term effects of energy and resource use on society and the environment and evaluate options for conserving energy and resources. (Science)

2. Use technological problem-solving skills to design, build, and test a device that transforms one form of energy into another. (Science)

3. Use a variety of forms to communicate with different audiences and for a variety of purposes. (Language)

KDB Umbrella for Conservation Clubhouse

Once Cathy decided that her broad-based standards were a good fit, she was ready to decide upon her KDB Umbrella. Cathy had a good understanding of the expectations for Grade 5 given her horizontal scan. As well, she had a good understanding of what was most important to know, do, and be given her vertical scans. She was now in a good position to determine the KDB and to consider Essential Questions to frame the unit.

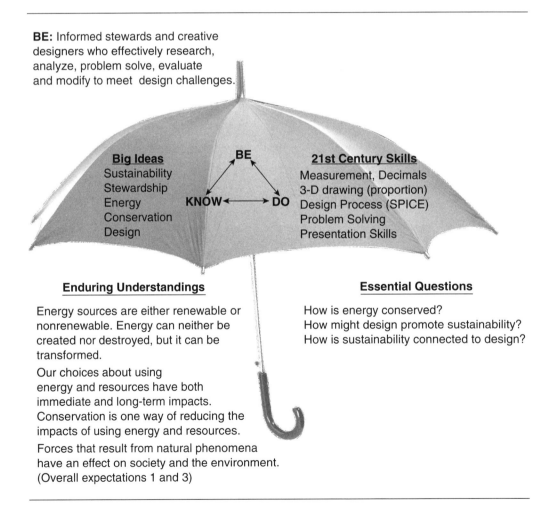

BE: Informed stewards and creative designers who effectively research, analyze, problem solve, evaluate and modify to meet design challenges.

Big Ideas
Sustainability
Stewardship
Energy
Conservation
Design

BE

KNOW ←→ DO

21st Century Skills
Measurement, Decimals
3-D drawing (proportion)
Design Process (SPICE)
Problem Solving
Presentation Skills

Enduring Understandings

Energy sources are either renewable or nonrenewable. Energy can neither be created nor destroyed, but it can be transformed.

Our choices about using energy and resources have both immediate and long-term impacts. Conservation is one way of reducing the impacts of using energy and resources.

Forces that result from natural phenomena have an effect on society and the environment. (Overall expectations 1 and 3)

Essential Questions

How is energy conserved?
How might design promote sustainability?
How is sustainability connected to design?

Rich Culminating Assessment Task:
Conservation Clubhouse Portfolio

Earth and Space Science, Math,
Visual Arts, Music, Media Literacy

The prime minister of Dilopriando wants to encourage students to conserve energy, so he is running a design competition for Grade 5 students across the country. Your task is to design a "Conservation Clubhouse" with energy saving features and a renewable energy source. (Note: Dilopriando is our class-created country, and we have elected a student prime minister.)

Your contest submission must include

- A SPICE design process log for your clubhouse (including design Scenario, Problem brief, Investigation focus questions and research notes, design idea diagrams including the one you Choose to construct, and your Evaluation and modifications)
- Blueprints of your clubhouse (floor plan and front view at least)
- A PMI (Plus, Minus, Interesting facts) analysis of three different energy sources: one nonrenewable, two renewable
- A comparison of at least three different energy-saving devices you considered putting in your clubhouse with an explanation of why you chose the feature you did (math problem-solving solution)
- A newspaper article from your local newspaper detailing what the energy-saving features and energy source are for your clubhouse, why they were chosen, and what their benefits are
- Two posters promoting your design to different audiences
- An advertisement (slideshow or video) and jingle promoting your design

Your responsibilities include observing and listening to your classmates' presentations and evaluating them using a rubric created by the class. You will also use the rubric and check-brick to evaluate your own presentation. There will be teacher evaluation of all parts of your presentation.

The following two assessment tools are selected samples used for the Rich Culminating Assessment Task. Figure A.3 is a checklist coconstructed with the students to ensure quality in creating the blueprints. Figure A.4 is the teacher's rubric for the blueprints.

The rubric in Figure A.5 looks at the concept development of the students for the Big Idea for the unit. Examples of this type of work can also be seen in Figures 5.6 and 5.7.

Figure A.3   Conservation Clubhouse Blueprint Checklist Created by Grade 5 Class

Title and Name	
I have drawn a bird's eye view diagram of each floor, including • Straight ruled lines • Accurately measured angles (e.g., 90° corners)	
The dimensions of each floor are • Labeled • Reasonable • Shown in correct units	
My rooms are • Labeled • Of reasonable dimensions	
All of my furniture and the contents of my rooms • Are labeled in a blueprint key • Are of reasonable size • Have repeated features that are of the same size and shape (e.g., doors)	
My energy saving features are • Labeled in separate key • Highlighted one light color	
I can explain • The importance of proportion in design • Examples and nonexamples • How my blueprint or other blueprints can be upgraded • How my design conserves energy	

Figure A.4   Teacher Rubric for the Blueprints—Grade 5

	Level 4	Level 3	Level 2	Level 1
Knowledge and Understanding (blueprint)	Demonstrates a thorough understanding of the blueprint text format. (see checklist)	Demonstrates an understanding of the blueprint text format.	Demonstrates some understanding of the blueprint text format.	Demonstrates a limited understanding of the blueprint text format.
Thinking (peer and self assessment, oral questioning)	Level 3 plus: Can link proportion to the concept of design. For example: Designers have to have a solid	Can provide examples and nonexamples of proportion in their blueprints and identify them in other student	Can identify examples and nonexamples of proportion in other groups' presentations.	Demonstrates the ability to paraphrase the definition of proportion.

	Level 4	Level 3	Level 2	Level 1
	understanding of proportion and measurement in order to design functional products.	blueprints and explain how to correct the problems.		
Communication	<ul><li>Highly effective, clear</li><li>Extremely logical organization of labels, symbols, and keys</li><li>Correct spelling and use of all terms and vocabulary</li></ul>	<ul><li>Effective, clear</li><li>Logical organization of labels, symbols, and keys</li><li>Correct spelling and use of most terms & vocabulary</li></ul>	<ul><li>Partially clear</li><li>Some organization of labels, symbols, and keys</li><li>Correct spelling and use of some terms & vocabulary</li></ul>	<ul><li>Unclear</li><li>Limited organization of labels, symbols, and keys</li><li>Correct spelling and use of few terms & vocabulary</li></ul>
Application (Audience = competition judges)	Knowledge of energy conservation is applied in a highly effectively manner to the blueprint design in order to persuade the audience, demonstrating excellent stewardship.	Knowledge of energy conservation is applied effectively to the blueprint design to persuade the audience, demonstrating stewardship.	Some knowledge of energy conservation is applied to the blueprint design in an attempt to persuade the audience, demonstrating some understanding of stewardship.	A limited knowledge of energy conservation is applied to the blueprint design in an attempt to persuade the audience, demonstrating a limited understanding of stewardship.

NOTE: Proportion in this figure refers to the relationship of the size and shape of the parts of a figure to the whole figure—the scale of one object compared to its surroundings, with indications of how close and how large the object is.

Figure A.5   Big Idea Rubric (for Know)—Sustainability

Beginning	Developing	Competent	Proficient	Expert
Communicated the term associated with abstract concept.	Can paraphrase the definition.	Can provide examples and nonexamples.	Identifies key attributes of concepts.	Links concepts to other related concepts.

(Continued)

Figure A.5 (Continued)

Beginning	Developing	Competent	Proficient	Expert
Sustainability	Sustainability is the concept of meeting the needs of the present without compromising the ability of future generations to meet their needs.	This action promotes sustainability. This one does not.	This action promotes sustainability. This one does not. • Renewable resources • Nonrenewable resources • Energy efficient devices • Energy wasting devices • Energy conservation • Energy wasting	The way we design has an effect on sustainability. To be a good steward of the environment, we must incorporate sustainability into the design process.

Reclustered Web

At this point, Cathy was ready to think about how to best enable students to be able to demonstrate the KDB in the Rich Culminating Assessment Task. Although she had previously brainstormed for possible activities in her Exploratory Web, that was exploratory work only. Now she knew much more about what needed to be included in her curriculum unit. Was there a better way to think about daily instructional activities? She used her two Essential Questions as headings to recluster possible activities that would lead to the KDB. In this way she created two potential miniunits for Conservation Clubhouse. In this reclustered version of a web shown in Figure A.6, the activities are driven by the questions and not necessarily by disciplines to make natural connections.

Daily Instructional Strategies/Assessment Leading to KDB Umbrella and Rich Culminating Assessment Task

Cathy could now determine what she would do each day. She completed the four-column chart shown in Figure A.7. In the first two columns, she identified an instructional activity with an appropriate assessment task (and tool) embedded in it. Her goal was to make instruction and assessment seamless. Sometimes the assessment was nothing more than thoughtful observation. Sometimes it was more formal. She was conscious to balance assessment *of*, *for*, and *as* learning, so she categorized what type of assessment she was planning.

All activities/assessments were connected to standards that she identified in the third column. These standards were usually the more specific ones that fell under the broad-based ones, and sometimes there was more

Figure A.6

Sustainability

How is energy conserved?

- Investigate the meaning, forms, and sources of energy.
- Identify examples/nonexamples of conservation of energy in terms of energy transfer, resource production and use, and energy use at home and school.
- Develop an ongoing Frayer diagram for sustainability to collect examples and nonexamples of bias. (A Frayer model is a vocabulary development tool to help develop understanding of what is and what is not an example of a complex concept).
- Read, analyze, compare, and rank data for energy conservation (e.g., cost of energy use, cost of energy sources, efficiency ratings, pollution rates).
- Read and analyze fiction and nonfiction, and watch videos to identify good energy conservation practices
- Identify and compare short- and long-term effects of sustainable and nonsustainable energy practices (e.g., in media arts, science issues, environmental issues, social issues).
- Create examples and nonexamples of sustainable practices in literature, advertising, graphs, and charts. (Students will first see this expectation modeled; then they will work in groups with shared responsibility for demonstrating learning, and finally they will be expected to work independently.)
- Write persuasive letters (in response to articles, issues that come up in real life).
- Explore ways in which artists use imagery, language, music (e.g., advertisements, posters, jingles) to persuade by drawing on their audiences' emotions and prior experiences.

How might design and construction skills promote sustainability?

- Explore the concepts of design, the design process, and inventors through reading and discussion of fiction and nonfiction (*Newton and the Giant, The Three Wolves,* biographies of inventors).
- Look at "mentor texts" for diagrams, problem briefs, advertisements, et cetera to make checklists and rubrics.
- Develop drawing and measuring skills needed for the design task.
- From the students' experiences with energy conservation, create and develop an ongoing Frayer model diagram for stewardship to collect examples and nonexamples.
- Work through two design projects: (1) a device that transfers one kind of energy to another using only renewable energy sources (first try at the design process, and (2) a conservation clubhouse (second experience with design process).
- Keep a design process log.
- Prepare a report of these projects for a "design contest."
- Prepare advertising for the "winning design" for promotion to two different audiences.

than one subject area standard included for an individual activity. Cathy also included her planning with the students as instructional activities.

Finally, in the last column, she circled back to the KDB Umbrella and the Rich Culminating Assessment Task. How did the activity/assessment connect back to the KDB? How did it enable students to demonstrate the KDB in the culminating task? If the instructional strategy did not fulfill these purposes, then it had to be rethought or replaced.

Figure A.7 shows Cathy's written plan to address one Essential Question, "How is energy conserved?" She completed another chart for her other Essential Question, "How might design and construction skills promote sustainability?" that is not included here.

Although this four-column chart was thoughtfully planned, it does not take into account every moment of scheduled teaching time. There are things that will inevitably shift and change. Cathy will encounter teachable moments where she may pause and shift direction momentarily. She will constantly be giving feedback to her students. She will learn from her observations and from listening to her students that there are places that she needs to return to and teach differently because her students did not learn as she expected them to. But grounded with her curriculum plan, she can be assured that all of her activities, whether planned or spontaneous, will lead back to the KDB.

INTEGRATED CURRICULUM REFLECTION PIECE

by Cathy Griffin

I chose to do an integrated curriculum because it was relevant to me. I am teaching a Grade 5 class at the moment and this unit is my current unit of study. My primary goal in this second run through the Drake integrated curriculum design model, however, was to incorporate student voice into the planning.

I have long been convinced of the importance of metacognitive development in students. It has been excellent practice to create integrated units outside the context of the classroom, but with this project I wanted to involve my students in the planning process as well as actually teach the unit so I could make upgrades after I see what works and what does not. Throughout my unit are actual artifacts from the planning stages of the unit, which the students have taken part in.

I have a story to tell about my journey with the metacognitive approach to learning and how I have arrived where I am now.

My Metacognitive Journey

My first teaching experience was in New Zealand where I was lucky enough to end up teaching in an extremely innovative school. Near the

Figure A.7 Essential Question: How Is Energy Conserved?

Instructional Activity	Assessment	Standards	Connection to KDB/Rich Culminating Assessment Task
What Is Conservation? • Begin with scenarios of conservation and think/pair/share discussions of what is conservation. • Begin ongoing Frayer model of conservation. • Read aloud *Just a Dream* and begin add to Frayer model/concept map as per Lesson 1 in *Beyond Retell* (Patricia Cunningham and Debra Renner Smith). • Begin chart that shows long-term and short-term effects of conservation. (These are ongoing charts that we will build on throughout the unit). Continue to have read-alouds like *The Lorax* or *10 Simple Ways to Help the Environment* throughout the unit. (See #6 as well)	Task: Discussion Tool: Teacher observation of participation and the students' ability to extract meaning from a listening experience. (*for*) Task: Class development of chart Tool: Anecdotal notes (*for*)	Analyze the immediate and long-term effects of energy and resource use on society and the environment, and evaluate options for conserving energy and resources	Leads to an understanding of energy conservation (examples and nonexamples) and the short-term and long-term effects of conservation. (Know)
Curriculum Connections and the Culminating Task • Look at overall outcomes of the science curriculum. • Brainstorm possible learning tasks/assignments that will help us achieve these outcomes. • Share a few culminating tasks from energy units found on the Internet (including energy audits and the Conservation Clubhouse). • In groups, have students choose a culminating task and make a mind map showing what skills and knowledge they would have to develop in science, art, math, language, and any other subjects they choose in order to be able to do the culminating task. Use their ideas to make a class mind map for posting. (My students chose the Conservation Clubhouse.)	Task: Develop curriculum connections Tool: Anecdotal (*for*)	Interconnected skills: Explain, with some support and direction, how their skills in listening, speaking, reading, and writing help them to make sense of and produce their media texts, writing, et cetera.	Leads to an understanding of design and the number of skills across disciplines required to meet design challenges (Know)

(*Continued*)

Figure A.7 (Continued)

Instructional Activity	Assessment	Standards	Connection to KDB/Rich Culminating Assessment Task

Guided Reading
• In guided reading groups develop/elicit guiding questions with students before, during, and after reading an introductory energy article. Sample questions:
  ○ What is energy?
  ○ What types of energy are there?,
  ○ What are energy sources?
  ○ What are renewable and nonrenewable energy sources?
  ○ How is energy conserved?
  ○ Where does energy come from?
• Continue to choose books for guided reading that answer these questions.
	Task: Development of guiding questions
	Tool: NA (*for*)
		Make judgments and draw conclusions about the ideas and information in texts, and cite evidence stated or implied from the text to support their views.	These tasks will build students' understanding of the basic science concepts (Know), develop research skills (Do), and reinforce their confidence as questioners, researchers and analyzers (Be).

Model Research Skills
  ○ The use of guiding questions as a prereading strategy
  ○ Scanning text for answers
  ○ Highlighting
  ○ Taking jot-notes—including in the form of a PMI chart
  ○ Writing up answers
• Gradually move the students to working on answering research questions in pairs and then by themselves. Differentiate by giving multileveled groups different books to answer the same questions.
	Task: Choose focus questions and do research; record answers in reading response journals (including PMI charts) to communicate answers to guiding questions.	Use a variety of forms to communicate with different audiences and for a variety of purposes; use technical vocabulary.	

Instructional Activity	Assessment	Standards	Connection to KDB/Rich Culminating Assessment Task
• This work leads up to an independent research task to compare alternative energy sources using a PMI to decide which alternative energy they wish to use in their clubhouse (if any). • Technology permitting, this work should include the introduction of assistive technology such as Premier Suites as well as an introduction to Web research.	Tool: Student-generated rubrics (*of, for, as*) (modeled, shared, independent)		
Science Experiments For different sources of energy (heat, electrical, chemical, potential): • Give demonstrations. • Have students experiment with energy transformation and conservation. • Assign design projects where possible. • Brainstorm real-life applications • Investigate ways this type of energy is conserved. • Research and compare actual products or devices that aim to conserve energy (e.g., energy efficient appliances.) (See math problem solving below.) • Have students keep a science journal detailing (with diagrams) which methods of conservation they think could be incorporated into their clubhouse. (modeled, shared, independent)	Task: experiment and design reflections—science journal reflections. Tool: student generated rubrics (*for, as, of*) (modeled, shared, independent) Task: Science journal reflections. Tool: See above. (Actual design process to be	Investigate energy transformation and conservation; demonstrate an understanding of the various forms and sources of energy and the ways in which energy can be transformed and conserved. Use a variety of forms to communicate with different audiences and for variety of purposes; use technical vocabulary.	This task will introduce students to the expectations of the final writing and media tasks and will be used as an opportunity for assessment as learning. It will prepare them for the peer evaluation involved in their final task. (Do/Know/Be) This task will allow students to build a bank of information they need for their final task (Know). They are also building their confidence as problem solvers meeting a design challenge (Do, Be).

(Continued)

Figure A.7 (Continued)

Instructional Activity	Assessment	Standards	Connection to KDB/Rich Culminating Assessment Task
(See "Energy Around Us" by Rainbow Publishing for demonstration and design challenges.) • Keep adding to the "examples and nonexamples of conservation" chart. Include posters and advertisements (video and print) as models (see Media Literacy below). • Preteach vocabulary.	assessed next unit, experimental process next term)		
Math • Concurrently in math, teach, practice, and reinforce the decimal and whole number skills needed to understand and manipulate energy conservation units (R factors, efficiency ratings, cost of energy use) through mini-lessons. • Integrate problem solving into the science. • The context of the problems should shift between home, school, business, and clubhouse settings. For example, "Which of these three insulators will be best for our clubhouse? Consider the cost of buying the insulation and the R factors of each in order make your decision." • Work through modeling, sharing, and independently problem solving. • Develop criteria for presenting answers.	Task: Math problem solving Tool: Rubric, checklist created by students and teacher (*for, as*) Students will choose one solution to add to their portfolio (culminating task). (*of*)	Read, represent, compare, and order whole numbers to 100,000, decimal numbers to hundredths. Solve problems involving the multiplication and division of multidigit whole numbers, and involving addition and subtraction of decimal numbers to hundredths, (variety of strategies).	This task will develop problem-solving skills (Do) as well as build an understanding of ways people conserve energy (Know). Students will continue to develop experience as designers evaluating and making informed choices.

Instructional Activity	Assessment	Standards	Connection to KDB/Rich Culminating Assessment Task
Media Literacy Explore ways in which artists use imagery, language, and music (in advertisements, posters, jingles) to persuade by drawing on their audiences' emotions and prior experiences by comparing two or three of each: print ads, TV ads. • Compare purpose, audience, techniques, effect on audience (the students). • Create a checklist of text or media features and language conventions for science design projects • Model how to make an ad using the checklist (print and video) Have students create ads in small groups.	Task: Advertisement Tool: Rubric, checklist created by students and teacher (for, as) In Unit 2, students will create two ads for their portfolio (culminating task). (of)	Make judgments and draw conclusions about the ideas and information in texts, and cite stated or implied evidence from the text to support their views and perspectives. Use overt and implied messages to draw inferences and construct meaning in media texts. Identify whose point of view is presented or reflected in a media text, ask questions to identify missing or alternative points of view, and, where appropriate, suggest how a more balanced view might be represented.	This task will give students practice with the media format necessary for their final task and with the techniques used to reach audiences and persuade. It will reinforce their identities as analyzers and evaluators of text. (Do/Know/Be).

(*Continued*)

Instructional Activity	Assessment	Standards	Connection to KDB/Rich Culminating Assessment Task
Long- and Short-Term Effects of Conservation and the Introduction of the Term Sustainability. • Have a final discussion about the effects of conservation or the lack of conservation. Add final ideas to the class chart. Review this and the conservation chart with list of examples and nonexamples of conservation. • Reread *Just a Dream.* • Have students think/pair/share about why conservation is important and what their role in conservation is or should be. Record answers (in a way that leads to the meaning of sustainability) and ask if any of them know the word for the ideas they are coming up with. This leads directly into Unit 2, focusing on how design might promote sustainability or why sustainability must lead design.	Task: Discussion Tool: Teacher observation of participation and the students' ability to summarize what they have learned (*of, for*)	Analyze the immediate and long-term effects of energy and resource use on society and the environment, and evaluate options for conserving energy and resources. In discussion, identify, with some support and direction, what strategies they found most helpful in making sense of the science unit.	
Reflection Piece: Have students respond to the discussion in their choice of one of the following: • Create a poster promoting sustainability. • Write a letter to your local MP, parents, principal, or mayor about sustainability. • Write a science journal reflection. • Create a mind map of what you have learned in this unit with sustainability as the central concept. Have the students share and respond to each other's work, and provide them with an opportunity to upgrade or add to their own reflection pieces.	Task: Reflection/ consolidation of unit. Tool: Student/ teacher created rubric (*of*)		This task will allow students to reflect on what they have learned (Know). They will also be able to reflect on their roles as conservationists or stewards (Be).

end of my four years there, I had the opportunity to present, with two of my colleagues, at the Ninth International Conference on Thinking in Auckland. The thrust of our presentation entitled, "Harry Potter and the Thinking Hats" was to give children power over their own learning by:

Making the program as transparent and relevant to the children as possible

Teaching the independent use of thinking tools

Teaching children to use information and communication technology (ICT) creatively

In the four years prior to this presentation, the school had integrated De Bono's Thinking Hats across the school, initiated teacher moderation and individualized professional learning, started two digital classrooms with two children per computer (I taught one of these classes), and begun whole school integrated planning. Although our planning process was not as structured as the Drake model, it shared the foundations of making connections in rich and relevant contexts while assuring *for, as,* and *of* assessment of learning were in place (although not called this).

It has been quite a journey getting back to the lofty standards of our presentation since my separation from the staff at Sherwood and my return to Canada eight years ago. The barriers I have faced include numerous changes of school (eight schools in eight years) and grade as well as perceived or overt pressure to conform to grade partner planning. However, the most depressing barrier has been the self-doubting that comes with being isolated in your beliefs and practices.

The past eight years have not been without professional development. In my struggle to replicate the teaching environment I experienced in New Zealand, I sought out professional learning with like-minded colleagues. I joined a differentiated instruction committee and became a "First Steps Tutor" for an Ontario school board. Then I gained valuable professional development and leadership experience as a math and then literacy contact teacher (MCT, LCT) for another Ontario school board. I continued my personal study with reading such as the Lens-Dagett model of rigor and relevance. These learning and leadership experiences were very rewarding personally and further cemented the importance of building connections in learning, integrated planning, differentiated instruction, and metacognitive teaching and assessment practices. But rarely did I find truly like-minded colleagues and never were we able to take enough time to delve as deeply as I wanted to go into the integrated planning.

Although there was no one "supreme ordeal" for me, I certainly felt anxious about what I was doing and if I was on the right path. Every year as I changed schools or grades I felt the conflict between what I wanted to do and my perception of what my "more experienced" colleagues were doing. In my leadership roles, I felt ill prepared to deal with pervasive negative attitudes toward change.

This year has been a return to a positive community of learners for me. I have found a supportive group in the masters cohort and am giving myself permission to take the time I need to learn, consolidate, and be the teacher I want to be. I feel I am back on the "journey of the path with heart."

In my school I now have the confidence and understanding to speak up and explain what I am doing and why. I am better able to look for and foster what I need in a community of learners in my school now that I have realized the journey I have traveled. I have more awareness of and compassion for the isolation, anxiety, and conflict all teachers feel now that I understand the roots of these feelings in myself.

Most importantly, I think my journey has taught me to be patient with my own learning and that of others. Although I thought I "knew it all" as a young teacher in an innovative school, I can look back now and see all the pieces I was missing then that I have learned in the intervening years. With more life experience I realize that this is a never-ending process and that life's trials often get in the way of learning. We never arrive at the point of perfection. The real "innovation" at my school in New Zealand was the development of a community of learners that brought everyone onto the same journey.

My challenge in teaching has been to bring my students together on the same journey. I have always wanted them to be able to see where they are, what they are doing, and why. I want them to help direct their own learning as well as assess their learning and set new goals. What I have realized is that I need to develop an understanding of the community we have when we are on this journey. Students need to be able to identify the ingredients of a successful learning community (i.e., trust, respect, safe debate, common purpose, the right to disagree) and gradually learn to replicate them independently.

Appendix B

A Standards–Based Grade 10 Curriculum Unit

Saga of Survival

S *aga of Survival* is an integrated unit of study involving science, math, and English for a Grade 10 academic class; it is modified from the work of Will Lammers and Laura Tonin.

1. Broad-based curriculum standards (http://www.edu.gov.on.ca) selected after a horizontal and vertical Scan and Cluster:

- Solve problems involving quadratic functions. (math)
- Solve problems involving the analytic geometry concepts involving lines. (math)
- Solve trigonometric problems involving right or acute triangles. (math)
- Use a variety of organizational techniques to present ideas and information logically and coherently in written work. (English)
- Sort and label information, ideas, and data; evaluate the accuracy, ambiguity, relevance, and completeness of the information, and draw conclusions based on the research. (English)
- Produce written work for a variety of purposes, with the purpose of analyzing information, ideas, themes, and issues and supporting opinions with convincing evidence. (English)
- Spell specific academic and technical terms correctly. (English)
- Examine the factors that affect the survival and equilibrium of populations in an ecosystem, including heat transfer in weather systems. (science)
- Examine how abiotic (nonliving) factors affect the survival and geographic location of biotic (living) communities, and investigate the effects of heat transfer on development of weather systems. (science)
- Plan and conduct research into ecological relationships. (science)

2. Exploratory Web:

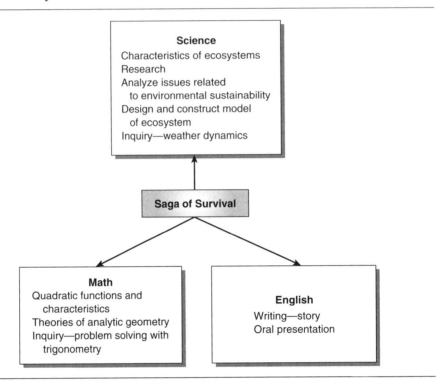

3. Know/Do/Be Umbrella:

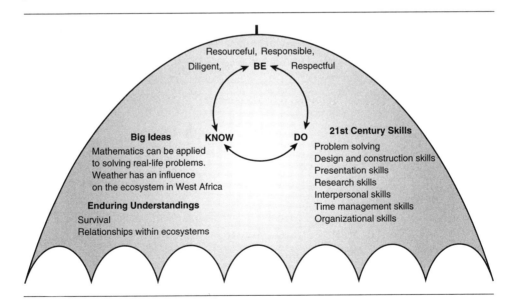

4. Essential Questions:

- How do natural forces affect survival?
- How can mathematics be used to solve real-life problems?

Unit question:

What difficulties did Polly face, and what resources did she need to survive?

5. Rich Culminating Assessment Task:

Polly, an avid traveler and sailor, fell into a predicament and has survived to tell about it. Last year, during a transworld solo sailing expedition, her sailboat sank during a storm. She managed to survive the disaster by swimming to the nearby island of Kwa Dratique, which is located in the tropics off the coast of West Africa. She has an incredible story to tell about her experiences, but it is sketchy. She is able to narrate to you the saga of her survival in general terms, but specifics are lacking.

You and a partner have been given the task of documenting Polly's story. You will be presenting her story as part of a community fair to commemorate her homecoming. A number of stands will be set up at the fair. Small groups of people from the community will visit you at your stand.

Your presentation of Polly's story should show the *process* you followed, as well as the *product* you created, as described in the following:

a. To fill in the details of Polly's story, your presentation should account for the following *processes:*

Show all of your research work in a learning log. Each entry should be dated.

Solve one of Polly's problems using trigonometry.

Solve one of Polly's problems using quadratic functions.

Solve one of Polly's problems using analytic geometry of line segments.

Show evidence of how Polly rationalized her food consumption, based on her environment and her resources.

Show how the weather systems on Kwa Dratique affected where and how she lived, given the geography of the land and its climate.

b. You should be prepared to present the following *products:*

Create an oral presentation of Polly's story.

Create a stand-alone display outlining the details of your story.

Organize information in two or more different ways (e.g., charts, graphs, text).

Document the references you used on your display.

Create a model that represents a typical ecosystem on Kwa Dratique.

Answer any questions for visitors, or provide any clarifying information they ask for.

Rubric for Rich Culminating Assessment Task

Criteria	Level 1 (below expectations)	Level 2 (barely meets expectations)	Level 3 (meets expectations)	Level 4 (exceeds expectations)
(/point total)	(points per level)			
Display: Creativity (/5)	Display does not catch the reader's interest. (2)	A small portion of the display catches the reader's attention. (3)	Most of the display catches the reader's attention. (4)	The whole display catches the reader's attention. (5)
Layout (/5)	Display is difficult to follow, **and** it has a sloppy appearance. (Lettering is unclear or illegible, and illustrations are not clearly presented.) (1–2)	Display is difficult to follow, **or** it has a sloppy appearance. (3)	Display is easy to follow, and it has a generally neat appearance. (4)	Display is easy to follow, has an excellent overall appearance, and makes good use of space allowed. (5)
Content (/5)	Display lacks information, **and** content is not self-explanatory. (0–1)	Display lacks information, **or** content is not self-explanatory. (2–3)	Display contains all relevant information and is self-explanatory. (4)	Displayed information is detailed, relevant, and self-explanatory. (5)
Learning log: Content (/5)	Entries are not titled or dated, log is an incomplete record of work done, **and** references are not documented. (0–1)	Entries are not titled or dated, **or** log is an incomplete record of work done, **or** references are not documented. (2–3)	Entries are titled and dated, log is a complete record of work done, and sources are referenced. (4)	Log contains all required content, and there is evidence of self-reflection as project progressed. (5)
Organization (/5)	Notebook **lacks all 3:** • names, date, and title on cover	Notebook lacks **2 of** • names, date, and title on cover	Notebook lacks **1 of** • names, date, and title on cover	Notebook **shows all 3:** • names, date, and title on cover

Criteria	Level 1 (below expectations)	Level 2 (barely meets expectations)	Level 3 (meets expectations)	Level 4 (exceeds expectations)
	• signs of being well used • neatness and legibility (0–1)	• signs of being well used • neatness and legibility (2–3)	• signs of being well used • neatness and legibility (4)	• signs of being well used • neatness and legibility (5)
Story: Inventiveness and mechanics of writing (/5)	The story lacks a coherent plot. (1)	The plot is coherent, but it is difficult to follow or not realistic. (2–3)	The plot is coherent and realistic. (4)	The plot is coherent, is realistic, and contains an element of surprise. (5)
Story: Grammar and spelling conventions (/5)	Writing contains more than five spelling and grammar errors. (0–2)	Writing contains three to five spelling and grammar errors. (3)	Writing contains not more than two spelling and grammar errors. (4)	Writing is free of spelling and grammar errors. (5)
Integration of content (/5)	Two (2) or more processes or products are missing from story. (0–2)	One (1) process or product is missing from story. (3)	All required elements of content are evident in story. (4)	All required elements of content are evident, and there is evidence of more analysis than expected. (5)
Use of terminology, units of measurement (/5)	Three (3) or more terms and units of measurement are either missing or used incorrectly. (0–2)	Two (2) terms and units of measurement are either missing or used incorrectly. (3)	One term or unit of measurement is either missing or used incorrectly. (4)	All terms and units of measurement are included and used correctly. (5)
Interpretation of data (/5)	There is little or no evidence that measurements and calculations were used to add meaning to the story. (0–2)	There is some evidence that measurements and calculations are used to add meaning to the story. (3)	Most measurements and calculations are used to add meaning to the story. (4)	Every measurement and calculation is used to add meaning to the story. (5)
Total:				50

6a. Reclustered Web: Standards reclustered according to miniunits.

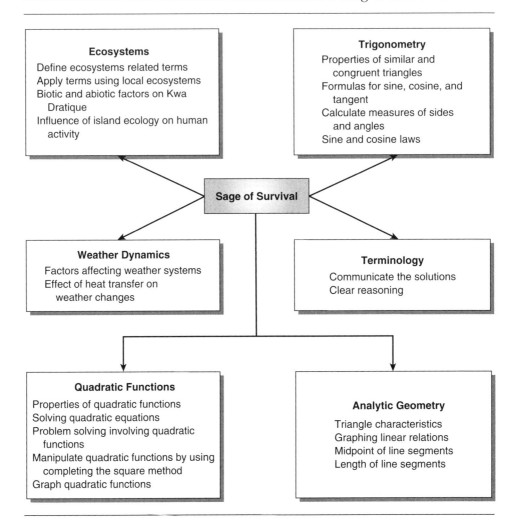

Ecosystems
Define ecosystems related terms
Apply terms using local ecosystems
Biotic and abiotic factors on Kwa
   Dratique
Influence of island ecology on human
   activity

Trigonometry
Properties of similar and
   congruent triangles
Formulas for sine, cosine, and
   tangent
Calculate measures of sides
   and angles
Sine and cosine laws

Sage of Survival

Weather Dynamics
Factors affecting weather systems
Effect of heat transfer on
   weather changes

Terminology
Communicate the solutions
Clear reasoning

Quadratic Functions
Properties of quadratic functions
Solving quadratic equations
Problem solving involving quadratic
   functions
Manipulate quadratic functions by using
   completing the square method
Graph quadratic functions

Analytic Geometry
Triangle characteristics
Graphing linear relations
Midpoint of line segments
Length of line segments

6b. Sample Miniunit: Ecosystems

Teaching/Learning Experience	Standard	Assessment
In groups, students brainstorm for roles that different people in a community need to play for the community to be self-sufficient. Teacher assigns each small group a role	Examine the factors (natural and external) that affect the survival and equilibrium of populations in an ecosystem. (science) Investigate potential topics by formulating questions. (English)	Each group shares its ideas, and teacher notes them on board for display. Teacher evaluates ideas for completeness. Teacher distributes a research rubric prior to activity.

Teaching/Learning Experience	Standard	Assessment
identified in the community. Small groups research using text or media-based resources to determine the name and description of the part of the ecosystem that plays a role similar to that identified in the community. Teacher shows visual display of Kwa Dratique and poses the following question: If you were to recommend that Polly reside in a particular location on the island, where would you locate her, and why? There are no roads on Kwa Dratique, and Polly must rely on the ecology of the land to survive.	Examine how abiotic factors affect the survival and geographical location of biotic communities. (science) Use a variety of organizational techniques to present ideas logically and coherently in written work. (English) Use the formula of length of a line segment to solve problems. (math) Use the formula of midpoint of a line segment to solve problems. (math) Focus on interpreting and analyzing information, ideas, themes, and issues and supporting opinions with convincing evidence. (English)	Students negotiate standards. Peer evaluation using rubric. Students generate a research- and problem-solving-skills rubric. Teacher collects and evaluates individual work.

SOURCE: Adapted from the work of Will Lammers and Laura Tonin.

Appendix C

A Rubric and Reflection Tool to Use as a Guide for Creating Your Own Standards–Based Interdisciplinary Curriculum

	Level 1	Level 2	Level 3	Level 4
Scan and Cluster	There has been no attempt to Scan and Cluster.	Horizontal and vertical scans are not complete and do not lead to meaningful clusters or do not address the meta-level.	Horizontal or vertical scan was done well and addresses the meta-level in most cases.	Both horizontal and vertical scans are thorough and include meaningful clusters of standards that work at the meta-level.
Selection of Broad-Based Standards	Broad-based standards are not chosen thoughtfully.	Broad-based standards act as an umbrella for the meaningful clusters in a hit-or-miss fashion.	In most cases, broad-based standards act as an umbrella for meaningful clusters.	Broad-based standards act as an umbrella for meaningful clusters.
Exploratory Web	No evidence to show the web was created using the standards.	Activities and assessments have some connection to standards.	Activities and assessments are connected to standards.	Activities and assessments are very well connected to standards.
Topic or Theme Choice	Illogical choice of topic with regard to Scan and Cluster.	Topic is not age appropriate or interesting to students.	Topic is age appropriate or interesting to students.	Topic is age appropriate or interesting to students and is backed up with informally collected student feedback.

	Level 1	Level 2	Level 3	Level 4
Construction of Know/Do/Be (KBD) Umbrella	Incomplete.	KDB elements (Enduring Understandings/Big Ideas, 21st Century Skills) are confused.	KDB elements clearly described.	Elements are concisely described, and the Be is insightfully linked to the Know and the Do.
Essential Question(s) Topic Questions	Questions are simplistic and require a single answer. Questions deal with a few parts of the unit.	Include topic and questions that could be more focused; questions tend to be simplistic, with few opportunities for multiple answers. Questions deal with individual parts of the unit.	Include topic and Essential Questions; questions encourage inquiry and multiple answers. Questions deal with substantial parts of the unit and reflect student input.	High level of relevance of Essential Questions and topic questions; questions encourage inquiry and use multiple answers as the focus of reflection. Questions reflect student input and have a high degree of relatedness to the unit.
Description of Rich Culminating Assessment Task	Minimal description of the task.	Description of the task but with few connections to the KDB Umbrella.	Clear description of the task with many connections to the KDB Umbrella.	Clear description of the task with many substantive connections to the KDB Umbrella.
Task-Specific Rubric	Rubric created with imprecise language and lacking meaningful and relevant indicators.	Rubric created with imprecise language and some meaningful and relevant indicators.	Rubric created in precise language with meaningful and relevant indicators in both teacher and student versions.	Rubric created with explicit, meaningful, and relevant indicators in precise language in both teacher and student versions.
Reclustered Web	No attempt at moving beyond the Exploratory Web.	Activities/assessments are still multidisciplinary. (This is fine if this	Activities/assessments are more integrated in nature.	Activities are integrated in nature (if appropriate).

(Continued)

(Continued)

	Level 1	Level 2	Level 3	Level 4
		is what is desired.) Activities/ assessments only partially answer the Essential Question(s). Some alignment with the KDB Umbrella and Rich Culminating Assessment Task	Activities/ assessments answer the Essential Question(s). Adequate alignment with the KDB Umbrella and Rich Culminating Assessment Task.	The web shows that the suggested activities/ assessments are strongly aligned with Essential Question(s). Strong alignment with KDB Umbrella and Rich Culminating Assessment Task.
Instructional Activities/ Assessments/ Standards/ Connection to KDB and Culminating Task.	Dull activities. Assessment disconnected from activities. No alignment.	Somewhat challenging and engaging activities/ assessments. Weak alignment.	Acceptably challenging and engaging activities/ assessments. Good alignment.	Challenging and engaging activities/ assessments. Strong alignment.
Assessment Tools	Poor assessment tools disconnected from the task.	Good assessment tools that fit the tasks.	Good assessment tools that fit the rigorous but engaging tasks.	Excellent assessment tools that fit the rigorous but engaging tasks.
Assessment *of*, *for*, and *as* Learning	No variety.	Some variation in *of*, *for*, and *as* assessment tasks.	Good variation in *of*, *for*, and *as* assessment tasks.	Rich variation in *of*, *for*, and *as* assessment tasks.

QUESTIONS FOR REFLECTION

Rich Culminating Assessment Task

- Does the assessment provide a way to celebrate learning? Is it fun?
- Does the assessment provide an external audience to witness or assess the performance or demonstration?

Daily Activities and Assessments

- Keeping the connection to the KDB Umbrella in mind, how do the daily activities align with the Rich Culminating Assessment Task?
- Choose two Big Ideas or 21st Century Skills, and discuss how you will know when the student has learned them. What will your assessments for these concepts and skills look like?
- Have you used any traditional assessments? Why or why not?
- If you used traditional assessments, describe the connections you made in format and skill level to the standardized testing students will be required to complete.
- Describe your first assessment and discuss the reasons for the choices you made, given what you know about assessment.
- Describe your second assessment and discuss the reasons for the choices you made, given what you know about assessment.
- What would you describe as your most significant learning from this process?

SOURCE: Adapted from the work of Glynnis Fleming, instructional coach, District School Board of Niagara.

References

Aikin, W. M. (1942). *The story of the eight-year study.* New York: Harper.

Albright, S. & Breidenstein, A. (2004). A school with a worldview. *Edutopia Online.* Retrieved November 16, 2005, from http://www.glef.org

Assessment Reform Group. (2002). *Assessment for Learning: 10 principles.* Retrieved from http://www.assessment-reform-group.org.uk/

Atkinson, Bishop, Beckett, Desmond, Kristoff, Moore, Tonner, et al. (2001). *The conservation clubhouse: Energy and control: An integrated unit for grade 5.* Retrieved from http://orgs.educ.queensu.ca/curr/ConsrvClb.pdf

Au, W. (2007). High stakes testing and curricular control: A qualitative metasynthesis. *Educational Researcher, 36*(5), 258–267.

Barseghian, T. (2011, September 21). YouTube launches site specifically for teachers. *Mind/Shift: How we learn.* http://mindshift.kqed.org/2011/09/youtube-launches-site-specifically-for-teachers/

Beane, J. (1993). *A middle school curriculum: From rhetoric to reality.* Columbus, OH: National Middle School Association.

Beane, J. (1997). *Curriculum integration: Designing the core of democratic education.* New York, NY: Teachers College Press.

Billig, S. (2000). *The impacts of service learning on youth, schools and communities: Research on K–12 school-based service learning, 1990–1999.* Denver, CO: RMC Research. Retrieved from http://www.servicelearning.org/library/resource/1699

Black, P., Harrison, C., Lee, C., Marshall, B., & Wiliam, D. (2003). *Assessment for learning.* Berkshire, UK: Open University Press.

Black, P. & Wiliam, D. (1998). Assessment and classroom learning. *Assessment in education, 5*(1), 70–74.

Bolack, K., Bialach, D. & Dunphy, M. (2005). Standards-based, thematic units integrate the arts and energize students and teachers. *Middle School Journal, 31*(2), 57–60.

Brookhart, S. (2010). *Formative assessment strategies for every classroom.* Alexandria, VA: ASCD.

Brown, D. F. (2006). It's the curriculum, stupid: There's something wrong with it. *Phi Delta Kappan, 87*(10), 777–783.

Caine, R., & Caine, G. (1997). *Education on the edge of possibility.* Alexandria, VA: Association for Supervision and Curriculum Development.

Carnegie Corporation. (1989). *Turning points: Preparing youth for the 21st century.* New York, NY: Carnegie Corporation of New York.

Committee on a Conceptual Framework for the New K–12 Science Education Standards. (2011). *A framework for K–12 science education: Practices, crosscutting concepts, and core ideas.* Washington, DC: National Academies Press.

Cornejo-Sanchez, D., & Wakefield, C. (2008). Superhero in the making. *Unboxed: A journal of adult learning in schools, 1.* Retrieved from http://www.hightechhigh.org/unboxed/issue1/cards/1.php

Curry, J., Samara, J., & Connell, R. (2005). *The Curry/Samara Model®: Curriculum, instruction and assessment yield statistically significant results.* Retrieved November 16, 2005, from http://www.curriculumproject.com

Darling-Hammond, L. (2004). Standards, accountability, and school reform. *Teachers College Record, 106*(6), 1047–1085.

Darling-Hammond, L. (2010 May). *What kind of change can we believe in? Toward an equitable system of good schools.* Distinguished Contribution to Education Research Award (2009) lecture at annual meeting of American Educational Research Association, Denver, CO.

David, J. L. (2011). High stakes testing narrows the curriculum. *Educational Researcher, 68*(6), 78–80.

Davidson, C. (2011). *Now you see it: How the brain science of attention will transform the way we live, work and learn.* New York, NY: Viking.

Dewey, J. (1938). *Experience in education.* New York, NY: Collier Books.

Dewey, J. (1966). *Democracy and education.* New York, NY: Macmillan/Free Press. (Originally published in 1916)

Doidge, N. (2007). *The brain that changes itself.* New York, NY: Penguin.

Drake, S. M. (1991). How our team dissolved the boundaries. *Educational Leadership, 49*(2), 20–22.

Drake, S. M. (1993). *Planning for integrated curriculum: The call to adventure.* Alexandria, VA: Association for Supervision and Curriculum Development.

Drake, S. M., & Burns, R. (2004). *Meeting standards through integrated curriculum.* Alexandria, VA: Association for Supervision and Curriculum Development.

Drake, S. M., & Reid, J. (2010). Integrated curriculum: Increasing relevance while maintaining accountability. *What works? Research into Practice.* Retrieved from http://www.edu.gov.on.ca/eng/literacynumeracy/inspire/research/WW_Integrated_Curriculum.pdf

Drake, S., Reid, J. L., & Beckett, D. (2010, May). *Exploring best stories of assessment experiences.* Paper presented at the Ministry of Education/Faculty of Education Forum, Toronto, ON.

Dubnar, S. (2010, May 12). How is a bad radio station like the public school system? [Web log post]. *Freakonomics: The hidden side of everything.* Retrieved from http://www.freakonomics.com/2010/05/12/freakonomics-radio-how-is-a-bad-radio-station-like-the-public-school-system/

Dukes, T. (2011, Sept 26). 'Angry birds' and teaching physics. *The News & Observer.* Retrieved from http://www.newsobserver.com/2011/09/26/1517619/angry-birds-and-teaching-physics.html#storylink=misearch

Earl, L. (2003). *Assessment as learning.* Thousand Oaks, CA: Corwin.

Elmore, R. F., & Rothman, R. (1999). *Testing, teaching and learning: A guide for states and school districts.* Washington, DC: National Academy Press.

Erickson, H. L. (1995). *Stirring the head, heart, and soul: Redefining curriculum and instruction.* Thousand Oaks, CA: Corwin.

Ferrero, D. J. (2006). Having it all. *Educational Leadership, 63*(8), 8–14.

Fogarty, R. (1991). *The mindful school: How to integrate the curricula.* Palatine, IL: Skylight.

Foley, A., & Condon, M. (2005, April). *Taking back ownership of curriculum standards.* Paper presented at ASCD Conference, Orlando, FL.

Flowers, N., Mertens, S. B., & Mulhall, P. F. (1999). The impact of teaming: Five research-based outcomes. *Middle School Journal, 29*(4), 38–41.

Hargreaves, A., & Earl, L. (1990). *Rights of passage: A review of selected research about schooling in the transition years.* Toronto: Ontario Ministry for Education.

Hargreaves, A., & Shirley, D. (2009). *The fourth way: The inspiring future for educational change.* Thousand Oaks, CA: Corwin.

Heller, L. (2011, September 19). Teaching the leaders of tomorrow [Web log post]. *Champions of Change.* Retrieved from http://www.whitehouse.gov/blog/2011/09/19/teaching-leaders-tomorrow

Herbert, M. (2011, September 19). Scofield welcomes teachers from China. *Stamford Patch.* Retrieved from http://stamford.patch.com/articles/scofield-welcomes-teachers-students-from-china

Hoachlander, G., & Yanofsky, D. (2011). Making STEM real. *Educational Leadership, 68*(6), 60–65.

Jacobs, H. H. (Ed.). (1989). *Interdisciplinary curriculum: Design and implementation.* Alexandria, VA: Association of Supervision and Curriculum Development.

Jacobs, H. H. (Ed.). (2004). *Getting results with curriculum mapping.* Alexandria, VA: Association of Supervision and Curriculum Development.

Jacobs, H. H., & Johnson, A. (2009). *Curriculum mapping planner: Templates, tools and resources for effective professional development.* Alexandria, VA: ASCD.

Jalen Rose Leadership Academy. (n.d.). *Academics.* Retrieved from http://www.jrladetroit.com/academics

Jensen, E. (2005). *Teaching with the brain in mind.* Alexandria, VA: Association of Supervision and Curriculum Development.

Johnson, L. F., Smith, R., S., Smythe, J. T., & Varon, R. K. (2009). *Challenge-based learning: An approach for our time.* Austin, TX: The New Media Consortium

Kahne, J. (1995). Revisiting the eight-year study and rethinking the focus of educational policy analysis. *Educational Policy, 9*(1), 4–23.

Kendall, J. (2011). *Understanding Common Core State Standards.* Alexandria, VA: ASCD.

King, K. V., & Zucker, S. (2005). *Curriculum narrowing.* Retrieved November 16, 2005, from http://harcourtassessment.com/hai/Images/pdf/assessmentReports/CurriculumNarrowing.pdf

Lachowicz, J. (2004). Curriculum mapping in alternative education settings. In H. H. Jacobs (Ed.), *Getting results with curriculum mapping* (pp. 97–111). Alexandria, VA: Association for Supervision and Curriculum Development.

Lankes, T. (2011, September 21). City schools find wiggle room in gym requirement. Rochester Democrat and Chronicle. Retrieved from http://pqasb.pqarchiver.com/democratandchronicle/access/2463201301.html?FMT=ABS&FMTS=ABS:FT&type=current&date=Sep+21%2C+2011&author=Tiffany+Lankes&pub=Rochester+Democrat+and+Chronicle&edition=&startpage=n%2Fa&desc=City+schools+find+wiggle+room+in+gym+requirement

Larmer, J., & Mergendoller, J. R. (2010). Essentials for project-based learning. *Educational Leadership, 68*(1). Retrieved from http://www.bie.org/images/uploads/useful_stuff/7_Essentials_PBL_EdLeaderSept10.pdf

Littky, D. (2004). *The big picture.* Alexandria, VA: Association for Supervision and Development.

Maiers, A. (2011, July). *Guidelines of passion-based learning* [Web log post]. Retrieved from http://www.angelamaiers.com/2011/07/guidelines-of-passion-based-learning.html

Manzo, R. K. (1996). Districts pare electives for core courses. *Education Week.* Retrieved from http://www.edweek.org/ew/articles/1996/12/11/15stand.h16.html

Martin, R. (2007). *The opposable mind.* Boston, MA: Harvard Business School Press.

Milentijevic, I., Ciric, V., & Vojinovic, O. (2008). Version control in project-based learning. *Computers and Education, 50,* 1331–1338.

Miller, L. (2004, September). Mapping the journey to school success. *Professionally Speaking,* 51–56.

Mitchell, F. M. (1998). *The effects of curriculum alignment on mathematics achievement of third grade students as measured by the Iowa Test of Basic Skills: Implications for educational administration.* Unpublished dissertation, Clark Atlanta University, Atlanta, GA.

Murray, T. & Bellacero, J., (2008). Students write tabloid tabulations in a math gossip magazine. *National Writing Project.* Retrieved from http://www.nwp.org/cs/public/print/resource/2738

National Middle School Association. (2004). *NSMA position on statement of curriculum integration.* Retrieved September 21, 2011, from http://www.ncmsa.net/NMSA-Curriculum.html

New Media Consortium. (2011). *The NMC Horizon Report: 2011 K–12 Edition.* Stanford, CA: Author. Retrieved from http://www.nmc.org/pdf/2011-Horizon-Report-K12.pdf

Ohio State Department of Education. (2001). *Office of regional school improvement services: A case study of key effective practices in Ohio's improved school districts.* Bloomington: Indiana Center for Evaluation, Smith Research.

Ontario Ministry of Education. (2000). *The Ontario curriculum, grades 11 and 12: Social science and humanities.* Available at http://www.edu.gov.on.ca

Ontario Ministry of Education. (2002). *The Ontario curriculum, grades 11 and 12: Interdisciplinary studies.* Available at http://www.edu.gov.on.ca

Ontario Ministry of Education. (2004). *The Ontario curriculum, grades 1–6: Social studies, and grades 7 and 8: History and geography* Available at http://www.edu.gov.on.ca

Ontario Ministry of Education. (2005a). *The Ontario curriculum. grades 9 and 10: Canadian and world studies.* Available at http://www.edu.gov.on.ca

Ontario Ministry of Education. (2005b). *The Ontario curriculum. grades 11 and 12: Canadian and world studies.* Available at http://www.edu.gov.on.ca

Parry, W. (2010, April 12). Stamford students study water quality with SoundWaters. *StamfordAdvocate.com.* Retrieved from http://www.stamfordadvocate.com/news/article/Stamford-students-study-water-quality-with-432491.php

Pink, D. (2009). *Drive.* New York, NY: Riverhead Books.

Prensky, M. (2001). Digital natives, digital immigrants. *On the Horizon, 9*(5), 1–6. Retrieved from http://www.marcprensky.com/writing

Ravich, D. (2011, October 11). What can we learn from Finland? *Education Week Bridging Differences.* Retrieved from http://blogs.edweek.org/edweek/Bridging Differences/2011/10/what_can_we_learn_from_finland.html

Root-Bernstein, R., & Root-Bernstein, M. (2011, March 16). Turning STEM into STREAM: Writing as an essential component of science education. *National Writing Project.* Retrieved from http://www.nwp.org/cs/public/print/resource/3522

Schmied, K. (2005a). *A view that matters: Understanding essential questions.* Allentown, PA: Performance Learning Systems.

Schmied, K. (2005b, April). *Did you ask a good question today?* Paper presented at ASCD Conference, Orlando, FL.

Small, G., & Vorgan, G. (2008). *iBrain: Surviving the technological alteration of the modern mind.* New York, NY: HarperCollins.

Smith, B. (2011). *The Jalen Rose Leadership Academy Research & Technology E-Lab Book.* Detroit, MI: The Rose and Carter Publishing Studio. Retrieved from http://www.jrladetroit.com

Smith, C., & Myers, C. (2001). Students take center stage in classroom assessment. *Middle Ground, 5*(2), 10–16.

Stahnke, D. (2011). Illuminated mathematics. *Unboxed: A journal of adult learning in schools, 8.* Retrieved from http://www.hightechhigh.org/unboxed/issue7/illuminated_mathematics

State of Vermont Department of Education. (2005). *Vermont's framework of standards and learning opportunities.* Retrieved November 16, 2005, from http://www.state.vt.us/educ/new/pdfdoc/pubs/framework.pdf

Stevenson, C., & Carr, J. (1993). *Dancing through walls.* New York, NY: Teachers College Press.

Strobel, J., & van Barneveld, A. (2009). When is BBL more effective? A meta-synthesis of meta-analyses comparing PBL to conventional classrooms. *Interdisciplinary Journal of problem-based learning, 3*(1). Retrieved from http://docs.lib.purdue.edu/ijpbl/vol3/iss1/4

Theirer, K. (2010, October) Imagine a school where all kids have an individual lesson plan. *Big Picture Learning.* Retrieved from http://www.bigpicture.org/2010/10/imagine-a-school-where-all-kids-have-individual-lesson-plans/

Thomas, D., & Brown, J. S. (2011). *A new culture of learning: Cultivating the imagination for a world of constant change.* CreateSpace: Authors. Available from http://www.amazon.com/New-Culture-Learning-Cultivating-Imagination/dp/1456458884/

Thompson, C. (2011, July 15). How Khan Academy is changing the rules of education. *Wired Magazine.* Retrieved from http://www.wired.com/magazine/2011/07/ff_khan/all/1

Tomlinson, C. A, Kaplan, S. N., Renzulli, J. S., Purcell, J. H., Leppien, J. H, & Burns, D. E., Strickland, C. A., et al. (2009). *The parallel curriculum: A design to develop high potential and challenge high- ability learners* (2nd ed.). Thousand Oaks, CA: Corwin.

Trilling, B., & Fadel, C. (2009). *21st century skills: Learning for life in our times.* San Francisco, CA: John Wiley & Sons.

Truesdale, V., Thompson, C., & Lucas, M. (2004). Use of curriculum mapping to build a learning community. In H. H. Jacobs (Ed.), *Getting results with curriculum mapping* (pp. 10–24). Alexandria, VA: Association for Supervision and Curriculum Development.

Udelhofen, S. (2005). *Keys to curriculum mapping.* Thousand Oaks, CA: Corwin.

Vars, G. (2001a). Can curriculum integration survive in an era of high stakes testing? *Middle School Journal, 32*(2) 7–17.

Vars, G. (2001b). Editorial comment: On research, high stakes testing and core philosophy. *Core Teacher, 50*(1), 3.

Volante, L. (2006). An alternative vision for large-scale assessment in Canada. *Journal of Teaching and Learning, 4*(1), 1–14.

Vygotsky, L. S. (1978). *Mind in society: The development of higher mental processes.* Cambridge, MA: Harvard University Press.

Watters, A. (2011a). Can a $35 tablet be as effective a learning tool as an iPad? *Mind/Shift: How we will learn.* Retrieved from http://mindshift.kqed.org/2011/10/can-a-35-tablet-be-as-effective-a-learning-tool-as-an-ipad/

Watters, A. (2011b). Distractions begone! Facebook as a study tool. *Mind/Shift: How we will learn.* Retrieved from http://mindshift.kqed.org/2011/09/distractions-set-aside-facebook-as-a-study-tool/

Watters, A. (2011c). The first "internet class" goes to college. *Mind/Shift: How we will learn.* Retrieved from http://mindshift.kqed.org/2011/08/the-first-internet-class-goes-to-college/

Wiggins, G., & McTighe, J. (2005). *Understanding by design* (2nd ed.). Alexandria, VA: Association for Supervision and Curriculum Development.

Wiliam, D. (2010). Standardized testing and school accountability. *Educational psychologist, 45*(2), 107–122.

Willis, J. (2006). *Research-based strategies to ignite student learning: Insights for a neurologist/classroom teacher.* Alexandria, VA: ASCD.

Willis, J. (2009). Teaching the brain to read: Strategies for improving fluency, vocabulary and comprehension. *Educational Leadership, 67*(4). Retrieved from http://www.radteach.com/page1/page8/page44/page44.html

Index

CORWIN
A SAGE Company

The Corwin logo—a raven striding across an open book—represents the union of courage and learning. Corwin is committed to improving education for all learners by publishing books and other professional development resources for those serving the field of PreK–12 education. By providing practical, hands-on materials, Corwin continues to carry out the promise of its motto: **"Helping Educators Do Their Work Better."**